The Social Structures of Global Academia

Higher education and research are now at the centre of economic and social policy in advanced information societies. Global networks of researchers, finance, students and policymakers invoke collaborative sociological perspectives. What it means to be an academic and to work in a technologically advanced knowledge industry has undergone transformations that cross national borders. The future of knowledge production, social development, prosperity and the freedom of ideas are caught in the swelling of global tides.

The Social Structures of Global Academia exposes readers to a variety of issues that are impacting academics across the globe. The volume includes contributions by leading social scientists and innovative research from emerging scholars. Its anchoring themes include academic ethics, the affective cultures of scholarship, changing funding structures and social control of the currents of scholarly life.

Giving readers an overview of the growing field of critical studies of academia, *The Social Structures of Global Academia* will appeal to students and scholars seeking to understand more of the burgeoning field of critical sociologies of higher education, and general readers interested in contemporary knowledge about universities, science and the people who make it their passion. It will also appeal to policymakers who are invested in trying to make universities more viable places to work.

Fabian Cannizzo is an independent researcher in Melbourne, Australia.

Nick Osbaldiston is a senior lecturer at James Cook University, Cairns, Australia.

Routledge Advances in Sociology

261 Horizontal Europeanisation
The Transnationalisation of Daily Life and Social Fields in Europe
Edited by Prof. Dr. Martin Heindenreich

262 The Marginalized in Genocide Narratives
Giorgia Donà

263 The Social Structures of Global Academia
Edited by Fabian Cannizzo and Nick Osbaldiston

264 Citizenship in the Latin American Upper and Middle Classes
Ethnographic Perspectives on Culture, Politics, and Consumption
Edited by Fiorella Montero-Diaz and Franka Winter

265 Youth and the Politics of the Present
Constructing the Future
Edited by Enzo Colombo and Paola Rebughini

266 Trade Unions and European Integration
A Question of Optimism and Pessimism?
Edited by Johannes M. Kiess and Martin Seeliger

267 Globalization, Modernity and the Rise of Religious Fundamentalism
The Challenge of Religious Resurgence against the "End of History" (A Dialectical Kaleidoscopic Analysis)
Dimitrios Methenitis

For more information about this series, please visit: www.routledge.com/Routledge-Advances-in-Sociology/book-series/SE0511

The Social Structures of Global Academia

Edited by Fabian Cannizzo and Nick Osbaldiston

Routledge
Taylor & Francis Group
LONDON AND NEW YORK

First published 2019
by Routledge
2 Park Square, Milton Park, Abingdon, Oxon OX14 4RN

and by Routledge
52 Vanderbilt Avenue, New York, NY 10017

Routledge is an imprint of the Taylor & Francis Group, an informa business

British Library Cataloguing-in-Publication Data
A catalogue record for this book is available from the British Library

Library of Congress Cataloging-in-Publication Data
Names: Cannizzo, Fabian, editor. | Osbaldiston, Nicholas, editor.
Title: The social structures of global academia / [edited by] Fabian Cannizzo and Nick Osbaldiston.
Description: Abingdon, Oxon ; New York, NY : Routledge, 2019. | Series: Routledge advances in sociology ; 262 | Includes bibliographical references and index.
Identifiers: LCCN 2019001316| ISBN 9781138610125 (hbk) | ISBN 9780429465857 (ebk)
Subjects: LCSH: Education and globalization—Social aspects. | Education, Higher—Social aspects. | Learning and scholarship—Social aspects. | Information society.
Classification: LCC LC191.9 .C36 2019 | DDC 370.116—dc23
LC record available at https://lccn.loc.gov/2019001316

ISBN: 978-1-138-61012-5 (hbk)
ISBN: 978-0-429-46585-7 (ebk)

Typeset in Times New Roman
by codeMantra

Contents

Chapter 1

An introduction to the social structures of global academia

Fabian Cannizzo and Nick Osbaldiston

Academia as a field of study

The form of social organisation that we call academia and the legal bodies that house it, such as universities and colleges, are today nearly mythological icons in wealthy nations. They are framed in public discourse not only as foundries of knowledge but also as economic resources, moral classrooms and facilitators of socio-economic mobility. As Steven Ward (2012, p. 131) notes, within popular Organisation for Economic Cooperation and Development (OECD) rhetoric, which heralds the emergence of a 'knowledge society':

> Universities occupy a particularly special place in this new economic configuration and the creation of these new national, regional and city-based "information systems." Knowledge society proponents envision universities as engines of economic growth... They are to do this by providing the new epistemic materials for post-industrial production, by becoming the setting for entrepreneurial innovation, business incubation and technology transfer and by providing a well-trained and flexible labor force that can continuously be retrained with useful skills as economic conditions and the needs of corporations change.

Although they are legislated at the pinnacle of nationally accredited education systems globally, universities are not reducible to the infrastructure and bureaucracies that give them materiality. Beyond the present focus on 'innovation, vocationalism, knowledge transfer, marketability, workforce needs and adherence to the cost-saving and moralizing discipline imposed by the bottom line' (Ward, 2012, p. 145), the university is vitalised by the idea that the rationalisation of knowledge is a public good, which also requires an appropriate form of social organisation. Debates about how such an organisation might manifest constitute the study of academia. This type of study is necessarily as concerned with systems of meaning (culture) as it is with systems of coordination (organisations) as the recognition and reproduction of academia are closely entangled with the identity of human agents.

This edited collection is framed through the reference point of 'global' academia to problematise contemporary studies of the academic in two ways. First, the understanding of academia that has emerged in English-speaking contexts has been shaped by a global political economy that has centred some perspectives and excluded others. Scientific and academic practice have always shared a relationship with political economy, which Raewyn Connell (2007) has shown to be well illustrated in sociology's own history. Early sociology naturalised intellectual distinctions between European empires and colonised societies through an optimistic narrative of social Darwinism that placed European culture at the height of social development (Connell, 2007, p. 17). Although this narrative has lost currency with contemporary social theorists, the structures of power that commingled with these ideas continue to shape global knowledge production. The 'Eurocentric curriculum' that has developed from this history is not limited to sociology but has come to reproduce the centrality of British, European and American academic scholarship across the globe (Connell, 2017). A focus on 'global' academia centres the history of political economy in narratives of knowledge production and the reproduction of inequalities in academia.

Second, by encouraging contributors to reflect on the global production of academia, this collection hopes to begin redressing the regionalism that has characterised much sociological research surrounding the academic. By juxtaposing different experiences and studies from across different contexts and regions, this volume invites thinking beyond national boundaries. While the complexity of a global political economy may mean that we may never cover as much terrain as might be required to achieve this aim, exploring different narratives across nations allows us to reimagine the university beyond the usual 'core' United Kingdom/North American focus. Furthermore, by examining places as diverse as Finland and Australia, we can perhaps start to witness and track the trickle down of policies, politics and rhetoric into peripheral developed nations within global academic labour.

Contemporary critical academic scholarship is, however, still largely drawn from the social theoretical and scientific giants of Europe and North America. We will now outline what we see as some of the ways in which these important contributions shape our discussions of academia. These all suggest possible pathways towards a more global study of the social structures of academia, even within regional contexts. We will begin by exploring the works of Pierre Bourdieu and Mary Henkel, and then examine the discipline focusses of Tony Becher and Paul Trowler. Following this the chapter will introduce the themes of the book and the individual contributions within it.

National academic systems

Pierre Bourdieu's (1988) sociology of French academia in *Homo Academicus* is an exemplar of the study of national academic systems. He mobilises his conceptual categories of capital to conduct a 'field' analysis of the Parisian-centred system of offices and associations, drawing a clear distinction between the cultural economy of the sciences and of academic posts. Bourdieu (1988, p. 48) claims that:

> the university field is organized according to two antagonistic principles of hierarchization: the social hierarchy, corresponding to the capital inherited and the economic and political capital actually held, is in opposition to the specific, properly cultural hierarchy, corresponding to the capital of scientific authority or intellectual renown.

These two economies reveal distinct social logics upon which 'academic' and 'scientific' value are realised among scholars. While these logics impact different areas of the university (i.e. distinct disciplines) in varied ways, both 'scientific competence and social [academic] competence' (1988, p. 59) must be demonstrated to manipulate power. The flow of power within the French academic system is nationally specific in that 'academic capital is obtained and maintained by holding a position enabling domination of other positions and their holders', the highest positions of which rest in the Universities Consultative Committee – the board of examiners to the Ecole Normale Supérieure (Bourdieu, 1988, p. 84; also see Altman & Bournois, 2004). Bourdieu is critical of the French academic succession examinations, claiming that the choice of academic 'head' (doctoral supervisor) and thesis are 'to some extent a relation of capital to capital' (1988, p. 94), that is, by demonstrating the 'correct' dispositions and citations, mutually produce value for both the supervisor and the pupil. He claims that this encourages a 'special form of anti-intellectualism… and which most often has no connection with the technical necessities of a true apprenticeship' (1988, p. 95). For Bourdieu, the socially codified power within French academia acts to reproduce the academic field, institutional hierarchies and capital.

Another approach to the national study of academia has emerged from Mary Henkel's (2000) study of academic identity in the changing UK policy landscape. Henkel focusses on how academics develop identities that are both 'distinctive and socially embedded' among disciplinary, institutional and work-based groups (Henkel, 2005, p. 156). While the framework adopted allows for a supra-national analysis of academic life, Henkel focusses on the importance of the policy context in which academic bureaucracies, organisations and funding mechanisms operate (Henkel, 2000). Because of the specificity of national higher education and research policy frameworks, Henkel (2005, p. 156) emphasises the need to 'be cautious about drawing broader conclusions' from her study of the United Kingdom, which has been transformed by regionally specific policies. Notably, while phenomena such as the massification of higher education and tighter budgetary constraints are widespread issues in higher education across national borders, Henkel (2000) describes the shift of organisational power in the United Kingdom as 'centralised decentralisation' (p. 57). Premised on the view that 'creative peripheries need strong central values and strategies' (p. 57), budgetary responsibility was devolved to departmental and other 'middle' managers without equal power to decide budgetary goals (p. 58).

For Henkel, research policies being pursued 'at national and institutional levels were raising fundamental questions for what it means to be an academic' (2005, p. 165). The 'academic manager' emerged in this period as an identity around which scholars could anchor their future planning and sense of organisational self. Managers in Henkel's study, who took their identities 'extremely seriously', experienced very loose role 'scripts' and 'no systematic training' for their newfound careers (Henkel, 2000, p. 237). Academic managers were hence taking on positions they were unfamiliar with while becoming encoded in an antagonistic dichotomy – 'between Them (managers) and Us (the workers)' (anonymous academic, in Henkel, 2000, p. 238). As Musselin (2008) notes, focussing on (regionally specific) policy developments allows for an investigation of new boundaries, such as those between the beneficiaries of new funding mechanisms and others, and a rethinking of assumptions about academic life, such as the tendency to treat academia as a 'special' domain of social life in which the transformation of academics into knowledge workers might be overlooked (p. 53). Both Bourdieu and Henkel encourage a focus on the transformation of regional systems that are themselves dependent on their relationships to state bureaucracies and institutional cultures.

The cultures of academic disciplines

A second means for approaching academia as a global entity has emerged from scholars who place professional cultures at the centre of academic identity and organisational life. In 'Science as a vocation', Weber (1919/1946) drew a contrast between what he described as 'the organization of science as a vocation' and the condition of science in Weber's time, which had 'entered a phase of specialization previously unknown' (p. 134). Far from being consumed by a breadth of scientific work, the modern scholar is a specialist who must bear certain qualities suited to their role in history, notably, 'enthusiasm' and 'passionate devotion' to discovery in the presence of a deep uncertainty about the ultimate result of one's efforts (Weber, 1919/1946, p. 136). Weber's polemic outlines character traits associated with an ethics of office (du Gay et al., 2018) which he deems appropriate to the role of the modern scientist. Leaders within different academic communities have attempted to either restate or reinvent a performative polemic such as Weber's; perhaps the most notable within the discipline of sociology are Robert Merton's (1942/1973) widely discussed ethos of science, which include the principles of Communism, Universalism, Disinterestedness and Organised Scepticism (abbreviated as CUDOS), and Edward Shils's (1984/1997) 'The academic ethic', which describes the moral duties of scholars within the context of the early 1980s United States. As Stephen Turner (this volume) notes, this genre of writing is likely a response to a communal crisis, when the values and morals being described are no longer able to operate as tacit, assumed knowledge and mores but rather are felt to be in need of codification and formal communication. While these performative texts offer insight into how different elite groups within academia conceptualise and contest professional boundaries and norms, they tend to be premised on exceptionalist arguments about what constitutes their professional or disciplinary grounding. That is, they are focussed on narratives and concerns internal to the group as the authors themselves admittedly have a vested interest in the future of their scholarly groups.

Another body of works focussed on professional norms presents professional comparisons or inter-disciplinary interactions that are helpful in exploring not only the internal consistency of disciplines but also how disciplines reinforce their interiors by reference to other social groups. Tony Becher and Paul Trowler's *Academic tribes and territories* (2001) is one of the most well-cited studies of disciplinary cultures and boundary-making between these 'tribes'. Employing their colourful metaphor, Becher and Trowler (2001, p. 47) argue:

> The tribes of academe, one might argue, define their own identities and defend their own patches of intellectual ground by employing a variety of devices geared to the exclusion of illegal migrants... To be admitted to membership of a particular sector of the academic profession involves not only a sufficient level of technical proficiency in one's intellectual trade but also a sufficient level of loyalty to one's collegial group and of adherence to its norms.

Disciplinary socialisation is hence central to this model of tribe-like affiliation as disciplinary ideologies and 'heroic myths' form a core of tacit knowledge, values and norms shared in common by 'tribal' members (pp. 48–49). However, if territories are the product of *organisational* boundary-making, rather than *epistemic* differences, then the specialisation that Weber argued was characteristic of his time may actually be, following Ruscio, 'an iron law [that] controls the progress of science and similarly the academic profession' (in Becher & Trowler, 2001, p. 66), which some argue have been especially detrimental to disciplines with porous boundaries, such as sociology (Holmwood, 2010). Steve Fuller (2016), taking this logic of territorial guarding into the competitive political economy of academic capitalism, describes the underlying knowledge incentives within academia as a form of 'rentier capitalism' (pp. 40–46). The proliferation of sub-disciplinary networks within national and international scholarly associations attests to the value of exploring this intersection of cultural and political economies. The role of leadership in professional tribes is an ongoing field of interest to organisational scholars in higher education. Michèle Lamont's (2009) study of grant review panels suggests that senior scholars from different 'tribes' not only engage in boundary-work when required to work with scholars from different disciplinary backgrounds but also draw on 'a lot of shared norms' that stem from common experiences as disciplinary leaders (p. 44). Disciplinary and professional norms are intertwined with the power structures through which territorial boundaries are contested and reproduced. As Lamont (2009) argues, the boundary-work at play here is embedded then into institutional practice. However, those within the conflict rather than consensus disciplines, such as the social sciences vs the harder sciences, tend to reinforce and perform their boundaries strongly (Hearn & Anderson, 2012). Disciplines across the globe are worthwhile entities to examine not simply because of this institutional battleground but also for their meaning-making for individual academics (Becher & Trowler, 2001) that can extend into understanding in everyday life.

Economic rationalisation, acceleration and the technopolitics of audit

Academic working conditions and career expectations have shifted significantly since Logan Wilson conducted his study of the United States' elite universities during the Second World War. In *The Academic Man*, Wilson (1942/2017) sought to investigate 'the special folkways and mores of the profession', whose function he defined as 'the conservation, dissemination, and innovation of knowledge' (p. 3). The elite US universities in 1942 supported a relatively informal job market (in comparison to the 1990s), which Altbach describes as resembling a 'medieval guild' where masters cared for their apprentices through access to 'semi-closed' marketplaces (Altbach, 1995, p. xvi). Far from rose-coloured images of the 'Golden Age' of scholarship (Cannizzo, 2018a; Ylijoki, 2005), Altbach notes that 'the academic market in 1942 was certainly not robust… [and] a significant number of new Ph.Ds could not find jobs in their fields' (1995, p. xvii). Several large-scale developments have been identified by sociologists since Wilson's modern universities, which have formed a third research approach for studying academia as a global phenomenon. The expansion of digital information communication systems, managerial authority over the everyday activities of the university and the presence of economics in imagining scholarly futures has led to claims that academic work has been transformed by a new mode of reasoning. We describe the sum of these logics here as the rationalisation of academia. While rational action is far from a stranger within scientific and scholarly life, several discourses of critique have emerged that take aim at what might be described as the dominance of means-ends reasoning over value-rational modes of action that define mythologies of scholarly work. We will describe these discourses here as economic, managerial and temporal rationalisation.

First, the discourse of economic rationalisation has received revived popularity in the wake of Foucault's 1978–1979 lectures on *The Birth of Biopolitics* (Foucault, 2008), linking the entrepreneurialisation of everyday life with the growing popularity of 'neoliberalism' as a political rationality. Prior to this discourse, a number of social and organisational changes to universities in the global metropole sparked new concerns and hopes for the future of higher education and research, such as the growth of national government intervention into the funding and missions of universities, the massification and eventual universalisation of access to higher education, the growth of the idea of a 'knowledge economy' within international organisations such as the OECD and the World Bank, and the expansion of many higher education sectors through the creation of new institutions (Ward, 2012). In *Labor and Monopoly Capital*, Harry Braverman (1974/1998) describes a transformation in the relationship between science and industrial capitalism – a scientific-technical revolution that began in the late nineteenth century. Braverman claims that this revolution emerged at a point where science ceased to be merely a 'social property' in 'the province of amateurs, "philosophers," tinkerers, and seekers of knowledge', and was transformed into a 'highly organized and lavishly financed state' in the 1970s as capital 'systematically organize[d] and harness[ed] science, paying for scientific education, research, laboratories, etc.' (1974/1998, p. 107). The desire to predictably organise science and scholarship for the benefit of stakeholders (whether the public citizen or the private investor) became central to attempts to transform the character of scholars and scientists into instruments of economic productivity. Since it came into the purview of the governmental rationalities, the university has become the subject of a supernova of scholarly comment and critique.

Central to the critique of neoliberal academia is that it effects a transformation of scholars into another permutation of *Homo economicus*, enacting a kind of 'everyday neoliberalism' (Mirowski, 2013; also see Cannizzo, 2018b). Whereas classical liberalism takes the view that the individual should be freed from interventions by the state, neoliberalism conceives of the state's role in producing freedom more positively: to 'create an individual that is an enterprising and competitive entrepreneur' (Olssen & Peters, 2005, p. 315). It is not only a discourse but also the reasoning of an ethos of government. Unlike classical liberalism, which championed the Hayekian premise that the spontaneous order of markets produces systemic stability, economists such as James Buchanan express 'a much greater faith in *conscious action*' and the capacities of the state to 'engineer a market order' (Olssen & Peters, 2005, p. 319). A key shift for academic practitioners emerges in the form of de-professionalisation as 'education is represented as an input-output system which can be reduced to an economic production function' within OECD and national policy discourses (Olssen & Peters, 2005, p. 324); Braverman's scientific-technical revolution comes full circle as the rationalisers lose grip on the reigns of rationalisation. Or as Slaughter and Rhoades comment in *Academic capitalism in the new economy*, 'Universities are difficult to separate from the new economy because they contribute richly to its development' (2004, p. 15). However, far from a monolithic model of economics-as-neoliberalism, the study of economic rationalisation is fragmented over forms of capitalism, as Olssen and Peters (2005, p. 559) have mused, as different meanings of knowledge within broad policy contexts imply different relationships between knowledge production and state economics.

Second, studies of managerial rationalisation often develop from premises similar to the literature on economic rationalisation but differ in their focus on the organisation of the labour process as the key site of conflict and transformation. Bureaucratic structures, institutional norms and technological infrastructure are variously centred as key motors in the transformation of academia in regimes such as the United Kingdom's New Public Management (Lorenz, 2012). Investigations of the forms of visibility and control produced by the introduction of metric assemblages into universities have been interlocutors between scholars and university managers (Burrows, 2012; Power, 1997). The development of 'quantified control' (Burrows, 2012) has seen not only new means of enacting managerial governance but also an affective transformation of academia, notably described by Rosalind Gill (2010) as a sense of harried, surveilled anxiety. Managerial control has been closely connected to the forms of visibility legitimised and institutionalised within labour control regimes, often described as 'accountability', 'efficiency' or 'transparency' programmes. The United Kingdom's Research Excellent Framework, Australia's Excellence in Research for Australia and Aotearoa New Zealand's Performance-Based Research Fund aim to not only distribute funding but also produce legitimacy for this distribution. The potential for the production of new forms of visibility and connections to managerially monitored data assemblages has invoked anxiety and even cynicism about the future of the digital academic, especially through social media spaces that allow for professional and private personas to become blurred (Carrigan, 2016; Lupton, 2014, 2015; Lupton et al., 2018). Managerial rationalisation here is creeping beyond the confines of professional roles and into digital realms, partially due to the collapse of work and non-work contexts.

Finally, temporal rationalisation is a critical concept that has emerged from the intersection of the study of sociotemporalities (Zerubavel, 1981/1985) and the political economy of knowledge. Filip Vostal's (2016) study of the variegated and transforming temporalities of academic life is perhaps the most articulated expression of this genre. Vostal's study is notable in that it attempts to overcome past reifications of temporal rationalisation (sometimes characterised as a telos of 'acceleration' – Rosa, 2013), problematising calls for '*general* slowness' in academic life (p. 196; cf. Berg & Seeber, 2017; Pels, 2003). Unlike studies of economic or managerial rationalisation, those focussing on the temporal dimension of rationalisation centre the processual properties of social action, resisting the reification of social life (in the form of a 'structure') in favour of ideal-type categories (Osbaldiston et al., 2016) and analyses of synchronisation or arrhythmia of actions and processes (Vostal et al., 2018). The growth of information and communication technologies (ICTs) has been central to studies of the temporality of academic life as these systems allow for faster access to information, growing and ethically challenging sources of data, especially for the social sciences (Lupton, 2015; Possamai-Inesedy & Nixon, 2017) and the more fluid experience of work places and times, which are both locked into laboratory infrastructure while also as mobile as laptops and smartphones.

It is clear that there is not enough space to do justice to the myriad methodologies that have been invested into understanding academia and, importantly, unpacking what might be transforming within it. One thing that stands out as a common belief in contemporary literature is the sense that academia is indeed changing. A big question now is why this is so and, of more importance to younger generations, what can be done about it. Frequently, academics studying academia have no shortage of reasons to answer the first question but unfortunately do not provide much response to the second. This volume is perhaps no exception to this as resisting the sorts of rationalisations that are occurring within the academy is no easy feat. We will return to this subject later in this introduction. There is still much more work to be done in order to outline, first, the different layering of institutional/individual inequality that exists within academia and, second, the appropriate and realistic response to it. This volume of work attends to this in some detail.

Overview of the book

The chapters in this collection represent a diverse set of individual themes and interests across different disciplinary backgrounds, each speaking to a facet of the structuring of academic life. These analyses of social structure have been organised here into four broad themes: **academic ethics**; **affective cultures**; **funding and metrics;** and, lastly, **agency and control**.

In **Part One: Academic Ethics**, John Holmwood and Stephen Turner take us through a historical overview of the changing nature of both the academy and the academic themselves. For Holmwood, it is imperative to understand the history of the university before we can engage with the present.

The university, and its history of elitism, has in the past been delivered to the public as a social good. The term 'multi-versity' describes the manner in which the university was seen as a contributor to the economic foundations of the state but also to the betterment of individuals through alleviating social immobility and improving democracy generally. However, as Holmwood charts out, the ramification for public investment into higher education is that it is vulnerable to political shifts. The widespread changes within the United Kingdom and the United States towards responsible spending has led to the marketisation of the university more generally and a gradual instrumentalisation of academic labour. The university has stopped, largely due to neoliberal politics, being seen as a public good and is now framed as an important contributor to private economies and corporate interests.

Holmwood's work dovetails into Turner's piece on the academic ethic. Following Shils's discussion of scientific ideals (such as independence, truth-seeking and respectability, both within and outside the university), Turner tracks the professionalisation of the university and the impact this had on academic ethics. He argues, convincingly, that this had the impact of turning science into 'patentable, impactful, and useable' knowledge, while the social sciences/humanities were unable to follow suit due to their inability to create items for corporate use. For Turner, the social sciences are under constant threat from the harder sciences and exist within a system that does not recognise their contributions to knowledge in the form of resources. Professionalisation of the university space, over time, has done little to realise Shils's academic ethic and instead has produced a highly competitive and narrowly individualised marketplace of knowledge and a lack of love for learning.

Following this, Nick Osbaldiston, Fabian Cannizzo and Christian Mauri offer an empirical investigation of the moral economy of service within the academy. This chapter provides some weight to Turner's arguments by inviting us to consider the pressure placed upon younger academics to increasingly work without pay. As is shown, for those in precarious roles especially, there is an investment of unpaid labour that is hoped will be paid out at a later date but which is also rationalised as something of a labour of love. The chapter argues that while academic citizenship may well be on the decline, a willingness persists among academics to work extra for the good of others, especially students. This chapter centres the political economy of academic labour and reveals a certain ethical dilemma wherein younger, often casual, academics work beyond capacity for the purposes of enhancing work security in the future. As this chapter argues, it is this sort of labour that is increasingly becoming the norm and as such (re)produces hierarchies and inequalities among academics.

In **Part Two: Affective Cultures**, Mona Mannevuo and Elina Valovirta, Fabian Cannizzo and Oili-Helena Ylijoki take us through some of the emotional and subjective states of academic life. In the first chapter from

Mannevuo and Valovirta, we are exposed to a localised context which produces certain emotions for academics. Coming from the Finnish perspective, this chapter traces the management of shame for academics who are in a 'peripheral place' and never 'international enough', displaying the inequality embedded in the political economy of European university systems. As the authors point out, this produces a highly competitive environment and an individualised workforce. Academics rationalise this space through love of work that 'normalises the exhaustive patterns' of labour relations. Mannevuo and Valovirta then offer their own experiences of micro-emancipation from these spaces through the pub quiz, a time which helps to 'put our lives in perspective'.

Following this, Cannizzo takes a look at the work of scholars through the cultural lens of authenticity. Using Richard Sennett's concept of craftwork, this chapter argues that the idea of genuine or real academic labour (namely research-orientated) tends to privilege certain structures. This is especially fractured for Cannizzo across class and gender lines, where, especially in the case of the latter, external structures to the university have reconstituted and enforced 'old social divisions'. Female academics in particular, due to gendered expectations and responsibilities, are left behind in the wake of the persistence of the ideal of academia as a lifestyle to which one must be wholly committed. In short, those who are unable to acquire the 'authentic' ideal of an academic life suffer as a result. Cannizzo calls for a rethinking of career and planning in order to deal with this issue further.

This contention that the 'authentic academic ideal' is afforded to only some lays at the heart also of Ylijoki's contribution. Unlike Cannizzo's chapter though, this chapter focusses on a narrative of happiness. Using empirical work from across elite universities, Ylijoki is able to show us that academics with capacity and resources actively reject a misery narrative that bemoans the state of academia. Rather, work is discussed as enjoyable; a privilege; successful; and, importantly, free. She concludes that there is a stratification of academics across the different 'life-worlds' where elites are able to distinguish their work from that of the 'complainers'. There is, as Ylijoki comments, a lack of empathy towards those who the successful see as failures. From this perspective, it would seem, the neoliberal mindset of blaming victims for their own mess is very much at play.

In **Part Three: Funding and Metrics**, Gaby Haddow and Björn Hammarfelt first examine the very real impacts of evaluative metrics on early career researchers in Australian universities. They show through empirical work that the intensification of metrics and benchmarking produce multifaceted reactions among academics. This includes a range of responses where early career researchers use an evaluative framework to either resist, play the game or give up. Importantly, Haddow and Hammarfelt argue, metrics can be used to both measure success and contribute to an academic identity but also to potentially undermine this process. This is especially the case for those in vulnerable positions within institutions. However, these authors also argue that embedded within metricisation is resistance and that intellectual pushback against measurement could well contribute positively to academic selves.

This question of success though, as others note, has to be tempered by a realisation of the increasingly casualised nature of academia. Thomas Franssen and Sarah de Rijcke expose this form of precarity further in their contribution on funding regimes within a Dutch research group. While research funding may have risen, they argue, this only serves to promote short-term contractual labour among postdoctoral researchers, thereby increasing ontological insecurity and anxiety within the labour force. Franssen and de Rijcke further claim that although collegiality and communitarian values within research groups are important for short-term contracted researchers, these are unlikely to solve the broader issue at hand, that is, the proliferation of research grants (small and large) which produce a structure/culture of short-term labour.

To complete this section, we are pleased to present a reprint of Ruth Müller's wonderful paper entitled *Racing for what? Anticipation and acceleration in the work and career practices of academic life science postdocs*. In this highly provocative piece, Müller explores the experiences of postdoctoral life scientists in Austria and argues that younger academics are working to their limits but also anticipating that competition for positions within academia will be increasingly more difficult to acquire. Postdoctoral researchers engage with what she terms anticipatory acceleration in that as a group they are involved in a 'vicious cycle' of competition where time and activity can always be further 'optimised'. Müller argues that one of the consequences of this type of informal structure is that postdoctoral researchers are less likely to engage with research topics of less certainty, that is, topics which are 'unpredictable' or 'speculative'. Concluding this, however, is an insightful discussion around the idea of slow science, not as a temporal reordering but rather as a reflexive reframing of the worth of research and knowledge (see the following).

In the final section, **Part Four: Agency and Control**, Christian Mauri lends another theoretical framework to the experiences of insecurity by exploring the contemporary academic precariat. In this grounded piece, Mauri argues that the precariat, mostly sessional academics, is defined by an existence of insecurity, unpaid labour, marginality and 'relative deprivation'. Structures, both formal and informal, within the academy serve only to weaken the mobility for the sessional staff member. As we are reminded in this chapter, the university is now thriving on this insecure labour, and sessional teachers are especially vulnerable to lack of opportunity. In this setting, sessional teachers not only find it difficult to acquire long-term work but also can be victims to hiring policies that are often informal, lack transparency and are less likely to be merit driven.

Additionally, Mauri exposes the idea that living and working in the university is experienced in diverse ways. This is the subject of Sarah Davies's chapter in this book. She explores the deep narratives that researchers, who are situated within competing spaces of institutionalised evaluation mechanisms and the ideals of being a good academic, draw upon to make sense and unpack their experiences of academia. Davies argues that universities today are lived in multiple, competing and fragmented ways, and provocatively argues that we should be reporting it in a similar fashion. She concludes, using ethnographic and autoethnographic work, that even bureaucratic attempts to responsibilise academics can be rethought and internalised through different paradigms of self-care. Practices of the self, mundane or otherwise, are a feature of everyday academic life used to make sense of our work and as such should be the focus of our analysis.

To conclude this section and this volume, Raewyn Connell offers us some of her thoughts on the history and changing regimes of knowledge production across the world. Similar to many of those chapters preceding her work here, Connell explores some fundamental and growing inequalities, including the rise of managerial control of teaching and research through technology. Importantly though for our work, Connell provides us with a departing comment on the rise of alternative approaches to the neoliberal university. This can be seen, for instance, in the 'Free University' movements across the West, which attempt to utilise public space for 'educational activities'. These ideas are important to consider, but as many others have argued in this volume, who can afford to be involved, and how does this challenge the vastness of the contemporary university today?

Reflections and departures

We conclude here by offering some reflections on the volume and perhaps some thoughts about stepping forward. At the beginning of this chapter, we described three broad approaches to a sociology of global academia that are found within academic labour studies. It is clear that among these there is disagreement, and it is also evident that we have not covered some important work in this space too. However, one of the fundamental features of current academic labour is the question of what academics do; how they experience the academy; and, further, how they make sense of the changing nature of work. We would like to offer another suggestion to this list of research questions that perhaps underpinned Shils's initial work on academic ethic – what can we realistically do now?

Müller (this volume) offers up a suggestion from the slow movement – where practices of knowledge generation can be reflected upon critically and open up space to ask, as she does, 'to whose benefit is it that we are racing?' This enquiry is worth following up on and thinking through from the slow perspective. The foundation for such a thought is not simply that academic work has sped up but also that there has been a 'cultural politics of immediacy' (Tomlinson, 2007, p. 154) which has penetrated the core of the academic institution. This includes the sorts of things discussed in this book, such as quick publications, engagement through social media, pressure on teaching practice to be flexible, less time to think and more time spent on easy research that requires little deliberation and can be more easily automated. We can see the culture of immediacy through technologies that update constantly one's citations and metrics such as the h-index. We can also see it in the 24/7 cycle of email availability that students now have with teachers and the rising expectation to 'be on call'. Of course, these things are spread throughout Western modernity, as plenty of scholars have commented (Agger, 2004; Parkins & Craig, 2006; Tomlinson, 2007; Vostal, 2016). We do not pretend here to know the answer to this problem. However, following Müller's considerations, we would depart with some comments on what investing in the 'slow' might mean.

Slow does not necessarily entail a temporal dropping out of society. Rather, as Parkins and Craig (2006, p. 3) offer, going slow means a 'conscious attempt to change the temporal order to one which offers more time [… and] having time for something means investing it with significance through attention and deliberation'. Recurring features of the slow movements (such as Slow Food, Slow Travel, Slow Towns) enact these changes in various everyday practices. It requires 'care' and 'attention' to action, where a 'reconfiguring of local social relations and identities' is engaged with in 'new reflexive ways' (Parkins & Craig, 2006, p. 11). From an academic perspective, this potentially could mean taking a moment to reopen thinking through what it means to be an academic (Cannizzo, this volume) and renegotiating that ideal/ethic at a local level. Slow Food advocates will also argue that there needs to be a deeper ethical motivation for their action – often seen in the embracing of local foods and a tie to questions of environmental degradation. What might a new academic ethic look like which could be a prime motivator for the slowing down of academia? Connell (this volume) suggests that maybe it's in the opening up and democratisation of knowledge. Turner (this volume) considers that maybe it is held in the recapturing of the 'love of learning' which is held back by the professionalisation of disciplines.

We do not claim to know what the answer is – or that there is necessarily a single answer at all. As Tomlinson (2007, p. 186) claims on the 'slow movement', 'it seems unlikely' that it can 'in any direct way challenge the institutional grip of the condition of immediacy'. It could be said that any attempt to slow down academia might be fraught and doomed from the outset. However, as Tomlinson (2007, p. 186) adds, 'we surely should reject inevitabilism' and explore the values/ethics of the slow and subsequently the 'conditions of their cultivation'. Attempts have been made (see Vostal, 2016). These are worth considering. Rather than adding the chorus of things that are wrong with academia, it might be necessary to ask questions about what is right; what is good; and what we can change, albeit slowly.

References

Agger, B. (2004). *Speeding up fast capitalism: Cultures, jobs, families, schools, bodies.* Boulder, CO: Paradigm Publishers.

Altbach, P. G. (1995/2017). The American academic profession: Persistent themes, escalating concern. In L. Wilson & P. G. Altbach (Eds.), *The academic man: A study in the sociology of a profession* (pp. ix–xxv). London: Routledge.

Altman, Y., & Bournois, F. (2004). The "coconut tree" model of careers: The case of French academia. *Journal of Vocational Behavior, 64*(2), 320–328.

Becher, T., & Trowler, P. (2001). *Academic tribes and territories: Intellectual enquiry and the culture of disciplines* (2nd ed.). Buckingham: TSRHE and Open University Press.

Berg, M., & Seeber, B. K. (2017). *The slow professor: Challenging the culture of speed in the academy.* Toronto, ON: University of Toronto Press.

Bourdieu, P. (1988). *Homo academicus*, P. Collier (Trans.). Stanford, CA: Stanford University Press.

Braverman, H. (1974/1998). *Labor and monopoly capital: The degradation of work in the twentieth century* (25th anniversary ed.). New York, NY: Monthly Review Press.

Burrows, R. (2012). Living with the h-index? Metric assemblages in the contemporary academy. *The Sociological Review, 60*(2), 355–372.

Cannizzo, F. (2018a). 'You've got to love what you do': Academic labour in a culture of authenticity. *The Sociological Review, 66*(1), 91–106.

Cannizzo, F. (2018b). Tactical evaluations: Everyday neoliberalism in academia. *Journal of Sociology, 54*(1), 77–91.

Carrigan, M. (2016). *Social media for academics.* London: Sage.

Connell, R. (2007). *Southern theory: The global dynamics of knowledge in social science.* Crows Nest, NSW: Allen & Unwin.

Connell, R. (2017). Southern theory and world universities. *Higher Education Research and Development, 36*(1), 4–15.

du Gay, P., Lopdrop-Hjorth, T., Pedersen, K. Z., & Roelsgaard, A. O. (2018). Character and organization. *Journal of Cultural Economy.* Advance online publication. doi:10.1080/17530350.2018.1481879.

Foucault, M. (2008). *The birth of biopolitics: Lectures at the Collège de France, 1978–1979*, G. Burchell (Trans.). New York, NY: Palgrave Macmillan.

Fuller, S. (2016). *The academic Caesar: University leadership is hard.* London: Sage Swifts.

Gill, R. (2010). Breaking the silence: The hidden injuries of neo-liberal academia. In R. Flood & R. Gill (Eds.), *Secrecy and silence in the research process: Feminist reflection* (pp. 228–244). London: Routledge.

Hearn, J. C., & Anderson, M. S. (2002). Conflict in academic departments: An analysis of disputes over faculty promotion and tenure. *Research in Higher Education, 43*(5), 503–529.

Henkel, M. (2000). *Academic identities and policy change in higher education.* London: Jessica Kingsley.

Henkel, M. (2005). Academic identity and autonomy in a changing policy environment. *Higher Education*, *49*(1–2), 155–176.
Holmwood, J. (2010). Sociology's misfortune: Disciplines, interdisciplinarity and the impact of audit culture. *British Journal of Sociology*, *61*(4), 639–658.
Lamont, M. (2009). *How professors think: Inside the curious world of academic judgement*. Cambridge, MA: Harvard University Press.
Lorenz, C. (2012). If you're so smart, why are you under surveillance? Universities, neoliberalism, and new public management. *Critical Inquiry*, *38*(3), 599–629.
Lupton, D. (2014). *'Feeling better connected': Academics' use of social media*. Canberra, ACT: News & Media Research Centre, University of Canberra.
Lupton, D. (2015). *Digital sociology*. London: Routledge.
Lupton, D., Mewburn, I., & Thompson, P. (2018). The digital academic: Identities, contexts and politics. In D. Lupton, I. Mewburn, & P. Thompson (Eds.), *The digital academic: Critical perspectives on digital technologies in higher education* (pp. 1–19). London: Routledge.
Merton, R. K. (1942/1973). The normative structure of science. In R. K. Merton & N. W. Storer (Eds.), *The sociology of science: Theoretical and empirical investigations* (pp. 267–278). Chicago, IL: University of Chicago Press.
Mirowski, P. (2013). *Never let a serious crisis go to waste: How neoliberalism survived the financial meltdown*. London: Verso.
Musselin, C. (2008). Towards a sociology of academic work. In A. Alberto & B. Ivan (Eds.), *From governance to identity: A festschrift for Mary Henkel* (pp. 47–56). Dordrecht: Springer.
Olssen, M., & Peters, M. A. (2005). Neoliberalism, higher education and the knowledge economy: From the free market to knowledge capitalism. *Journal of Education Policy*, *20*(3), 313–345.
Osbaldiston, N., Cannizzo, F., & Mauri, C. (2016). 'I love my work but I hate my job'—Early career academic perspective on academic times in Australia. Advance online publication. doi:10.1177/0961463X16682516.
Parkins, W., & Craig, G. (2006). *Slow living*. Oxford: Berg.
Pels, D. (2003). *Unhastening science: Autonomy and reflexivity in the social theory of knowledge*. Liverpool: Liverpool University Press.
Possamai-Inesedy, A., & Nixon, A. (2017). A place to stand: Digital sociology and the Archimedean effect. *Journal of Sociology*, *53*(4), 865–884.
Power, M. (1997). *The audit society: Rituals of verification*. Oxford: Oxford University Press.
Rosa, H. (2013). *Social acceleration: A new theory of modernity*, J. Trejo-Mathys (Ed.). New York, NY: Columbia University Press.
Shils, E. (1984/1997). The academic ethic. In D. Grosby (Ed.), *The calling of education* (pp. 3–128). Chicago, IL: University of Chicago Press.
Slaughter, S., & Rhoades, G. (2004). *Academic capitalism and the new economy: Markets, state, and higher education*. Baltimore, MA: John Hopkins University Press.
Tomlinson, J. (2007). *The culture of speed: The coming of immediacy*. London: Sage.
Vostal, F. (2016). *Accelerating academia: The changing structure of academic time*. Houndmills: Palgrave Macmillan.
Vostal, F., Benda, L., & Vortová, T. (2018). Against reductionism: On the complexity of scientific temporality. *Time and Society*. Advance online publication. doi:10.1177/0961463X17752281.

Ward, S. C. (2012). *Neoliberalism and the global restructuring of knowledge and education*. New York, NY: Routledge.

Weber, M. (1919/1946). Science as a vocation. In H. H. Gerth & C. W. Mills (Eds.), *From Max Weber: Essays in sociology* (pp. 129–156). New York, NY: Oxford University Press.

Wilson, L. (1942/2017). *The academic man: A study in the sociology of a profession*. London: Oxford University Press.

Ylijoki, O.-H. (2005). Academic nostalgia: A narrative approach to academic work. *Human Relations*, *58*(5), 555–576.

Zerubavel, E. (1981/1985). *Hidden rhythms: Schedules and calendars in social life*. Berkeley, CA: University of California Press.

Part I

Academic ethics

Chapter 2

The public good of higher education

John Holmwood

Introduction

In 1963, the President of the University of California and important figure in the development of the California Master Plan for Higher Education (which launched in 1960), Clark Kerr, delivered his Godkin Lecture on 'The uses of the university' (1963/2001). Much re-published and revised, he used the term 'multi-versity' to indicate the changes that higher education had undergone with the rise of the modern research university and the expansion of public higher education. The university had changed from being an institution of elite recruitment and reproduction, concerned with the development of character, to being central to the economy and an instrument of social mobility and democratic inclusion. Higher education, he argued, necessarily had multiple functions, but the increased importance of public funding was likely to entail greater political scrutiny. However, as we shall see, one of the consequences of the increased political significance of higher education has been to subject it to the nostrums of governing political ideologies. In the 'anglosphere', these have been dominated by neoliberalism and the aim to marketise public functions.

I

Historically most universities began as religious or private foundations. The publicly funded university is by no means the most typical of university forms and it is not even the most prestigious. For example, the United States has a history of private foundations alongside 'land grant' universities. The latter represent the first public universities, following the Morrill Act of 1862 that provided a federal endowment of land to establish state universities. But private ivy-league colleges and liberal arts colleges preceded them and continue to be among the most prestigious in the United States. Many of those private colleges were formed from endowments from wealth derived from plantation slavery (Wilder, 2013). The situation was not much different for early public universities. Indeed, the very term, 'land grant' indicates that they were part of a settler-colonial project involving the extension of the United States' border to the west and building up local infrastructure to exploit lands from which native Americans had been dispossessed.

Many state universities founded under the land grant system were segregated institutions that denied entry to African American students; they were part of the 'Jim Crow' arrangements that subverted equality after initial Civil War reconstruction (Du Bois, 1935). Separate institutions for black students were founded around the same time – frequently by religious bodies – and the provisions of the Morrill Act were not extended to black students until 1890, when states that operated segregation were required to provide separate public institutions for black students. Segregated public education in the United States was not ended until Brown versus Board of Education (1954) and the Higher Education Act of 1965, which was implemented alongside other achievements of the Civil Rights Movement, such as the Voting Rights Act of 1965 (itself dismantled in 2013).[1] It is precisely these developments which are regarded as extending social rights and moving towards the democratisation of higher education and which we might also consider as a move towards the decolonisation of higher education, however incomplete (for further discussion, see Holmwood, 2018).

The Higher Education Act of 1965 also extended financial assistance to students as part of President Lyndon Johnson's 'Great Society' programme (Wilder, 2013). The California Master Plan, with its careful setting out of tiers of higher education from the research universities of the University of California, through state colleges delivering undergraduate education (and a smaller research/scholarship role for academic staff) to community colleges providing non-degree and pre-degree education, represented a new approach to higher education. It was a system with low fees and clearly demarcated possibilities for students to move between its different levels. Private universities like Stanford and University of Southern California lay outside the system, but, at its apex, the University of California, Los Angeles and Berkeley provided an equivalent education available on the basis of merit.

At more or less the same time in the United Kingdom, the Robbins Report (1963) proposed an expanded system of public higher education. The racialised character of United Kingdom's universities was much less visible than that of the United States. This was because Empire served to 'externalise' race as an issue of the relation between the metropole and dominions (Shilliam, 2018), whereas racial structures in the United States were necessarily 'internal' structures of domination and exclusion. For example, in the case of the United Kingdom, higher education institutions were exported to the dominions (typically, the Scottish model of higher education was introduced by Scots-descended civil servants) and served the consolidation of Empire, especially in white settler colonies such as Australia, New Zealand, Canada and South Africa. Domestic universities in the United Kingdom also served the education of colonial administrators (Steinmetz, 2014). However, the wider context of the Robbins reforms was the gradual dismantling of Empire and the United Kingdom readying itself to turn its back on a political economy of Commonwealth as a consequence of taking up membership in the European Union, itself a political system founded on amnesia about the colonial heritages of its member states (Bhambra, 2016).

The Robbins Report proposed a system without fees and supported by means-tested grants to meet the living expenses of students. It identified four aims, or public benefits, that warranted a new system of public higher education. These were the public benefit of a skilled and educated workforce (1963, para. 25), the public benefit of higher education in producing cultivated men and women (1963, para. 26), the public benefit of securing the advancement of learning through the combination of teaching and research within institutions (1963, para. 27), and the public benefit of providing a common culture and standards of citizenship (1963, para. 28). In addition, the report stated that, 'courses of higher education should be available for all those who are qualified by ability and attainment to pursue them and who wish to do so' (1963, para. 30).

Both the US and UK systems of public higher education are now experiencing their final moments. By 2012, it was widely acknowledged that the California Master Plan no longer functioned as it was designed. From the start, there had been pressure to increase tuition fees and, as Newfield (2016) argues, this was part of a pattern across the United States which accelerated after the financial crisis of 2008. However, at the same time as spending on higher education was cut (and replaced by tuition fees at an even higher level), so state spending on prisons increased five-fold (Kroll, 2012, October 2). A similar development occurred in the United Kingdom (more properly England, given that education had become a matter of devolved government after the creation of the devolved assemblies in 1998). Public funding of undergraduate degrees in humanities and social sciences was scrapped in 2011 and replaced by fees (together with a system of publicly supported loans). The last vestige of the system of subsistence grants was converted into loans and the Higher Education and Research Act of 2017 marked the final step in a shift to a competitive, market-oriented system of higher education with the creation of a 'level playing field' for the entry of for-profit providers (which, by 2010, had come to represent about 12% of post-secondary enrolments in the United States, but close to 70%, in India, Malaysia and South Korea where the 'interruption' of public higher education had taken place earlier). Indeed, following other accounts of the early introduction of neoliberal policies as part of structural adjustment in non-Western countries, Mamdani (2018) has argued that the African university was an early victim and, in consequence, the movement to decolonise the university is necessarily a movement against fees.

II

How should we understand these developments and their sociological significance? I shall suggest that they represent a shift from higher education being understood as a *social right* to it being seen a *personal responsibility* of individuals and their families and investments in human capital (see Holmwood & Bhambra, 2012).

There is an extensive sociological literature on the idea of social rights beginning with T. H. Marshall's (1950a) important essay on 'Citizenship and social rights'. However, while school education was a central part of his argument of the need to address social obstacles to full participation in liberal democratic rights of civil and political citizenship, higher education was not mentioned. It is not difficult to see why. Higher education is not something that can be made universal in the same way as secondary education and there can be little doubt that it also confers private benefits on those who participate in it, for example in terms of labour market advantages. Since Marshall, there have been few who have applied the argument to higher education. A notable exception was the American sociologist, Talcott Parsons. He developed Marshall's argument in the context of what he called the 'modern citizenship complex' (Parsons, 1971) and extended it to higher education in a book-length study of the American University, written together with Gerald Platt (Parsons & Platt, 1973).

Parsons set out an account of citizenship and membership in what he called the 'societal community'. Civil rights provide the framework of the boundary relations between the societal community and the state in terms of free expression and assembly, while political rights determine participation in the selection of government through the extension of the franchise. Social rights, for their part, address the welfare of citizens, 'treated as a public responsibility' to secure the 'provision of realistic opportunities to make good use of such rights' (Parsons, 1971, p. 21). Social rights seek 'to ensure that adequate minimum standards of "living", health care, and education are available' (1971, p. 22). Parsons goes on to argue that 'it is particularly notable that the spread of education to ever wider circles of the population, as well as an upgrading of the levels of education has been closely connected with the development of the citizenship complex' (Parsons, 1971, p. 22).

On the one hand, Parsons's argument was similar to that of Kerr. Like the latter, he saw the university as having multiple functions although he was more sanguine than Kerr about their mutual consistency and complementarity. The modern 'multi-university', according to Parsons and Platt, is a 'bundle' of functions with the cognitive function of a societal responsibility for the production and reproduction of research and scholarship, the function in dominance. This cognitive function is increasingly important in the transition from industrial to post-industrial society, which is in effect a *knowledge society*. Those who do not attend university nonetheless derive positive benefits from the role of knowledge in the development of employment structures and the adaptive upgrading of all jobs. According to Parsons – and Kerr makes similar arguments – economic growth is increasingly dependent on an effective university system, but economic growth is understood to be inclusive. Indeed, the latter 'truth' was understood to be expressed in the famous Kuznets curve which purported to show declining economic inequality (understood in terms of percentile shares in national income) as modern societies matured (Kuznets, 1953). In effect, Parsons suggests that employment itself comes to be incorporated within the citizenship complex and, in that way, the benefits of higher education are generalised.

Parsons also traces the 'civil', 'political' and 'social' development of organisational forms. This occurs first in terms of orientation to the market, where increased scale introduces distinct occupational roles associated with management. This is initially found in the rise of bureaucratic forms of organisation. However, with the development of the citizenship complex, 'associational' forms of organisation also emerge. These extend throughout the societal community and become increasingly important in the 'fiduciary boards' of large corporations. Parsons identifies employment as a form of membership of a collectivity (beyond a simple contract). Different forms of associative membership both define a modern societal community and interpenetrate with other organisational forms.

What is significant about this account is that Parsons explicitly understands the core structure of the university to be 'associational' (i.e. 'collegial') and uses its mode of organisation to understand wider developments. In other words, if the modern university becomes like a corporation, this is also because, at the same time, the corporation becomes more like a university. In part, Parsons attributes this to the separation of ownership from the functions of management. This latter development assigns to managers a 'political' role in the corporation, reconciling different claims upon it. In this way, management is able to take on the status of a 'profession' similar to the rise of other 'professions'.

The development and transformation of the profession was, for Parsons, one of the key features of associative membership in the modern societal community. Professions enjoy a monopoly of practice in the light of claims for special expertise requiring considerable trust on the part of clients who are not able to judge services provided in terms of a principle of *caveat emptor* that might operate in other contractual relations. This poses a moral hazard, or information asymmetry, where clients may be vulnerable to a self-interested professional's pursuit of profit. However, according to Parsons, professional associations serve to regulate the relations between practitioners and clients and do so both by certifying knowledge and by codes of practice that establish a 'professional ethics' (something he develops from Durkheim). The point is not that the professional person is less driven by self-interested motivations, but that these are constrained by new social structures towards a reconciliation of private and public interest in terms of self-conscious duties and responsibilities.

Once again, this is an argument also set out by Marshall (1950b). In an article first written in 1939, but specifically selected by him for publication alongside his more well-known 'Citizenship and Social Class', he makes the point that the development of rights also requires special occupational groups to deliver them, namely professions. Under the dominance of civil and political rights, the professions are associated with an 'individualist' form of transcendence of self-interest related to pecuniary advantage. This involves,

> the belief that the individual is the true unit of service, because service depends on individual qualities and individual judgement, supported by an individual responsibility which cannot be shifted on to the shoulders of others... it is not concerned with self-interest, but with the welfare of the client.
>
> (1950b, p. 140)

With the development of social rights and services provided directly through public authorities, however, this involves that, 'the professions are being socialized and the social and public services are being professionalized' (1950b, p. 147). With regard to the first aspect, professions are brought to connect the welfare of the individual client with obligations to the wider public. With regard to the second, the professionalisation of services means that they are provided in a manner befitting social rights of citizenship. They are provided as a service to individuals regarded as equal members of the political community, rather than as recipients of charity.

To some extent, then, the development of the professions follows the track of the university itself. Just as the professions once recruited from those with high status backgrounds because they served people of a similar status (an argument that goes back to Adam Smith), so the university was initially associated with the reproduction of elite culture. However, with the development of the 'citizenship complex', as the professions are democratised, so, too, is the university. This is not the democracy that might be claimed by a student movement concerned to disrupt all hierarchies, a movement that was very active when both Kerr and Parsons were writing (and which had led to Kerr's sacking as President of the University of California by Governor Ronald Reagan). According to Parsons and Platt, the student movement was a symptom of changes to the university and not in itself the direct expression of the new meaning of the university for democracy.

This is so not least because the university is responsible for what Parsons calls the 'cognitive complex' and its normative significance within modern societies. While the professions are the 'outward' face of the knowledge society and its demand for specialised expertise, the university is increasingly the guarantor of the knowledge base of that expertise and its development through research. Professional associations continue to regulate practice, but increasingly the knowledge they certify is credentialised through universities and their professional schools (including business schools). At the same time, for Parsons, this means that the 'profession of higher education, and of scholarly research, has also been acquiring greater relative importance' (1971, p. 26), along with the notable fact that the educational revolution has begun to 'transform the whole structure of modern society. Above all, it reduces the relative importance of the two major ideological concerns, the market and bureaucratic organization. The emerging emphasis is on associational organization, especially its collegial form' (1971, p. 98).

Within his general theory of modernity, Parsons placed the United States as its 'lead society' and associates the development of modernity to three constitutive revolutions. These are the 'democratic revolution', the 'industrial revolution' and the 'education revolution'. With regard to the latter, Parsons and Platt write that, 'the modern university, especially in its American version, is the current culmination of the educational revolution. It has become the lead component of an extensive process of change permeating modern society at many levels' (1973, p. 3). The 'autonomy' of the university, then, has a specific meaning within the citizenship complex. Its knowledge is at service to a societal community in which

> the principle of equality has broken through to a new level of pervasiveness and generality. A societal community as *basically* composed of equals seems to be the 'end of the line' in the long process of undermining the legitimacy of ... older, more particularistic ascriptive bases of membership.
>
> (Parsons, 1971, p. 119)

According to Parsons, a university is not the same as a business organisation, although it does have its business side (e.g. it has to generate revenues and make material provision for its activities and this requires a distinctive – functionally specific – type of employee different from the academic). In a similar way, the business organisation has its aspects similar to the university, but with a different ordering under the pursuit of profitability over the long term, while the university is defined by its pursuit of cognitive rationality and its contribution to the realisation of social rights.

III

What is evident is that the situation of universities in the Unites States and the United Kingdom is now radically different from what Kerr and Parsons envisaged. In the United Kingdom much has been written about the importation of business practices and the role of audit measures to evaluate research and teaching. The latter has been justified by the advocates of new public management as a way of providing a transparent accounting of public spending (see Barzelay, 2000; Dunleavy & Hood, 1993). However, from the perspective set out here, these techniques of public governance have not themselves been transformative. What has been transformative has been the direct marketisation of the university. This has also been associated with the widespread decline of 'associative' forms of management in private companies as they have been redirected towards short-term shareholder value (Bartzell, 1989). There has been a marked shift in collegial governance in universities and its replacement by managerial hierarchy. In the United Kingdom, for example, only the Universities of Oxbridge and Cambridge retain collegial governance. In the United States, Ginsberg (2011) has written of the 'fall of the faculty'.

More widely, there has been a neoliberal assault on social rights of citizenship and a corresponding widening of inequality such that economic growth can no longer be represented as inclusive (see OECD, 2015; Piketty, 2014). At the same time, social mobility has declined, with the World Bank (Narayan et al., 2018) reporting that the United States and the United Kingdom offer few opportunities for children from the poorest families to progress and that current generations have worse chances than their parents. In this context, it is not surprising that higher education is no longer a means of social improvement and has returned again to being an instrument of the reproduction of social inequality.

Equally significantly, the demise of social rights has now been brought directly into the university, which in the United States and United Kingdom is now directly subordinated to neoliberal public policies (see Berman, 2012). Parsons and Platt described the modern university as a 'bundle' of functions. It is striking that recent advocates of marketisation (such as the new head of the regulatory Office for Students in England, Sir Michael Barber) refer to the need of its 'unbundling'. In this way different activities can be subjected to market disciplines and, more specifically, competition from for-profit providers (Barber et al., 2013). As Cottom (2017) has argued the latter directly target students from disadvantaged backgrounds – especially those from racialised minorities – as they target the revenue possibilities of student loans and offer cheaper degrees.

Kerr (1963/2001) warned of the way in which increased public funding would make universities more vulnerable to political interference. However, while he anticipated competition from lobbyists on behalf of other good causes for public spending, he did not anticipate a major transformation of the university itself. Newfield (2016) describes how politicians, policy analysts and university leaders in the United States have given up justifying higher education as a public good in favour of its private benefits of investment in human capital and service to the corporate economy. A similar pattern has been evident in the United Kingdom since 2008. Arguments about the public benefits of higher education have been wholly absent from policy documents and no Vice Chancellor has sought to defend universities as a public good. At the same time, academics have been converted into employees, and, all too frequently, precarious at that.

In this context, it is perhaps salutary to revisit arguments from radical sociologies in previous decades that the professions represent a form of monopoly power (see Collins, 1990; Johnson, 1972; Larsson, 1977). While in many cases, these accounts were designed to serve a further democratisation of knowledge production, they have been appropriated by neoliberal policy-makers as a justification of the marketisation of higher education.[2] However, on the earlier analysis, the professions do not represent a self-interest derived from their monopoly of warranted knowledge but a public interest, organised under democratic values of a society of equals. In contrast, under neoliberalism, private interests aggregated through the market have become the definition of the public interest, while claims of public benefits realised through the public funding of higher education are represented as an ideological cover for the sectional interests of faculty (operating as a profession).

The primary self-understanding of knowledge production in the modern university is that it should be produced through dialogue and collegiality, obeying norms of what Habermas (1987) calls communicative rationality. Although the knowledge produced can be marketised through various kinds of application, the point is that it is, at its core, produced in a process unconstrained by the market or direct political power. To the extent that it is so constrained, then its status as public knowledge is reduced to instrumental interests or political authority.

The wider context is the application of neoliberal policies to all public services, including universities themselves. This can be illustrated in the introduction of the 'impact agenda', where all publicly funded research should show a direct benefit for identifiable users. Whereas the logic of the teaching reforms was that *the beneficiary should pay*, the logic of the impact agenda is the opposite. There should be no publicly funded research without a beneficiary, *but the beneficiary should not pay*. It might be argued that the taxpayer is the ultimate beneficiary of economic growth but this would require the latter to be inclusive.[3] Neoliberal public policies, in contrast, as we have seen, are associated with widening inequalities.

The impact agenda, for example, recommends that research should be co-produced with beneficiaries (see Research Councils UK, n.d.). In consequence, it proposes that research should be aligned with the interests of those beneficiaries and modified in order better to realise them. The intention of the impact agenda was to speed up the commercialisation of research, or the time from idea to income. However, it does allow the beneficiaries to be non-commercial. In principle, this suggests that research might also be directed towards democratic ends, even where the democratic functions of universities are demoted. However, this misses the significance of wider changes to the public sphere.

Neoliberal policies have also encouraged public authorities to become commissioners of services rather than direct providers. The providers of public services are increasingly for-profit companies and charities. The latter, for their part, are also recommended to co-provide services together with for-profit companies. For example, academy schools are frequently set up as charities with back-office services provided by for-profit companies and consultancies. In this context, the putative 'public good', or 'social justice', focus of charities becomes attenuated, at just the moment that co-production becomes a requirement of the impact agenda.

This changing nature of civil society is well expressed in a report for the National Coalition for Independent Action (2014, p. 2):

> the force of entering the welfare market, increasingly as bid candy, has had disastrous consequences for voluntary services and their ability to respond to community needs. The capitulation by many in the voluntary sector, including its national and local leadership bodies, to these government agendas has done much damage to the ability of voluntary organisations to work with and represent the interests of individuals and communities under pressure. Privatisation and co-option into the market is driving down the conditions of staff working in voluntary services, diminishing their role in advocacy and jeopardising the safety of people using such services.

In effect, the impact agenda requires academics to align their research with private interests, rather than a general public interest. For the most part academics have acceded to the wider environment that has eroded academic freedom and non-utilitarian claims about the public value of research. For example, the UK Academy of Social Sciences sponsored a Campaign for the Social Sciences which lobbied MPs at the time of the last general election. However, the value of social science it promoted was its benefit to policymakers and commercial organisations seeking to understand different aspects of the public's resistance to their endeavours.[4] It will be recalled that this was an election in which the Conservative Party manifesto committed a Conservative Government to holding a referendum on leaving the European Union, yet there was no mention of social science research facilitating public debate.

In Donald Trump's campaign for the Presidency (and his conduct of office since) and the campaigns for the United Kingdom to leave the European Union, expertise was disparaged as self-interested and social media used to promote fake news, much to the dismay of many commentators, perhaps, especially, academics. Yet, I have suggested that the attachment of expertise to interests has been a gradual process within the academy as neoliberal policies for higher education have been promoted.

The general process of neoliberalism, as well, involves the hollowing out of the public sphere and the replacement of associational relations with the market. Yet it is associational relations of civil society that provide a defence against populism, at the same time the neoliberalism requires populism as its supplement. Thus, Donald Trump promotes corporate interests in the name of populism, while, in the United Kingdom, a hard neoliberal Brexit is promoted in the name of 'taking back control'. The problem at hand is not that of the potentially malign role of social media, but of a broken public sphere, which includes the undermining of the democratic functions of the university.

IV

David Goodhardt (2017) has coined the terms 'somewheres' and 'nowheres' to characterise a new political division between those rooted in place (and nation) and those who represent unrooted elite values. This makes it difficult to understand how a populism grounded in the former can be made to serve corporate interests. However, his distinction echoes an older one put forward by the sociologist Alvin Gouldner (1957), in order to understand the new 'associational' corporation, that of 'cosmopolitans' and 'locals'. The former were those with professional expertise deriving from outside the corporation, while 'locals' were those whose careers depended on the corporation. The latter were integrated with the hierarchy of the corporation and suspicious of the former. In this context, academics are the quintessential 'cosmopolitans', but we are increasingly under pressure to be 'locals' (acting to sustain our corporate 'brand'). As such, our 'professionalism' is increasingly transformed into a form of self-interest expressed through market relations. The new populist 'localism' is one that subverts 'cosmopolitanism'. However, it is not 'elites' that are its target but public values, including those of the university and its functions for democratic publics.

Notes

1 Of course, higher education was also gendered, with women frequently excluded, and associated with the development of education outside the university, as in the 'settlement house' movement in the United States and the United Kingdom. See Deegan (1988). In brief, this exclusion was overcome by the expansion of higher education represented by the Robbins reforms and by the California Master Plan.

2 Collins was ambivalent between the market and social democratic understandings of education, as should be evident in his account of professions in terms of 'market closure'. Fuller (2018, July 19), previously an advocate of social epistemology, has recently endorsed marketisation for its capacity to undermine academic monopolies.

3 In its advocacy for inclusive growth, the OECD, for example, argues that

> Inclusive growth is economic growth that creates opportunity for all segments of the population and distributes the dividends of increased prosperity, both in monetary and non-monetary terms, fairly across society. In many countries, people have not seen their incomes rise for years. The gap between rich and poor has widened, with those at the top capturing the 'lion's share' of growth.

See, OECD Inclusive Growth. No date, no pagination. Available at: http://www.oecd.org/inclusive-growth/

4 See Academy of Social Sciences (2015). Among its statements are, 'Advancing and applying science depends on profits, policies, markets, organisations and attitudes' (from the executive summary); 'The study of public values and attitudes is vital, too, especially when innovation prompts uncertainties and concerns, as with genetically modified crops or shale gas extraction' (p. 6); and 'without a better grasp of people, technological advances may be frustrated, or blocked, and fail to realise their potential' (p. 5).

References

Academy of Social Sciences. (2015). The business of people: The significance of social science over the next decade [Web page]. Retrieved from https://campaignforsocialscience.org.uk/businessofpeople/

Barber, M., Donnelly, K., & Rizvi, S. (2013). *An avalanche is coming: Higher education and the revolution ahead.* London: IPPR. Retrieved from http://www.ippr.org/publications/an-avalanche-is-coming-higher-education-and-therevolution-ahead

Bartzell, Y. (1989). *The economics of property rights.* New York, NY: Cambridge University Press.

Barzelay, M. (2000). *The new public management: Improving research and policy dialogue.* Berkeley, CA: University of California Press.

Berman, E. P. (2012). *Creating the market university: How academic science became an economic engine.* Princeton, NJ: Princeton University Press.

Bhambra, G. K. (2016). Whither Europe? Postcolonial versus neocolonial cosmopolitanism. *Interventions: International Journal of Postcolonial Studies, 18*(2), 187–202.

Collins, R. (1990). Market closure and the conflict theory of the professions. In M. Burrage & R. Torstendahl (Eds.), *Professions in theory and history* (pp. 24–43). London: Sage.

Cottom, T. M. (2017). *Lower ed: The troubling rise of for-profit colleges in the new economy.* New York, NY: New Press.

Deegan, M. J. (1988). *Jane Addams and the men of the Chicago school 1892–1918.* New Brunswick, NJ: Transaction Books.

Du Bois, W. E. B. (1935). *Black reconstruction: An essay toward a history of the part which black folk played in the attempt to reconstruct democracy in America, 1860–1880.* Philadelphia, PA: Albert Saifer Publisher.

Dunleavy, P., & Hood, C. (1993). From old public administration to new public management. *Public Money and Management, 14*(1), 9–16.

Fuller, S. (2018, July 19). Academic monopolies are nothing to be proud of. *Times Higher Education.* Retrieved from https://www.timeshighereducation.com/opinion/academic-monopolies-are-nothing-be-proud

Ginsberg, B. (2011). *The fall of the faculty: The rise of the all-administrative university and why it matters*. New York, NY: Oxford University Press.
Goodhardt, D. (2017). *The road to somewhere: The populist revolt and the future of politics*. London: Hurst and Company.
Gouldner, A. (1957). Cosmopolitans and locals: Toward an analysis of latent social roles. *Administrative Science Quarterly*, *2*(3), 281–306.
Habermas, J. (1987). *The theory of communicative action, volume II: Lifeworld and system*. Cambridge, MA: Polity.
Holmwood, J. (2018). Race and the neo-liberal university: Lessons from the public university. In G. K. Bhambra, D. Gebrial, & K. Nişancioğlu (Eds.), *Decolonising the university* (pp. 37–52). London: Pluto Press.
Holmwood, J., & Bhambra, G. K. (2012). The attack on education as a social right. *South Atlantic Quarterly*, *111*(2), 392–401.
Johnson, T. J. (1972). *Professions and power*. London: Macmillan.
Kerr, C. (1963/2001). *The uses of the university*. Harvard, MA: Harvard University Press.
Kroll, A. (2012, October 2). The slow death of California's higher education. *Mother Jones*. Retrieved from https://www.motherjones.com/politics/2012/10/california-public-university-higher-education/
Kuznets, S. (1953). *Shares of upper income groups in income and savings*. Cambridge, MA: National Bureau of Economic Research.
Larsson, M. S. (1977). *The rise of professionalism*. Berkeley, CA: University of California Press.
Mamdani, M. (2018). The African university. *London Review of Books*, *40*(14). Retrieved from https://www.lrb.co.uk/v40/n14/mahmood-mamdani/the-african-university
Marshall, T. H. (1950a). Citizenship and social class. In T. H. Marshall (Ed.), *Citizenship and social class: And other essays* (pp. 1–85). Cambridge, MA: Cambridge University Press.
Marshall, T. H. (1950b). The recent history of professionalism in relation to social structure and social policy. In T. H. Marshall (Ed.), *Citizenship and social class: And other essays* (pp. 128–155). Cambridge, MA: Cambridge University Press.
Narayan, A., Van der Weide, R., Cojocaru, A., Lakner, C., Redaelli, S., Mahler, D. G., … Thewissen, S. (2018). *Fair progress? Economic mobility across generations around the world*. Washington, DC: World Bank. Retrieved from http://www.worldbank.org/en/topic/poverty/publication/fair-progress-economic-mobility-across-generations-around-the-world
Newfield, C. (2016). *The great mistake: How we wrecked public universities and how we can fix them*. Baltimore, MD: Johns Hopkins University Press.
OECD. (2015). *All on board: Making inclusive growth happen*. Paris: OECD Publishing. Retrieved from http://www.oecd-ilibrary.org/development/all-on-board_9789264218512-en
Parsons, T. (1971). *The system of modern societies*. Englewood Cliffs, NJ: Prentice Hall.
Parsons, T., & Platt, G. M. (1975). *The American university*. Cambridge, MA: Harvard University Press.
Piketty, T. (2014). *Capital in the twenty-first century*. Cambridge, MA: The Belknap Press.

Research Councils UK. (n.d.) Excellence with impact [Webpage]. Retrieved from https://www.ukri.org/innovation/excellence-with-impact/

Robbins Report. (1963). *Higher education: Report of the committee appointed by the prime minister under the chairmanship of Lord Robbins 1961–63* (Cmnd 2154). London: HMSO.

Shilliam, R. (2018). *Race and the undeserving poor: From abolition to Brexit*. London: Agenda Publishing.

Steinmetz, G. (2014). British sociology in the metropole and the colonies, 1940s–1960s. In J. Holmwood & J. Scott (Eds.), *The Palgrave handbook of sociology in Britain* (pp. 302–337). London: Palgrave Macmillan.

Waterhouse, P. (2014). Homes for radical action: The position and role of local umbrella groups [Working paper]. Retrieved from http://www.independentaction.net/wp-content/uploads/sites/8/2014/08/Role-of-local-umbrella-groups-final.pdf

Wilder, C. S. (2013). *Ebony and ivy: Race, slavery, and the troubled history of America's universities*. New York, NY: Bloomsbury Press.

Chapter 3

Beyond the academic ethic

Stephen Turner

Introduction

In the early 1980s, Edward Shils, together with others, undertook the task of defining what he called 'The Academic Ethic' and elaborated these ideas in a report on principles and considerations governing academic appointments at the University of Chicago (1982/1997) and in his Jefferson Lecture on the relation between the University and the State (1979). It is perhaps best to think of this task in terms used by Alasdair MacIntyre in many of his writings, in which he observes that the explicit formulation of an ethical doctrine typically came at the point where it was no longer a matter of general tacit acceptance, but was becoming lost, as when heroic virtue of Agammenon is articulated by Thrasymachus in the non-heroic world of fifth century BC Athens (MacIntyre, 1981, p. 130), or the public virtues of honour of Roman society, which have been rendered obsolete by social disorder, are articulated by the Stoics, in a burst of ethical writings, as private virtues (MacIntyre, 1966, p. 108). Shils's exchanges with his friends and collaborators who commented on the project bear this out: they understood the changes in circumstances that had made what they took to be the traditional academic ethic obsolescent if not obsolete and were formulating it in order to defend it in the face of these changes.

Shils understood science in terms of what might be called 'the liberal theory of science', which treated scientists, and by extension all of academia, as independent agents seeking truth in their own ways, governed by their own sense of what was promising to research, bound together only by their mutual dependence as scholars and teachers and by a strong tradition of truth-seeking and mutual respect. At the time he was writing, the threat could be understood in terms of the problem of the relation of the university to the state, and the conflicts between the intrinsic aims of the university and the temporary aims of the state.

Today we have a new problematic, which is being defined, in an outpouring of writings by academics about the audit or performance culture, as the rule of universities by administrators, and their effects on science and academic life generally. These writings typically also appeal to a vestigial form of the liberal theory of science. Although there are attempts to replace this theory, none of them adequately express the new situation. And like Shils nearly 40 years ago, this is an 'owl of Minerva flying at dusk' moment. The authors recognise that the damage has been done and is irreversible. They protest against it. They are also paralysed by it.

What is the relevance of these 'traditional' academic values today? If the liberal theory of science is dead, what are the reasons, and what are the practical realities that have replaced it? Answering these questions takes us to the heart of problems of the organisation and financing of academic life, the audit culture, and the question of truth itself. It also requires avoiding nostalgia for an imagined past, and gaining a realistic understanding of the past, and of the reasons it cannot be returned to. For those who are happy with the present, and there are many beneficiaries of the current order of academic life who are (despite their complaining about not getting enough of what they want quickly enough), these are non-issues. For those who are not, there should be a way of self-understanding that is an alternative to pure despair.

Understanding the present also requires a deeper understanding not only of the 'traditional' academic past of the mid-twentieth century but also of the status quo ante the world of academia and learning prior to the research university and to the spread of the German model of the late nineteenth century which inspired the research university. This prior, and much older, model still can be detected in a few formal features of academic life, and prowls around, as Weber puts it, like the ghost of dead religious beliefs. It is this prior model, or so I shall claim, that perhaps provides the best answer to the question of what sort of vocation or calling for the life of the mind exists and should exist today.

The liberal theory of science

The academic ethic as Shils described it was a complex of rights and responsibilities that served to define the morality of action within an institutional arrangement. It is perhaps best to begin with the arrangement and what it entailed, and what variations existed. The institutional arrangement was between universities and various other bodies, of which the state was, in European countries, the most important. The model for this arrangement was the German academic system of the late nineteenth century, which became the model for the modern research university. The university professed to be, as Shils put it, 'the methodical discovery and the teaching of truths about serious and important things' (1982/1997, p. 3). Unlike other tasks, however, such as producing food or providing services, this task had no natural connection to a market, nor to a place in a stable economic division of labour. It depended instead on indirect connections, notably to the professions, in which learning made the recipient of this knowledge more valuable for the tasks of that profession, or served as a cultural value that universities could turn into income.

Much of the change with which we will be concerned is quite recent. It was only with what Christopher Jenks and David Reisman described in *The Academic Revolution* (Jencks & Riesman, 1968/1977), the changes of the 1950s and 1960s, that expectations for ordinary academics included a significant, or any, amount of 'research'. The triad of teaching, research and service which is at the core of many evaluation systems in universities derives from the teaching, research and extension triad of the American land grant universities of the nineteenth century. But in its original form, these were largely separate functions: research took place at an experimental farm, often located hundreds of miles from the university; extension was training for farmers that occurred largely where the farmers lived; teaching was done at the university by people who did little or no 'research' of any kind. Colleges and Universities focussed on training. Harvard University, for the first three centuries of its existence, was essentially a training school for congregational ministers, a task it still performs. The ministry was a paradigmatic profession: a calling but also a source of income and a status in an established institution, in this case the church. The same could be said for Cambridge and Oxford, which not only produced for the religious market but had religious tests for entry late in the nineteenth century, and whose presses still rely on revenue from the Bible market. One could multiply examples indefinitely. On the continent, the market relation was to the state – which needed educated administrators. The value of the university was not for its pursuit of truth, but for its ability to provide some sort of educational experience and some sort of certification which the market, in the Harvard case the congregations hiring the minster, valued. To be sure, there was a small minority of students who valued knowledge for its own sake and were able and willing to pay for instruction. But this small minority would never be large or rich enough to support a university, and there were never enough academic jobs for them to constitute an academic class of the scale of present academia.

The relationship with the professions produced a particular kind of university which persisted and grew over a millennia, with typical groupings of 'faculties' associated with the professions, and some sort of core liberal arts faculty which provided instruction that was considered to be more elementary and general. Until the nineteenth century these faculties were more concerned with the transmission of dogma than 'discovery' and were often strikingly retrograde in relation to the knowledge available outside the university. The logic of exclusion was central to the traditional university: it was a means of certifying that those trained within it conformed to the accepted truths. This fits with the demands of certification, and exclusion helped make the certification valuable.

It is important to understand how the university and academia related to intellectual life at large. Universities were places where people were learned, and went through various tests to show they were learned. A dissertation in the sixteenth century was a recapitulation of the professor's notes – the real test was the *viva,* in which the candidate demonstrated an ability to defend these views on his feet. In Britain, college fellowships were awarded based on exams, not production – and production was largely optional and in many cases non-existent, well into the postwar era. At the same time, there was a lively non-academic world of learning, and also of production – indeed, this is where the ideas normally emerged. This dual world was somewhat permeable until what William James called 'the Ph.D octopus' (1903) strangled the university – as evidenced by the career of James himself. But until the academic revolution, which occurred over a long period, led by the 'research universities', the qualifications of a professor were learning, not production. And one can see this even in the institutions of the German university, where the *Habilitationsschrift* must be in a different specialty than the PhD dissertation, and where there was originally no expectation that professors produce beyond this demonstration of learning.

This system began to break down in the nineteenth century with the emergence of chemistry as a valuable form of knowledge not directly linked to a profession. The transformative figure is the chemist Justus Leibig, whose chemical discoveries launched an international business in agricultural products, attracted students from all over the world and made him into a business magnate as well as a professor with a large and lively laboratory. This was knowledge that was valuable for a market other than the professions, and although its value was in a sense indirect as well, the users applied the knowledge and used the products themselves. The process of discovery could be tailored to the needs of the agricultural market. A new model was born. Liebig was not obliged to produce 'impact' or monetise his research, but he did. Chemistry research itself became valuable, and science generally became valuable, whether or not there were practical applications. It was enough that sometimes something came out of it, or that training in science benefitted someone. Soon enough it did, with applications of chemical knowledge to medical issues.

It was not until the late nineteenth century that a new model emerged based on the granting of PhDs and the creation of the modern set of disciplines. In the United States the origins of the modern category of research universities dates from 1915. The list has barely changed since then. But these universities were still primarily teaching institutions, with heavy teaching loads, and a scattering of productive 'research' faculty most of whose 'research' consisted of cataloguing existing knowledge in textbooks. Pressure to publish was very limited. The choice to write was largely voluntary. Peer-review was not burdensome. Book publishing outside of the textbook market was difficult, usually subsidised, and relatively rare, and there were few journals.

Decisions to publish were typically made by editors, without advice. These were the conditions under which the following was true:

> In the traditional university, professors were "unaccountable." The university was a sacred space where they were at liberty to pursue with students and colleagues their fields of inquiry without coercion or interference. This doesn't mean they were free without qualification, of course. Professors were deeply accountable, but in a sense that went far beyond the reach, ambition, and perhaps even the interests of the administrative caste — they were accountable to discover and then to tell the truth, and to encourage their students to do the same.
>
> (Srigley, 2018, February 22, n.p.)

This passage was taken from one of the many responses to the new regime of administrative control of the university through metrics and 'goals'. It reiterates ideas that Shils also expresses. And it is a source of confusion because much of the same language is used ideologically to describe the more recent past, the period after the academic revolution. This period was not free of coercion, but the coercion took a particular form.

Professionalisation

What changed? In a word, professionalisation. The description on the back of Jencks and Reisman's (1968/1977) book describes its message as follows:

> academic professionalism is an advance over amateur gentility, but they warn of its dangers and limitations: the elitism and arrogance implicit in meritocracy, the myopia that derives from a strictly academic view of human experience and understanding, the complacency that comes from making technical competence an end rather than a means.

Philosophers went from modestly saying, accurately, that they 'taught philosophy' to saying they were 'philosophers' or even 'professional philosophers' to distinguish them from other things that go by the name of philosophy. In sociology, the name of the American Sociological Society was changed to the acronymically less anatomical American Sociological Association to reflect the new status of 'profession'. Political sciences became 'scientific', with the behaviouralist revolution, whose leaders are now mercifully forgotten. The term 'scholar' was consistent with knowing and expounding, and with the value of learning as an end in itself: the term 'profession' implied not merely 'professing' but possessing a specific set of skills and body of knowledge that was in some sense exclusive – unlike the mere learning of the amateur.

Why did it change? The story varies from country to country and field to field, but much of it had to do with the rapid expansion of universities in the two decades after the Second World War. In much of Europe this meant the transformation of universities from sleepy places with scholars who pursued their own arcane interests to places brimming with students. In the United States something similar happened. In both cases a new model of the academic career emerged, which was less individualistic and more tied to the idea of a discipline of judging and evaluating peers. In science, there was a different process, more closely related to funding, which eventually came to affect the rest of the academy.

The point of professions is to exclude and gain benefits from excluding. And the transition to professionalisation was marked by a kind of punitiveness towards not only amateurs but also deviants, people who failed to get with the new programme and so forth. Andrew Abbott discusses the reign of Peter Blau and Peter Rossi at the *American Journal of Sociology* in the 1950s, before the transition to the later dependence on peer-review (Abbott, 1999, pp. 140–148). Decisions were not arbitrary, but depended on conformity to the standards that they self-confidently set. There was a strong, and strongly self-justifying, sense of professional standards that just happened to be their standards, and included themselves and their friends and excluded the scholars of the past, as well as most of the 'profession' of which they were a part. Something similar happened in all the fields of the humanities and social sciences.

In a sense the Old Boys' network which the revolutionaries overthrew became more insidious than before. In the older system, it was taken for granted that appointments were culturally coded, and that merit was secondary. But because academic life itself was less oppressive, the system was less oppressive. No one could reasonably hope to be an Ivy-League professor who could not act the part; but there were other places they would fit in without being excluded from scholarship. The combination of the Old Boys' network and disciplinarisation relegated those outside the network to humiliation as well as exclusion, all in the name of professionalisation.[1]

At the time of the professionalisation of humanities and social science disciplines there was consciousness of the change and laments about it. These typically came in the form of criticism of the flight from teaching that this system allowed in elite universities and the declining status of teaching. Jacques Barzun was a typical but highly visible example (Champion, 2018). The flight from teaching was of course hierarchical: it was a feature of elite institutions that only slowly spread to their imitators, and rich institutions mitigated the change by continuing to provide a more traditional 'liberal arts' education to its younger students, though over time the number of people not caught up in professionalisation who could do this in the old way dwindled. So, the flight from teaching reinforced hierarchy and intensified the pressure to conform to the new idea of 'professional'. Competition also affected salaries. For the first time academics who were considered disciplinary leaders or celebrities received enormous salaries: one chair of political science was rumoured to be making $100,000 in the mid-1970s, a salary equivalent to more than $600,000 today. The era of celebrity academics had arrived, though now they needed only to be disciplinary celebrities, who were only read by other academics. The political scientist who cashed in on this status at the University of Chicago, David Easton, was not at all a public intellectual, nor did he even write about politics in a way that was remotely relevant to actual politics, despite working in the heart of the south side of Chicago, home of one of the most corrupt and powerful political systems in the country.

Professionalisation as a power system

With the rise of professionalisation or disciplinary control there became a sharp sense among many scholars that the demands of disciplinary competition were inimical to genuine scholarship, to thought and to the examination of serious questions – even the serious questions of the disciplines themselves. The criticisms made by Barzun with regard to the decline of teaching were interlaced with comments on the triviality of much of what came to pass as 'professional research' as well as its subordination to political agendas (Champion, 2018). Professionalism put paid to the standard of 'serious things' by erecting a new standard: acceptability in the academic labour market. If a graduate student, or tenure-seeking junior colleague comes to you with a serious and deep project, one is compelled to advise him or her that in order to be employed one must produce, that a modest but doable project would be better, and that one should take care to check the journals to see what is fashionable in the area of this project and therefore needs to be cited and if need be praised – this is the standard of the peers to which disciplinarisation makes the hopeful student subject. At the beginning of the project of professionalisation, when the professionalisers themselves were trained in the older fashion, the gap between the two standards was not terribly obvious. The flush job market of the 1960s following the expansion of the universities and the students of the baby-boom allowed for a freedom that was unprecedented and never to be repeated. When the contraction occurred – in the early 1970s in the United States – not only did disciplinary standards become more coercive, a new set of ascriptive criteria was imposed on hiring.

The history of disciplinarisation has been written many times, for many disciplines, but for what follows a brief summary is useful in order to understand what followed the failure of these projects. At the time of the formation of these disciplines, science had already taken a more or less modern disciplinary form, and by virtue of its practical applications, especially in chemistry, had established a 'professional' identity apart from the academy. In the United States, and at roughly the same time in other countries – the United Kingdom preserved amateurism longer, and preserved a kind of museum of academic eccentrics at Cambridge and Oxford immune from outside influences. Ironically, this last group was the source of many of the professionalising ideas in the humanities (cf. for philosophy, Searle, 2015). The first wave of professionalisation in the United States was at the time of the formation of disciplines, roughly 1890–1905. This was followed in the 1920s by a series of 'news': the new history, the new political science, and by large changes in related disciplines, as well as the humanities. This generation asked variations of the question Robert Merriam, *consigliere* of the Rockefeller philanthropies and proponent of the new political science, asked about political theory: 'will our older friends have to go?' For the time being political theory, which was included in the field as part of the original construction of the discipline, survived. Similarly, for the other fields – pockets of less professionalised scholarship persisted, though often in a lower status.

The postwar period saw a reinvention of the impulse to scientise, which treated the previous attempt as a failure. 'Behavioural science', and its hallmarks of quantification, attitude studies and a different set of statistical techniques, taken mostly from social psychology, dominated this effort. Previously, social science statistics had required a staff with rows of calculators to produce correlations, so quantification at this level was rare; now a set of tables and Chi-square tests of significance sufficed. With computerisation this changed again, and new methods requiring more number-crunching power were used, and the older kind of correlational analysis returned because it no longer required the human labour of the past. This movement was a 'success' in academic terms, inasmuch as it attracted foundation funding, and then government funding, and quickly came to dominate the labour market in the relevant fields. There was a self-conscious sense of ridding these fields of 'intellectuals'. As W. F. Ogburn put it,

> There are a number of criteria which have been considered of high value in the past which I think should be of decreasing value in the future. If we agree that the goal of sociology is too scientific I would not pay too much attention to scholarship as such in the Department of Sociology. Obviously in the humanities its place is at the top. I would be inclined to subdue interest in social philosophy though of course it has a place somewhere in the university curriculum. My guess is that the role of theory as formerly held is due for some deflation. Scientific theory is of course not. The old time conception of theory is really something of a grand synthesis or system of ideas, none of which are ever set up in the form that can be demonstrated scientifically. Theory in both sociology and economics has largely been a system of ideas.
>
> (Ogburn, ca. 1953)

The subsequent history of this department and the rest of academic social science proved to be the realisation of this ideal – scholarship was out, and 'science' was in. And the conflict between the two was evident: scholarship belonged somewhere, but somewhere else.

These newly configured fields recruited students with intellectual or broadly 'political' and reformist interests and turned them, with a certain amount of bullying, into professionals. The original flame of intellectual interest did not completely die out among the students, but there was no question of who had the status and power in these fields. And there was no return to the past: this generation of postwar scientisers obliterated the older kind of scholarship by ignoring it. Even the canonical classics were reduced to snippets, as was done by the Columbia sociology department, which taught them by providing sheets of out-of-context paragraphs that were selected because they related to the new vision of the field. Something similar happened in field after field: in philosophy the great thinkers of the past were reduced to simplified argument forms, and those forms were what was taught.

The younger generation rebelled against this new order. They installed Pitirim Sorokin as the President of the ASA, and Hans J. Morgenthau as president of the APSA, in defiance of their elders. And they read and identified with C. Wright Mills's *The Sociological Imagination* (1959), a book that has still not lost its power. But this was not a success story; it was a tragedy. As Edward Shils pointed out in a brutal review of the book in *World Politics* (1961), there was no intellectually realisable programme there but instead a reversion to historicism and an endorsement of works of 'a degree of pompous vagueness which', Shils says, were reminiscent 'of the windy formalities of the University of Frankfurt before Hitler closed down German sociology in 1933' (1961, p. 613). Shils was an idiosyncratic product of the 1930s, an amateur sociologist who never received a degree in the subject, an admirer of European intellectuals, and initially an enthusiast for the post-war professionalisation of sociology, an enthusiasm that soon waned. In this review he acknowledges and agrees with much of Mills's critique of the sociology of the time. But both the review and the book are better understood as a lament for academic values that were already fading into irrelevance.

The 1960s was thus a decade of institutional triumph for the professionalisers, and of creeping intellectual failure. The students they attracted and kept, once it became clear that the projects had failed, were either careerists who believed in the project only to the extent that it advanced their careers or were intellectually and politically inclined against the project and openly hostile to it. Thus it came to pass that the generation of 1968, clever and energetic, found themselves in the 1970s and 1980s with a collapsed job market and a collapsed and dying programme of professionalisation. This core fact extended to the whole of the humanities and social sciences with the exception of economics and perhaps linguistics. The emergence of post-modernism was not the cause of the failure of all of these professionalising programmes but a symptom and a restatement in flowery language of the obvious: that the programmes had fractured into pieces that no longer fit together nor made sense apart from the larger failed programme that had originally generated them. There was going to be no 'science of society', or of politics or culture, nor were any of the systematising projects of philosophy going to be any more than academic games.[2] The post-modernists were assigned the blame for this failure. But to quote Cavafy, 'Those people were a kind of solution' (1904/1992).

Degenerate professionalisation

While this drama was playing out, the institutional ground was shifting. By looking at Shils's strictures written during this period, we can get a better sense of what the new compulsions of the academic world would be. Shils was attempting to show how much of what was emerging in his own time conflicted with the pre-professional academic ethic of the past, which he nevertheless professed to discern continuing in the professionalised practices of his own time. And the comparison can give us a way of inferring the significance of the changes for the question of what sort of 'vocation for science', to use Weber's phrase of a century ago, is possible today. The ethic described by Shils pointed even farther back, to the period before professionalisation – before what William James called 'the PhD octopus' (1903) – and before Shils's ideal of 'distinguished contributions', to a period in which learning itself was a value. The mark of this change, for me, is exemplified by the story of the candidate for a position in Trinity College Dublin, who sent in a package of reprints. One of the members of the committee on appointments responded by commenting 'bloody pamphleteer'. The pamphleteers ultimately won.

To understand this change, and its effects, it is necessary to address some painful issues. The key issue is this: science professionalised successfully, though not without its own issues of overproduction and waste. But the standards of science and the standards and reality of non-science fields differ dramatically. The use of science standards for non-science fields is an inevitable consequence of the need to balance the claims of each. But because science is the tail that wags the dog of the university, and also the source of its main claims to public utility, science sets the standards for everyone. These standards are, however, impossible for the humanities and social sciences to meet. The money is not there for large grants, there are no patents or marketable technologies, or very few. And we come to a basic fact. The project of professionalisation in the humanities and social sciences failed, and the analogous project in the sciences succeeded. In both cases the effects on traditional academic values were devastating.

The intellectual side of this failure in the social sciences and philosophy is a familiar story. Both were influenced by Logical Positivism, which promised to make each of them into sciences or something like science. In each field, the project ran into trouble, then critics, then to the collapse of the very idea. This is traditionally ascribed to post-modernism and Kuhn (1962/2012), and both placed a mark on what followed and constitutes the present situation, but post-modernism was less a cause than a symptom: the corpse of the professionalisation project was already rotting. Within Logical Positivism there had already been a debate that had surfaced fatal criticisms. The Kuhnian alternative provided a way of thinking of science that avoided these criticisms. In the postwar era the scientisation of the social sciences had been significant as a way of getting rid of traditionally minded scholars: the motto of Whitehead quoted by Merton at the time was 'a science that hesitates to forget its founders is lost' (Merton, 1957/1968, p. 38).

But the positive project of making social science into science was a disaster. The 'laws' and confirmed theories that were supposed to be the hallmark of science never appeared, and the statistical methods that were supposed to underpin this science produced many 'results' and an empowered class of researchers, but nothing like science. In science itself there was also a failure: the Unity of Science movement, which provided an intellectually serious goal for science and a model of science as a project, disappeared as science itself professionalised into separate domains.

The consequences of this for the present are simple enough. Science is no longer a possible model for the humanities and social sciences. The truths of professionalised science are not the all-embracing ones posited by the unity of science movement, but truths that are patentable, impactful, and usable for regulation or policy decision-making, and objective in a practical, technological sense rather than a transcendental sense. This is a model that is not available to social science or the humanities, except perhaps in areas like demography, economics, machine cognition and so on. But without this model of truth the humanities and social sciences, organised as professions but incapable of being professions in the originally intended sense, nevertheless are faced with the basic realities of intellectual life. About this we need to be clear: the basic fact of intellectual life is that it does not pay for itself. All knowledge regimes, of which professionalism is only one, need for there to be a source of income and support that derives from something other than the intellectual work itself. The academic regime in science derives this support from grants and teaching. In the humanities and social sciences it derives from teaching, and for a few highly exceptional people – public celebrities – from lecture fees and writing for the public, or writing widely used textbooks. Professionalisation was a way of marketing teaching in which the students did not become merely learned, but mini-professionals in their field.

The love of learning in a time of academic cholera

The system that emerged from the failure of professionalisation is brutally hierarchical. The division of labour stretches the notion of teacher-scholar to the limits. In the 1980s Shils could still write, speaking to the University of Chicago, that 'There should be no appointment in which the appointed person is expected to spend most of his time on classroom teaching' (Shils, 1997, p. 144). This is of course the fate of most 'professors' in the United States. Those who have time assigned to 'research' are members of a bizarre kind of aristocracy, and the inequality is increasing. Currently in the United States, nearly half of all college-level teaching is done by 'adjunct' faculty who do nothing for their pay but teach, and there is a growing number of 'lectureship' appointments that amount to adjunct positions added together, and allow for little or no advancement and miniscule pay.

For the people on the bottom, the relentless demand for teaching of the pre-professional period has changed only by the introduction of ever more scrutiny, in such forms as student evaluations, and the casualisation of this labour and the attendant impoverishment and insecurity. In the older world of impoverished academia before the First World War, professors at least had to be paid enough to be kept alive. In the new world of adjuncts and oversupply, they did not: teachers who had worked for decades for small amounts of pay could be and were casually dismissed, and the pay is often below subsistence levels. This class of academic proletarians enabled institutions to compete with one another in research by off-loading the work of teaching so that research could thrive. But this system did not benefit the humanities and social sciences, except marginally. The money went to the natural sciences and to supporting its research.

Yet there is a certain similarity between the teachers of the pre-professional order and present adjuncts, if one ignores the basic features of their existence – the boredom of teaching elementary classes repetitively, the large classes, the need to police unmotivated students and so forth. These adjuncts are free from the constraints of the professional system and can join movements against it – such as the movement against professional philosophy. Having no status and nothing to lose, they can choose to live the life of the mind as they please, to be learned without producing, and pursue projects if they wish, or decline to do so. They are also free in their intellectual life from the limits of disciplines and can read what they want. People without families to support can even enjoy this freedom, despite the lack of status and the poverty, if they can survive. All that is needed for a certain kind of happiness is to give up the hope of a tenured academic position.

The situation in science is only slightly better since a PhD scientist normally has skills that can be put to use elsewhere. The normal career in academic science is, however, just as marginal: if a person is lucky enough to get into the academic system at all, it will be in the form of a succession of poorly paid post-docs in which one performs routine laboratory tasks as part of someone else's research. The opportunities for tenure-track jobs are scarce, the competition is highly internationalised and fierce, and the level of desperation is high.

Academic life is selective, and the grounds for advancement at each stage are not clear, except for degree requirements, and depending on the system and the point in history, many are called who are not chosen. So the question of what sort of calling academic life has become is also a question about the calling of those who fall by the wayside. This has recently become a hot topic as a result of an op-ed by an historian who was giving up on academia, after having failed, despite some short term contracts, to gain a tenure-track job. She writes that

> Giving up on something that you thought was your life's calling hurts like hell. When you experience rejection from the entire institution of academia after devoting years of your life and thousands of dollars to become an academic, betrayal and rage sometimes become your only emotions for a good long while.
>
> (Munro, 2017, May 14, n.p.)

This comment has gone viral, and there are dozens of sites devoted to 'leaving academia'. They tell a bitter story about the myth of academic life and its seductions. One website describes its orientation as reflecting 'a belief that the current system is flawed, cruel, unsustainable and therefore impossible to directly engage with'. As a commentator explains, 'In this view, Ph.D. programs, with their false promises, lure students to serve as cheap labour, first as teaching assistants, then as poorly paid adjuncts when tenure-track jobs elude them' (Tuhus-Dubrow, 2013, November 1, p. 32). Many of the comments and contributions reflect the fact that the education that the injured academics have received is highly specialised – to leave academia is to face the impossible task of repackaging their achievements as marketable skills.

We can ask what relation this sense of 'calling' has to the academic ethic described by Shils. Are these cries of pain merely laments for a lost opportunity to pursue a career and to acquire the glittering prizes of the academic aristocracy? Certainly it is a part of current academic experience that students with high hopes gradually realise that the system is not based on merit, and suspect that they lack the qualities to succeed in it. And while these victims of the system realise that the promises were false, and that the system is cruel, the cruellest consequence is that the model of the 'professional' discipline in which they were trained gained them little beyond an introduction to the life of the mind that was limited and flawed.

The tragedy

The generation of which Shils was a junior member, born around the turn of the century, was a particularly extraordinary one, academically. Their prominence was perhaps enhanced by the accident of the rise of Hitler and the great German emigration. This posed challenges to academic establishments across the West and infused local intellectual traditions with new ideas. They were flexible and had to be. Many of them changed fields, changed orientations, and all of them had to adapt to succeed. But this was also the generation that constructed the post-war disciplinary world, without having been trained under it. They produced students who were different from them, responded to different career contingencies and a different academic labour market.

In a sense, it is the world of this younger generation, the one that started academic life in the middle of the century under a newly stabilised scheme of disciplines that Shils is describing in his writings on the academic ethic. They are the generation that both accepted and enforced the disciplinary order. Their legacy was a rigid disciplinary hierarchy, a narrow definition of professional and a form of training for students that was itself narrow, focussed on the job market and the academic hierarchy, and the demands of peer-review in the journal system. There was resistance, but the resistance was futile. Their legacy was intellectual failure. But the disciplines and institutional structures they created were a straitjacket that was impossible for subsequent generations to remove.

The logic of disciplinarisation had a dynamic that went beyond the aims of its creators – markets constrained teaching, competition constrained hiring, peer-review constrained publication, all with the result of the creation of a new kind of winner. The expansion and enrichment of the universities, and the democratisation of entry, made the jobs of the winners especially desirable. The market rewarded a certain kind of cleverness and the peer-review system rewarded conformity. The winners were, accordingly, clever and conformist, though they would deny this, and point to their minor technical achievements as evidence of their innovative thinking. Nor could they be challenged within the system, which was increasingly unequal. The system of disciplinary enforcement that had been imposed as a personal mission by the generation of the mid-twentieth century now was a machine that simply perpetuated itself – an enforcement mechanism that did its enforcing impersonally and therefore apparently objectively and without authoritarianism.

It was, however, a machine that had no direction. It disciplined without a common intellectual purpose – Shils's sense of 'serious and important things'. And it was soon metricised in ways that entrenched the winners and whatever made them winners. Education became, tacitly, education to succeed in the system. Peer-review became predictable as an affirmation of the hierarchy. Merit was no longer a matter of debate, but a matter of counting. What counted varied, but the importance of the top journals remained and was confirmed by such things as impact factors.

The system that remained was thus long on discipline, long on constraint, but short on intelligible purpose. The scientising generation of the mid-twentieth century at least had that, and it was a purpose that could be and was subject to withering critique. But the system that replaced it had no purpose. And, ironically, it was therefore vulnerable to ideological capture.

For Shils, the point of the academic ethic was that it was an integral part of an institutional order that successfully produced truth. Today his notion of truth and of serious and important things would be challenged by critics who would argue that it excluded the interests and experiences of women, oppressed races, the victims of colonialism, the global south and so on. Some Critical Race theorists deny any supra-individual notions of truth; all of them oppose 'merit', which they dismiss as a magical concept, denying that test scores, elite credentials and so forth have any intrinsic connection to anything called merit (Crenshaw, 2011, p. 1228). For them, and for many others, appeals to merit, or to older notions of what is serious and important, are taken as an ideological front for white male supremacy. The institutional order has also changed, to one driven almost entirely by metricised standards of quality, together with calculated administrative responses to public issues. These were outcomes Shils would have considered abhorrent. But they raise the question of what can an individual do today in the face of these changes in order to recapture some remnant of the academic ethic? Or whether it is simply no longer relevant, or whether the institution itself is fatally flawed.

Learning as a value

In addressing this bundle of questions I will make no gesture in the direction of institutional reform. I will also ignore the case of the celebrity scholar who has been able to transcend the limitations of the peer-review system by virtue of high academic status or membership in a high-status clique. The dominance, not to say destruction, of the university by the implementation of the professional model and the metricisation and politicisation of merit is for the foreseeable future irreversible. The social sciences and humanities have in any case shrunk to insignificance in the contemporary university and are under constant assault by the well-funded partisans of STEM. They can at best adapt to survive. As they decline, the distortions will become more rather than less extreme. But there remains the question of what the individual can, or should, do in the face of this institutional situation. Even the most relentless institutional order provides for opportunities to resist or escape. My concern will be to identify, if possible, the remnant of the academic ethic that is worth saving, that is accessible to the intelligent and intellectually inclined person, and to ask how it can be realised in the present.

What is worth saving? The academic ethic was preceded by and depended on a different, pre-professional ideal. We can call this the ideal of learning and the personal goal of being a learned person – which in earlier times was also a socially respected status.

This was a status with social support and recognition. Professors in the pre-professional era were learned persons, primarily, specialists secondarily, if at all. They embodied the ideals of what is now called slow academia and craftsmanship – these were the norms of academic production at the time. But they were never the only learned persons – unlike 'professionals' this was not a status based on exclusion. Moreover, there was a vast body of intelligent and interested readers, without specialised academic training, who read 'Great Books'; participated in reading groups and programmes; bought the *Encyclopædia Britannica* and the *Encyclopædia Americana* (which had contributors like Weber and Robertson Smith) and other imitators; proudly displayed, and even read, the Harvard Five Foot Shelf; and did not think of the university as having a monopoly on either knowledge or wisdom. Indeed, Charles Eliot, the president of Harvard, gave a speech to an audience of working men in which he declared that a five-foot shelf of books could provide 'a good substitute for a liberal education in youth to anyone who would read them with devotion, even if he could spare but fifteen minutes a day for reading'.

When Shils speaks of serious and important things, he is using the language of the pre-professional learned person. And it was this language, and these goals, that professionalisation supplanted. But for at least some of those seduced or bullied into professionalisation, some version of this older ideal still remained salient. And sometimes, for those who soured on the professional model, it was turned against the professional ideal. In philosophy, for example, there is an active movement *against* professional philosophy (http://againstprofphil.org/), and there are efforts to preserve a connection with philosophy among the academically dispossessed – people who have gone on to make their living outside academia. So there is something alive in the idea of learning, despite the hegemony of 'professionalism' in academia and the hegemony of the university over intellectual life.

Becoming learned is a goal open to everyone. It is not hierarchical – one can learn from anyone, whether they are discoverers or just learned people, or people who simply know things you do not. To be learned is not to be an expert on a canon, even a liberal arts canon. It is not to be a specialist: to be learned is to be able to integrate different kinds of knowledge. To be sure, being learned was a status that had an association with snobbery, but this association was largely a product of academia and *its* snobbery and exclusions, not something intrinsic to learning. People are learned, and if there is hierarchy, it is a hierarchy that is personal: the Harvard Five Foot Shelf, despite its limitations, was nevertheless a vast collection of ideas and perspectives, which inclined the mind to tolerance and difference, rather than dogma. And one might add that the kinds of readers that the 'shelf' attracted were themselves eager to learn beyond the shelf. One might cite the Tagore craze, the fascination with Indian religions that followed from the Columbian Exposition, the vogue of Zen Buddhism and the mid-twentieth century obsession with East-West relations, including such figures as Nobelist and best seller Pearl Buck. On a more elevated level, F. C. S. Northrop's 1946 book, *The Meeting of East and West,* has been continuously popular and in print ever since. This, not learning as some sort of covert ideology, is what has been lost in the present university.

With this we come to questions of value. To re-establish learning as a value is as difficult as any other reform of values. It needs social support, institutional acknowledgement and opportunities that correspond to it. The professionalisation of the humanities and social sciences undermined all three. But the much discussed 'crisis of the humanities', and the crisis that should afflict the social sciences as a result of such things as the replication and p-hacking crisis and the internal critique by John P. A. Ioannidis of the statistical practices that the social sciences rely on, may present an opportunity for reconsidering the professional model itself (2005). We will not pry the winners away from it. But for those outside the charmed circle, this is an opportunity we need to take. The distortions of the present system, and what Gloria Origgi correctly describes as our 'voluntary epistemic servitude' to it, are obvious (Origgi, 2015, p. 216). The institutional alternatives are not obvious. But learning is a value that is moribund but not dead. And if we value it we have a basis for resisting the professional machine, and perhaps for something more.

Notes

1 There is a fascinating book on the much loved sociologist *Austin Porterfield, A Man's Grasp Should Exceed His Reach: A Biography of Sociologist Austin Larimore Porterfield*, by Leonard Cain (2005), which describes the way in which Porterfield created a journal of medical sociology and importuned leading figures, such as Merton, to support it, only to be condescended to and humiliated, and eventually to have the project expropriated.

2 Richard Rorty chronicles the collapse of the project of analytic philosophy in the two retrospective essays in the reprints of *The Linguistic Turn* (1967/1992). Professionalised philosophy of course continued as a Zombie discipline despite the loss of purpose, as did the other professionalised disciplines of the humanities and social sciences.

References

Abbott, A. (1999). *Department and discipline: Chicago sociology at one hundred.* Chicago, IL: University of Chicago Press.

Cain, L. (2005). *A man's grasp should exceed his reach: A biography of sociologist Austin Larimore Porterfield.* Lanham, MD: Rowman & Littlefield.

Cavafy, C. P. (1904/1992). Waiting for the Barbarians. In G. Savidis (Ed.), *C.P. Cavafy: Collected poems,* trans. E. Keeley and P. Sherrard. Princeton, NJ: Princeton University Press. Retrieved from https://www.poetryfoundation.org/poems/51294/waiting-for-the-barbarians

Champion, R. (2018). Jacques Barzun and the classical liberal agenda. Manuscript submitted for publication.

Crenshaw, K. W. (2011). Twenty years of critical race theory: Looking back to move forward. *Connecticut Law Review, 43*(5), 1253–1352.

Ioannidis, J. P. A. (2005). Why most published research findings are false. *PLoS Med*, *2*(8), e124. doi:10.1371/journal.pmed.0020124

James, W. (1903). The Ph.D. octopus. *Harvard Monthly*, *36*(March), 1–9. Retrieved from https://en.wikisource.org/wiki/The_Ph.D._Octopus

Jencks, C., & Riesman, D. (1968/1977). *The academic revolution*. Chicago, IL: University of Chicago Press.

Kuhn, T. (1962/2012). *The structure of scientific revolutions*. Chicago, IL: University of Chicago Press.

MacIntyre, A. (1966). *A short history of ethics: A history of moral philosophy from the Homeric age to twentieth century*. New York, NY: Macmillan.

MacIntyre, A. (1981). *After virtue: A study in moral theory*. Notre Dame, IN: University of Notre Dame Press.

Merton, R. K. (1957/1968). *Social theory and social structure* (enlarged ed.). New York, NY: Free Press.

Mills, C. W. (1959). *The sociological imagination*. Oxford: Oxford University Press.

Munro, L. (2017, May 14). Leaving academia: Loss, grief, and healing [blog post]. Retrieved from http://www.lisamunro.net/blog-1/2017/5/14/leaving-academia-loss-grief-and-healing

Northrop, F. S. C. (1946). *Meeting of East and West: An inquiry concerning world understanding*. New York, NY: Macmillan. Retrieved from https://archive.org/details/in.ernet.dli.2015.184650

Ogburn, W. F. (ca. 1953). Some criteria for appointment to the Department of Sociology University of Chicago. Philip W. Hauser papers. (Box 14, Folder 11, Department of Special Collections). The Joseph Regenstein Library, The University of Chicago.

Origgi, G. (2015). *Reputation what it is and why it matters*. S. Holmes & N. Arikha (Trans.). Princeton, NJ: Princeton University Press.

Rorty, R. (1967/1992). *The linguistic turn*. Chicago, IL: University of Chicago Press.

Searle, J. (2015). Oxford philosophy in the 1950s. *Philosophy*, *90*(2), 173–193.

Shils, E. (1961). Professor Mills on the calling of sociology. Review of *The sociological imagination*, by C. Wright Mills (New York: Oxford University Press, 1959). *World Politics*, *13*(4), 600–621.

Shils, E. (1979). Government and universities in the United States: The Eighth Jefferson Lecture in the Humanities: 'Render unto Caesar…': Government, society and the universities in their reciprocal rights and duties. *Minerva*, *17*(1), 129–177.

Shils, E. (1982/1997). The academic ethic. In S. Grosby (Ed.), *The calling of education: The academic ethic and other essays on higher education* (pp. 3–128). Chicago, IL: University of Chicago Press.

Shils, E. (1997). *The calling of education: The Academic Ethic and other essays on higher education*, Steven Grosby (Ed.). Chicago, IL: University of Chicago Press.

Srigley, R. (2018, February 22). Whose university is it anyway? *LA Review of Books*. Retrieved from https://lareviewofbooks.org/article/whose-university-is-it-anyway/#!

Tuhus-Dubrow, R. (2013, November 1). The repurposed Ph.D.: Finding life after academia—and not feeling bad about it, *The New York Times*. Retrieved from http://www.nytimes.com/2013/11/03/education/edlife/finding-life-after-academia-and-not-feeling-bad-about-it.html

Chapter 4

Academic service

Attachment, belief and hope

Nick Osbaldiston, Fabian Cannizzo and Christian Mauri

Introduction

> Don't forget that we are called, or at least I hope so, to have an influence, that we must stimulate work around us, that we will be influential less by the perfection of our own work than by the activity of our thought, that by the need, the desire, the sacred fire of organized work that will emanate from us.
>
> (Hubert in Riley, 2010, p. 189)

What this volume seeks to provide is discussion around the narrative of discontent with the changing nature of academic labour. Belonging, identity and the craft itself are now removed from the supposed 'golden age' of knowledge creation. Neoliberalism in particular is touted as moving us towards a far more individualised and competitive culture wherein the pressures and intensities of academic life, particularly for the precariat, are defining this vocation as less valuable than in previous generations (see Mauri, this volume; Davies & Bansel, 2005; Parker & Jary, 1995). Nuanced accounts of academic life drill down further into the reflexive lives of individuals through narratives of care, planning, rationalisation and authenticity (Archer, 2008a, 2008b; Cannizzo, 2018; this volume). Nevertheless, today, as Turner (this volume, p. 36) notes, several authors lament at the decline of our university culture 'protest it' but 'are also paralysed by it'.

One of the areas less discussed but arguably impacted on greatly by this is academic service (Macfarlane, 2005, 2007; Pfeifer, 2016). In particular, the nature of the academic ethic, perhaps first touted by Weber (1919/2016, p. 339; see also Shils, 1997; Turner, this volume; Cannizzo, this volume) as the 'inner experience' or 'passion' of being in the service of science, is becoming increasingly divided between needs of disciplines, universities and personal ambitions. From a Weberian perspective, it is not surprising that this has happened.

Rationalisation was never a one-way street (Gane, 2001; Mommsen, 1992) but something that accords to the priorities of differing spheres of modern life. As Mommsen (1992, p. 164) explains,

> ... history was the embodiment of a plurality of competing processes of rationalisation, directed either by the immanent dynamic of material conditions and institutional structures, or by ideal interests which draw their energy from otherworldly and subjectively absolutely binding ideal values anchored in particular world-views which have found a concrete base in the life-conduct of social groups. These world-views are in a perennial struggle with one another.

In terms of academic service, we cannot simply attribute voluntary labour as a source of passion, nor as simply an act of obligation to the institution (either science or university). Rather, we could understand this all as a competing set of values or life-spheres that all demand attention and all provide impetus to do voluntary work.

While there has been little specifically written on this, MacFarlane (2005, 2007) provides us with a significant body of work to build on. Specifically, perhaps tapping into Weber's ideals on science and vocation, MacFarlane (2007) suggests us that academic citizenship is in decline. This is perhaps reflective of the broader cultural retreat from voluntarism where we 'live in an age of civic disengagement' (MacFarlane, 2005, p. 296). It is then not surprising that academics have followed and removed themselves from the sort of collegiality that underpins the institutional and campus life (Lawrence et al., 2012). For MacFarlane (2005, p. 309, *italics added*) however, we can also attribute this to the fractured nature of academia in the present:

> [E]vidence suggests that the collegiality of faculty life has been replaced by a less communal and more isolated existence. Institutional communities are strained by the growth in the size of universities; discipline-based communities are ever more fractured and specialised; and academic relations with students have become increasingly impersonal in the wake of massification. It follows that if you do not feel part of a community, *you are unlikely to know the moral obligations of kinship.*

In recovering this citizenship, MacFarlane (2005, p. 310) calls upon the senior leaders of universities, such as the 'Professoriate', to step in and act as 'role models' to younger generations. Only through this can we recover some of what was lost.

Literature on how to solve this issue is multifarious. Lawrence et al. (2012, p. 346), who follow a trend in exploring the decline of campus life, argue that 'campus attachment flows in large part from exchanges (social and organisational) underscoring the importance of research'. Commitment to the university (not simply the campus) can be accentuated through 'exchanges and socialization experiences' where faculty members feel 'departmental and campus level administrators' are fulfilling their part of the 'social contract' by delivering on their research needs. It is this which needs to be well valued and resourced. MacNeil (2016, p. 174) furthers this by arguing that collegiality can be built through 'more inclusive definition of the college so that it includes students and our communities', which would include casual/sessional staff as well. Embedded in this is the idea that civility can be renewed when mutual appreciation is shown between traditional and the new precariat in an inclusive faculty design. This acknowledges that non-faculty sessional and also 'professional staff' are 'increasingly performing roles traditionally performed by academic staff (and vice-versa)' (MacNeil, 2016, p. 174; see Pfeifer, 2016).

The premise that academic citizenship or collegiality is in decline is important to critique before moving forward. First, as Marini and Reale (2016) show us in Europe, collegiality still exists and can survive the turn to managerialism in universities. However, they conclude that in order for collegiality to survive, 'managerialism [...] must also accommodate and guarantee room for some forms of collegialism, particularly to govern academic issues such as research and teaching' (Marini & Reale, 2016, p. 123). How this occurs though is not as clear.

Second, MacFarlane's (2007) disengagement thesis suggests that at some point academics were more *engaged* in their citizenship compared with today. The quotation from early Durkheimian scholar Henri Hubert positioned at the start of this chapter exhibits the sort of collective effervescence and obligation that perhaps MacFarlane (2007) refers to. The institutional changes that have occurred within the university might call into question whether we could truly ever have that sort of emotional connection the Durkheimians felt (Riley, 2010). However, we cannot ignore that these times were also punctuated, especially within and between the disciplines, by intellectual territorial boundary-making and an active attempt to dissuade students/academics from different schools of thought (Gieryn, 1983; Lamont, 2009). Even today, the demarcation between disciplines serves to provoke a type of bordering where 'beliefs and perceptions' about 'producing and evaluating knowledge' are absorbed by scholars through socialisation practices (Becher & Trowler, 2001; Lamont, 2009, p. 53). The soft sciences in particular, which are not driven by consensus but conflict, are susceptible to boundary maintenance through cultural norms (Turner, 2014). Hearn and Anderson (2002, p. 520) find, using statistical work, for instance, that conflict within departments over promotion is weighted more heavily to the supposed 'soft' sciences compared with the 'hard'.

We have to remind ourselves that the sciences (both hard and soft) were built on a less collegial approach even though the harder sciences have shifted into post-normal science or consensus models today (Turner, 2014).

We only have to look at the manner in which the Durkheimians mentioned earlier, in a very non-collegial manner, attempted to push competitors to the fringes of academic life. Durkheim (1900/1979, p. 328), for instance, repeatedly described the German theorist Simmel's methodology as 'hybrid-illegitimate speculation' which he explicitly instructs not to attach 'a very high price' to. This sort of narrative displays the external ways in which disciplines, like sociology, were founded on boundaries between legitimate and illegitimate dependent on who were the power brokers at the time. This was governed internally as well where disengagement with *profane* thinkers such as Nietzsche was discouraged among the Durkheimians in favour of Kant and others (Riley, 2010).[1] Methods, theories and concepts that did not advance the moral, political and social orientation of the *sacred* in everyday French society were eschewed. Similar themes can be found across the world. For instance, Turner (2003, 2014) shows us that the direction of American sociology was driven by Parsons and Merton's projects, which colonised and pushed out anything or anyone they saw as illegitimate. Even in the early days of the Chicago School, as Cavan (1983, p. 408) recalls, students were 'expected to fall into line, to contribute to the unfolding discipline' and 'were not generally innovative' instead uncritically accepting the wishes, concepts and methods of leaders like Thomas. Similarly in Australia, other soft science disciplines like anthropology and political science looked upon the introduction of sociology with severe criticism and sought to delegitimise it from the outset (Harley & Wickham, 2014).

Despite this we can accept that academic citizenship does provide social and individual goods. As MacFarlane (2007, p. 55) argues, academic service feeds back into a broader set of obligations and duties that foster good collegiality and are 'vital to nurturing student welfare and the continued learning of both academic staff and students'. In short, academic service is important to 'sustaining the well-being of the learning community and in maintaining the wider compact between universities and society' (MacFarlane, 2007, p. 55). On the ground however, service is not so clear cut. Rather, it is divided between different states and identities, sometimes ascribed and sometimes chosen. MacFarlane (2007, p. 90, *italics added*) expresses this in the following:

> Service activities are inspired by a *complex series of emotions and attitudes*. These relate to our sense of security as university workers, our desire to lead professionally stimulating lives, to contribute to the maintenance and, sometimes, radical re-shaping of established academic and professional communities and our aspirations for change in society more widely. Service is about idealism but it is also about a *pragmatic response to the modern conditions of university life*. Hence, the 'call of service' is not, as might be supposed, exclusively connected with *altruism or the desire to promote social justice*.

Again, we should not be surprised about the complexity of the lived experience of academia as Weber perhaps predicted this better than anyone else. We are torn as MacFarlane's (2005, 2007) research shows between different life-worlds that draw us towards security, stability but also pull us in the direction of love for discipline and passion for our labour (cf. Cannizzo, 2018, this volume; Archer, 2008a).

In this chapter, we aim to explore the work of 'service' further by following the understanding and imagining of service among young early career academics (ECAs) and mid-career academics in Australia. Following MacFarlane's (2007, p. 71) model of academic citizenship/service, we contend that, for this new generation, forms of academic service are not necessarily easily tiered but intersect and at times conflict. Especially among those whose careers are fractured and tenuous, service is defined in part by a hope for future security. This hope is not necessarily based upon a sound assessment of future prospects or possibilities but, as we demonstrate, is rather premised on a ritual of security: résumé building. Service is bound to context in terms of both the position of the academic individually within the structure of the university and the temporal ordering of academies nationally where 'the uneven distribution of qualities of time' has meant some have fallen behind, while others' careers accelerate (Spurling, 2015, p. 386).

Methods

It is important first of all that we define and operationalise what we term as service in this chapter. MacFarlane (2007, p. 70; also see Pfeifer, 2016) conceptualises service as voluntary labour to 'students, colleagues, their institution, their discipline or profession, and the public'. Within this framing however, he argues that 'it is clear that there are fundamental differences in the status of different service activities' (MacFarlane, 2007, p. 70). From his work interviewing academics, he constructs a pyramid of service according to the values that academics place on different types of activities. The defining features of each type of service can be outlined in the following table (Table 4.1).

Different work can be understood as academic service. This ranges from pastoral care of students (largely invisible) right through to high level engagement with government agencies (largely visible). The status and prestige offered to the highest form, public service, is for MacFarlane (2007, p. 72) a reflection of the esteem that institutions place on visible and recognisable service. For instance, obtaining a place in a forum on national television is likely to draw more interest in a promotion panel than the coaching of a recently graduated PhD student in the interview process. The latter perhaps fed by a love and/or obligation for mentoring new academics, the former a response to publicly recognisable expertise.

Table 4.1 The service value hierarchy (adapted from MacFarlane, 2007, p. 71)

Academic service type	*Description/example*
Student (lowest value)	Pastoral care – e.g. feedback, coaching, references
Collegial (second lowest)	Working with colleagues – e.g. mentoring, staff development, team teaching
Institutional (middle)	Official positions in universities – e.g. committees, working groups, leadership
Discipline (second highest)	External focus on discipline groups – e.g. organising conferences, peer-reviewing
Public (highest value)	Scholarly expertise – e.g. media engagement, government reports, advising and/or developing skills with public

In our research, as will be shown, this model provides a good baseline for understanding the different types of activities academics undertake. However, we would complicate this further by arguing that each level of labour needs to be contextualised within the structures the academic is presently found in, which includes not simply position within the university (e.g. sessional/adjunct versus established professor) but also the ways in which our labour is used temporally. In particular, the hope that is embedded in our service is at times driven by the desire to strive towards security and a positive social identity.

This research is based on interview work conducted from 2015 to 2017 with academics across Australia. In total, during this time we interviewed 45 academics, mostly ECAs (n=34) and those from the soft sciences (social science, humanities) (n=35). The division between genders is also heavily weighted to females (n=31). Further to this, we also sought to open the structures and statuses between universities and as such interviewed academics from regional/rural universities (n=11) to examine their experiences in comparison to others.

The first iteration of the research conducted in 2015 sought to examine the temporalities of academic labour by examining how ECAs experienced and negotiated work/life balance (Osbaldiston et al., 2016). We were able to note that there was a significant division between labour spent in instrumental tasks (such as administration) and subjective tasks (such as writing and research) with the latter being privileged. Following this then, we were keen to examine the manner in which individuals devoted their labour to service to discipline. As such, a follow-up study was conducted with 20 sociologists in Australia (2016–2017) to unpack their times spent and emotional engagement with service to discipline. While this research was designed to unpack sociologists' experience of service, within the narratives there were several recurring themes that deserve comparison with the initial study of 2015. This chapter explores some of these themes later. We take here especially themes that traverse the pyramid of service from MacFarlane (2007) and cause us to think through the temporalities and contexts of academic labour.

Theme one: 'It's good for your résumé' – the labour of hope

We begin our analysis with the theme of career security – or more correctly put in the context of ECAs, service in the hope of security. From the Weberian standpoint we have used before, this is bound to the idea of subjective rationalisation where time spent in discipline especially satisfies the potential career prospects of the desired future (Osbaldiston et al., 2016). Here, however, we wanted to change tact a little and focus on the idea of hope – that service, or voluntary labour, might have some sort of capital/identity payoff in the future (Kuehn & Corrigan, 2013). Before engaging with this idea theoretically, it is worthwhile drawing out some of these narratives from the participants themselves.

Emma[2] is an ECA from a medium sized regional university in Australia and comes from the soft sciences. When we interviewed Emma, she was on the cusp of completing some important institutional service work, which, unfortunately for her, was less recognised than some colleague's more public service work. In particular, Emma laments that the service she does takes more time than those of her peers, but does not have the same level of 'showiness' to it. However, she does concede that:

> It's good for your CV because it shows you are actively involved and have these skills and whatever [...] people will say it'll be good for your career. Which I think is true to an extent, I think it's probably better if you're looking to apply for a job elsewhere than it is if you want to get promoted internally.

She argues further that service, especially in discipline and the public, is good initially, but does 'plateau' indicating that 'if you do more service [...] it doesn't add anymore to your CV because you should be spending that time writing papers instead'.

It is this narrative of career advancement and service for the hope of reward that we want to explore. Emma was told that service is 'good for your CV', indicating a reflexivity in the process of creating career and advice on what makes an attractive résumé. Sandra, a PhD student at the time of our interview, as another example desired to work in academia in the future. As a social scientist working in a large city based university, she had been taught to 'do service because it helps and it will help you' but added that it also 'helps others'. However, despite whatever deeper connection to service she feels, there is an element of hope in her voluntarism. In discussions about her work in social media for different public and disciplinary organisations, she considers that 'people see that I do that and they respond very positively to that and also people *know who I am* because of that'. Similar to Emma, there is an element of strategy in her work which perhaps she is more aware of:

> I think, in the future and when I'm applying for a job and someone sees Sandra, she is that woman who does the admin for that organisation, that it's probably a good thing [...] and I do see people responding favourably to the service that I do. I can tell people appreciate it. *They look at you a better* way because you do that. *So I think it will have positive impacts in the future.*

Sandra is here relating to more public than invisible types of service such as student or collegial support. However, it is evident that in her service, she imagines some future trade-off for her time. She remarks, in a self-deprecating way, 'I sound really mercenary like I'm doing this (service) just to get ahead'. From other discussions it is clear that Sandra is not simply doing labour for her ambitions but that it has some deeper authenticity for her. However, while she acknowledges that 'service is something you do to support or advance the field [...] it looks good on your résumé'.

Similar to these two, Bethany, who is an ECA from a medium sized city based university, invites us to consider hope labour. In discussing a relatively new role she took on within the institution, she contemplates (*italics added*),

> People say academia is an in-game and not kind of cynically [...] I just want to meet everybody I can, so that everybody knows my name. *I hope that through a role like this*, one positive outcome other than achieving good things with the role itself, would be that I could demonstrate that *I could successfully hold an academic job and be a useful member*, be a *proactive worker*, not be a wanker.

We can see within this a sense of protecting and projecting a type of identity to the community of scholars who might one day take an interest in employing her. While at the moment a sessional staff member, Bethany takes on roles to show she can do the 'academic job' well and be a team-member – presenting her identity as a good person. This is an example of the CV going beyond the paper and into the minds of others – the résumé as persona.

The idea of service work (especially institutional, disciplinary work) being good for the CV is a recurring narrative amongst many of our ECAs. However, even in some of the ideas espoused by our later career academics there is an element of hope and strategy in building service credentials. Nina, a late career academic from a large city based university, demonstrates this through an analogy:

> academic work is a bit like agricultural work: there are times when you're sowing seeds, there are times when things are bubbling along and you can do some maintenance work and then there are times when it's harvest and you just have to work.

While there is some cynicism in her thoughts later on some of those who do service, especially in the visible domains, she makes it clear that her career has been planned with service seen as something of accumulative importance:

> [Y]ou do have to be strategic and not take on too much and take on things that you're interested in [...] There's no point in being a member of something if you're just there and not actually making a difference. And someone did say to me earlier in my career, so I was on the ethics committee and that's a hard-working university committee [...] She said, *you've done that now, that's on your CV now*, you don't have to stay there now, you don't have to do it again [...] so the *light went on: these things are cumulative.*

Nina here espouses similar themes to our previous participants where career is cobbled together with service as a component. She has hoped though, and still hopes, that her labour is 'cumulative' in impact. Again, this relates to those things which are visible to the community/institution. In one of her final comments, Nina argues that the institution she belongs to encourages service, especially if it is 'kind of international service' and 'anywhere that you can *show* leadership'. This cuts to the heart of the idea of hope in relation to voluntary academic work – the desire for it to be visible, counted and potentially rewarding into the future.

This issue of it being counted is one that we will return to later, as well as the idea that this is not purely a case of being a careerist. Service labour is mixed with themes of short-term/long-term personal gain, obligations/duty and also desire/love for work. However, we cannot ignore the hope labour here. We borrow this term from Kuehn and Corrigan's (2013) work in the world of online social production. Here, producers of content (especially in the creative fields such as video making) rationalise their labour as self-actualising and subjectively rewarding, despite being largely unpaid. Individuals feel as though their labour is autonomous, creative, collaborative and controllable and subsequently not alienating in a Marxist paradigm (Kuehn & Corrigan, 2013). Despite this, Kuehn and Corrigan (2013, p. 13) find that producers in this space 'hoped that their current contributions would translate into future opportunities'. Neither self-actualisation nor hope dominates as the primary motivator; rather, these coexist:

> Socially recognised self-actualization is not an unimportant motivator for voluntary online content production [...] Our interviews indicate, though, that the pursuit of future employment opportunities should also be accounted for in explaining contributors' freely volunteered time and energy. One does not necessarily preclude the other. Hope labor, then can serve as one important motivator for free labor online, which, when commodified, reproduces the structural conditions which sustain digital capitalism.
>
> (Kuehn & Corrigan, 2013, p. 15)

This final point is of interest to us. As hope labour feeds back into the structural inequality of this digital space, perhaps it also feeds the circuits that sustain inequalities within the academy. In particular, the extra unpaid and *invisible* labour that is conducted by those in the precariat (see Mauri, this volume), could be described as hope labour, which Kuehn and Corrigan (2013, p. 20) themselves describe as potentially the 'guiding logic behind the academic internship'.

As our early career participants demonstrate (especially those in the very cusps of entering academia), hope labour is seen as a way of becoming employable, having an identity and building a career. This is recognised by another ECA from a medium sized metropolitan university, Vanessa, who argues:

> There's increasingly this idea that *we do things that we love for work*. That things aren't just a job anymore; you're doing it because you're passionate about it. So I think I can sort of see that seeping into my own ideas about work and life. I actually think it's quite a dangerous thing, because it does mean [...] *you end up doing a lot of unpaid work basically.*

We have noted these ideas in our own academic careers. In one circumstance, one of the authors can recount a moment when a senior manager of an institution spoke eloquently about life as an academic as passionate, engaged and caring (especially to students) and then gestured to the sitting crowd that this is why we work on weekends. Of course, academics are not always as accepting of this. But institutionally, there is an expectation of unpaid labour which has trickled down to ECAs. As Rachel, a mid-career academic, argues, 'Early Career Academics and those people who are desperate for their first appointment, *are in a highly vulnerable position and in an easily manipulated position*'. In short, these are people willing when asked to fulfil certain roles in the hope that it will lead to career stability and identity. There is, as Rachel points out, a power imbalance: younger academics are 'exuberant and vibrant' while also seeking security, making them more open to unpaid labour. What our respondents here have discussed mostly thus far are the visible roles. What we have not discussed yet, as one participant describes it, is 'all the shit we don't get paid to do', which is less visible and less easily transcribed onto a résumé.

Theme two: the labour of unrecognised service and the workload model

Across the interviews we conducted, there is a recurring complaint about the ways in which service is counted. While the institution values some visible service work, as Rachel points out, 'they're not going to *count* it'. This leaves some academics in a type of quandary where they have to weigh up costs/ benefits when work hours committed to other institutions/organisations is left off the workload spreadsheet. Rachel, at the time of interview, was facing a similar situation where she was invited to be a director of a national committee in her research area which was a 'no-brainer' in developing her 'network' but which is 'just not counted anywhere' in her workload model. She complains that 'they're (the institution) going to give me more teaching to make up for my lack of service (counted), which is an absolute bullshit situation'. Similar narratives were heard across our sample with some advocating to 'play the game' better by making service work visible to department heads (Emma) while others rationalised their time accordingly to do all the 'enjoyable' things in their private times (Vivian). Some even argue, such as Nigel, an ECA from a smaller metropolitan based university, that in order to be successful you have to accept that 'you do need to take on extra stuff', but that he actively evaluates each invitation on whether it is a 'thankless task' or not.

From this perspective, service is tempered by the failure of the institution to recognise and contribute hours to the day to perform it. The service that rarely gets counted, as many of our participants suggest, are activities involving service to discipline, some engagement (public) activities and mentoring students. These types of service however come, as a late career academic (James) argues, not simply from a 'careerist' mentality but a 'deep commitment' to one's passion. Bethany, who we introduced earlier, demonstrates this eloquently by arguing that she gets 'a sense of fulfilment out of' service and it provides alternatives to 'sitting at your desk, little jobs to work towards'. Most of her service, at the time of interview, revolves around organising mentoring and social networking opportunities for higher research degree students. She takes her cues from others and mentions people who are very 'active in service roles' who are for her 'crazy passionate about the research that they do, that they want to do the service as well'.

This idea of passion as a contributing motivator to service appears frequently in the messages we received from academics. Georgina, a recent ECA in a regional university, makes this point but also tempers it with a bit of warning, perhaps to herself;

> if I'm writing a blog or writing a piece with the Conversation [...] again that's something that kind of comes out of your personal time [...] it's becoming your hobby, it's the fun thing that you're doing in your spare time [...] but it is also actually work, and I think because we're passionate [...] we're not very good at realising that, we're doing service as a hobby.

Of course, Georgina here is describing some of that public engagement activity which is highly visible and rewarding to her personally. However, others make the point that those parts of invisible service such as 'mentoring' and 'collegiality' are a significant part of their experience of service.

This is especially relevant to our discussion of hope labour as a significant portion of those arguing for teaching as service come from late/mid-career academics whom younger generations take their cues from. Rachel, for instance, suggests that as a social scientist, she represents her 'discipline' to her students which makes teaching a form of 'service'. This pushes her to work hard and embody that identity as she performs her duties. A retired academic, Charles, argues similarly by arguing that one much perform,

> Teaching (as a service) interestingly and engaging students, exciting their minds, and supervising postgraduates so they go out and they too, insofar as they're able to, excite anybody's minds [...] being engaged in the community.

Along with this narrative, Richard, a retired social scientist, makes the point that,

> I think creating knowledge is one thing, disseminating that knowledge and the knowledge of others is a separate thing. I think that teaching is often downplayed [...] I love teaching [...] as academics we're paid to teach.

He then proceeds to argue that looking for opportunities to remove oneself from teaching through research grants is not 'giving back to the students your enthusiasm for the discipline'. In short, both Charles and Richard illustrate a view that teaching passionately and with purpose is a form of service especially to the community itself.

In addition to this, mentoring others (especially PhD students) is considered by some to be an important service component that academics draw passion from. A mid-career academic, Penny, makes this point about her own journey:

> I think mentoring young people, in terms of developing their career, ensuring students engage with the discipline and understanding how they can articulate themselves in a relationship to the discipline, *being an incredibly passionate educator,* I think, is an important service [...] So we have a national conference, we run a PhD prize very 2 years [...] I don't know how I manage it. I see it as really important. *It's nourishing for me. I just do it.*

The difficulty with this is that younger academics are acutely aware that mentoring and providing passionate teaching requires more work than is counted in their workload models. An ECA from a regional university, Beck suggests that 'a lot of work we do is not accounted for' and then provides an important point on this further,

> For example, the three courses that I needed to develop got no recognition at all [...] I spend two to three days a week developing courses, and it's not accounted for.
>
> Interviewer: Would you be interested in articulating these concerns to your superiors?
>
> Beck: Well they've just opened it up for commentary, so I think I will give feedback and write an email. But they don't know how to solve it. That's the thing.

The point here is that teaching passionately is seen as an important component of service (including time outside of counted hours) but which requires much effort. This is the argument of several ECAs, such as Genevieve, an ECA from a medium sized metropolitan university on a research only position, who contends that 'it is possible to do all of these things (research, teaching, admin), *but it's not possible to do all of them well at the same time*'. She continues by stating that 'something loses out, either your research loses out or you short change your students by not being engaged in the classroom'.

Unfortunately, as has been demonstrated repeatedly in academic labour literature (Coates et al., 2009; Mauri, this volume). The roles of teaching and even mentoring undergraduate students are shifting towards unstable sessional academics, such as some of those mentioned earlier. This movement is not necessarily equitable or formal, with these precarious workers having to compete for very short-term contracts with others. Casual labour, in this respect, creates a pressure on younger academics to teach well, present a good identity, with a hope that this will convince more stable academics to continue with their services later. When pressure to teach 'passionately' is not met with appropriate workloads for those inside formal positions in the academy, but which is an internal social structure, this presents problems for those with no 'formal' workload at all. Expectation, hope and passion for teaching drive sessional academics to work beyond remunerated labour hours.

Discussion: service within different spaces and times

It is difficult to provide all of the different ways in which academic service is narrated by our participants in this short space. Needless to say there is for ECAs (and even mid-career academics) a sense of hope in their work which revolves around the unwritten aspects of the CV that includes the ascribed identities potential employers give them. In short, ECAs hope that their work will demonstrate their standing as a good academic citizen. In this final concluding section, we want to tease this out and provide some discussion points around this notion of service and citizenship within the academy.

First of all, we argue that the academic disengagement thesis of MacFarlane's (2007) needs to be tempered with a discussion and description of the structure it apparently resides in. In our work, as well as that of others (Marini & Reale, 2016), there is evidence of academic collegiality/citizenship surviving in various forms. Unfortunately, as noted, there is a lack of institutional recognition of this in a formalised setting. As we shift further into an audit culture within universities (Kelly & Burrows, 2012), it is clear academics are feeling pressure to be strategic about their service activities. Rachel, our previous participant, exemplifies this in her thinking about whether to take on a new service role that was important to her career and research, but which would only serve to increase her workloads and impinge on work/life balance. However, as she also notes, these are the activities that the university also applauds and which feeds into their own image and organisational status. This leads us to acknowledge there is a growing disparity and inequality between visible (and counted) service and those opportunities which do not count in workload models.

Australian universities are now beginning to be measured on engagement activities through national metric systems. As politicians push rhetoric on value for money with public funding, institutions are now required to supply a portfolio of engagement activities for consideration in the Excellence in Research Assessment (ERA) rounds as they were for the United Kingdom's 2014 Research Excellent Framework (REF). Work that academics such as Rachel do, largely unpaid for and uncounted, will be important in these types of audits. However this is not how the university gains capital – and as such teaching realistically is the fundamental aspect of labour that is counted in workloads.

The second and related point is that universities are increasingly becoming dependent on this free labour that is rationalised by our participants as something they will do as it is their passion on one hand, but which on the other is based on hope for future trade-offs. Service, especially in relation to high visible, institutional service (such as committees) but also invisible service (such as mentoring and teaching), is described as an important contributor to identity and duty. Underlying this, though, is a hope that this sort of work will eventually be rewarded later. Kuehn and Corrigan (2013, p. 17) suggest that hope here can be understood as a 'projection into the future of a better, more challenging, or different state of being'. However, these 'future-orientated projections' are not always about changing one's relationship, but the maintenance of certain identities. For established academics, this can involve the consolidation of an academic identity in the now, and also an orientation towards what sort of academic they want to be later. Two examples demonstrate what we mean here. First, Yvette, a very early researcher working at a smaller metropolitan university, when we interviewed her she had reservations about her 'value' within the department she worked in. When asked about the idea of asking for potential changes to her workloads and personal plans for having children, she points out:

> I will probably wait a longer period of time until I felt that I had earned enough, not respect, but I suppose enough value within the workplace [...] to build up my value from my department's perspective, for them to see me as someone that has contributed and can contribute, *that is an important kind of person for us.*

The 'kind of person' she is describing here is no doubt a mixture of different attributes including research capacity and teaching ability. However, later she suggests, her identity ambition is wrapped up in academia and her ideal is to one day reach Professor so she can be part of the 'cultural change' required in workload management. In order to achieve this, as she concedes earlier in the interview, she will be required to take on leadership roles, something which is part of her future academic identity.

Similarly Emma, who we discuss earlier, describes her ideal career as one of success in 'research' and eventually promotion. She wants to avoid the 'stagnant teaching only' role but also avoid presenting herself to others as someone seeking 'fame and fortunes' alone. In the end, Emma proposes that she is 'trying to balance those things' that will forge her ideal career but also accomplish this 'while being a nice person'. In other words, Emma strives to protect her identity as a good academic citizen while also seeking future growth in her career. This, combined with her passion for volunteering to help colleagues where she can, presents her as an ideal candidate to offer free labour in the name of service.

Much of the hope labour that is undertaken in academia then is what is described as 'free or under-compensated' work, especially in relation to service that the university draws significant gain from but which, in turn, also produces expectations or norms (Kuehn & Corrigan, 2013, p. 20). We have discussed this especially in relation to sessional academics where the future collides with their present positions. As we have shown, academics who are at the beginning of their careers or developing their identities further seek to complement their research through service and write their future opportunities through these labours. The cost of service work to the individual can be measured in time. As Kuehn and Corrigan (2013, p. 20) argue, 'the hope labourer assumes other costs of production', including the 'costs of time that could be spent in some other useful way'. In the case of the sessional academic, for instance, the effort and time needed to provide teaching that is passionate also promotes the extra unpaid labour which denies them other career development time such as writing research papers – which arguably provides more potential opportunities than other activities. This sort of 'hope labour' is two-fold – first, to secure short-term employment and second, to present oneself as a good academic citizen. Unfortunately, 'hope labour thus contributes, in part, to the precarity of contemporary work' (Kuehn & Corrigan, 2013, p. 20). In other words, universities are now thriving on the provision of teaching services that are often under-paid to ensure their own success, which reverts back into a cycle of continuous sessional teaching and a significant power imbalance.

Conclusion

Service is a difficult topic to investigate with academics. As we have shown, there are cross-overs between activities that teachers and researchers do, which in an audit culture do not always count as service categorically. Furthermore, there is a sense of obligation and duty among some of our participants in relation to service that we have not explored thoroughly earlier. Rather, we sought to focus on how universities may tap into 'hope labour' to increase visibility and consolidate performance within and outside of institutional settings. Unlike MacFarlane (2007), we see less a decline in academic citizenship within our participants and more a structural inequality where the more precarious one is, the more likely service labour is open to manipulation and power imbalance. This is a temporal issue, especially where unpaid and uncounted labour is motivated by a desire to project a certain identity which will yield opportunities into the future but also where teachers volunteer their time beyond the remunerated rate. Of course, any discussion around temporality needs to consider the position of the person, the place the person is in and the structure that they work into (Spurling, 2018). However, broadly speaking, increasingly it appears that universities have tapped into the hope labour market to perpetuate this power inequality.

Notes

1 However as Riley (2010) argues, Hertz did take up some of the writings of Nietzsche and made them his own.
2 Pseudonyms are used throughout to maintain interview participants' privacy.

References

Archer, L. (2008a). The new neoliberal subjects? Young/er academics' construction of professional identity. *Journal of Educational Policy, 23*(3), 265–285.

Archer, L. (2008b). Younger academics' constructions of 'authenticity', 'success' and professional identity'. *Studies in Higher Education, 33*(4), 385–403.

Becher, T., & Trowler, P. R. (2001). *Academic tribes and territories.* London: Open Universities.

Cannizzo, F. (2018). 'You've got to love what you do': Academic labour in a culture of authenticity. *The Sociological Review, 66*(1), 91–106.

Cavan, R. S. (1983). The Chicago school of sociology, 1918–1933. *Urban Life, 11*(4), 407–420.

Coates, H., Dobson, I., Goedegebuure, L., & Meek, L. (2009). Australia's casual approach to its academic teaching workforce. *People and Place, 17*(4), 47–54.

Davies, B., & Bansel, P. (2005). The time of their lives? Academic workers in neoliberal time[s]. *Health Sociology Review, 14*(1), 47–58.

Durkheim, E. (1900/1979). Durkheim's review of Georg Simmel's *Philosophie des Geldes. Social Research, 46*(2), 321–328.

Gane, N. (2001). *Max Weber and postmodern theory.* Basingstoke: Palgrave Macmillan.

Gieryn, T. F. (1983). Boundary-work and the demarcation of science from non-science. *American Sociological Review, 48*(6), 781–795.

Harley, K., & Wickham, G. (2014). *Australian sociology: Fragility, survival, rivalry.* Basingstoke: Palgrave Macmillan.

Hearn, J. C., & Anderson, M. S. (2002). Conflict in academic departments: An analysis of disputes over faculty promotion and tenure. *Research in Higher Education, 43*(5), 503–529.

Kelly, A., & Burrows, R. (2012). Measuring the value of sociology? Some notes on performative metricization in the contemporary academy. In L. Adkins & C. Lury (Eds.), *Measure and value* (pp. 130–151). Oxford: Blackwell Publishing.

Kuehn, K., & Corrigan, T. F. (2013). Hope labor: The role of employment prospects in online social production. *The Political Economy of Communication, 1*(1), 9–25.

Lamont, M. (2009). *How professors think: Inside the curious world of academic judgment.* Chicago, IL: Harvard University Press.

Lawrence, J., Ott, M., & Bell, A. (2012). Faculty organizational commitment and citizenship. *Research in Higher Education, 53*, 325–352.

Macfarlane, B. (2005). The disengaged academic: The retreat from citizenship. *Higher Education Quarterly, 59*, 296–312.

MacFarlane, B. (2007). *The academic citizen: The virtue of service in university life.* New York, NY: Routledge.

Macneil, J. (2016). On the role of collegiality, civility and collectivism in shaping academic identity. *Labour and Industry: A Journal of the Social and Economic Relations of Work, 26*(3), 165–178.

Marini, G., & Reale, E. (2016). How does collegiality survive managerially led universities? Evidence from a European survey. *European Journal of Higher Education, 6*(2), 111–127.

Mommsen, W. (1992). *The political and social theory of Max Weber: Collected essays.* Chicago, IL: University of Chicago Press.

Osbaldiston, N., Cannizzo, F., & Mauri, C. (2016). 'I love my work but I hate my job': Early career academic perspective on academic times in Australia. *Time and Society.* Advance online publication. doi:10.1177/0961463X16682516

Parker, M., & Jary, D. (1995). The McUniversity: Organization, management and academic subjectivity. *Organization, 2*, 319–338.

Pfeifer, H. L. (2016). How to be a good academic citizen. *Journal of Criminal Justice Education, 27*(2), 238–254.

Riley, A. (2010). *Godless intellectuals: The intellectual pursuit of the sacred revisited.* New York, NY: Berghan Books.

Shils, E. (1997). *The calling of education: The academic ethic and other essays.* Chicago, IL: Chicago University Press.

Spurling, N. (2015). Differential experiences of time in academic work: How qualities of time are made in practice. *Time and Society, 24*(3), 367–389.

Turner, S. (2003). The maturity of social theory. In C. A. Camic (Ed.), *The dialogical turn: New roles for sociology in the postdisciplinary age* (pp. 141–170). New York, NY: Rowman and Littlefield Publications.

Turner, S. (2014). *American sociology: From pre-disciplinary to post-normal.* Basingstoke: Palgrave Macmillan.

Weber, M. (1919/2016). Science as a profession and vocation. In H. H. Bruun & S. Whimster (Eds.), *Max Weber: Collected methodological writings* (pp. 335–354). London: Routledge.

Part II

Affective cultures

Chapter 5

Affective infrastructures of global academia

Mona Mannevuo and Elina Valovirta

Introduction

'Finland repeatedly sets the highest standards, and it [higher education] is free there as well', remarks Noam Chomsky in an interview on neoliberalism and higher education (2018, p. 60). It is true that university education in Finland is free for its citizens now, but the introduction of tuition fees to non-European Union (EU) students in 2017 can be foreseen as a gateway to enforcing tuition at a cost for all in the future. Coincidentally, Finland's downfall from the 'highest standards' of quality education is taking place simultaneously: its celebrated Programme for International Student Assessment (PISA) results are waning and the 2018 QS rankings no longer included any Finnish universities inside top 100. In recent years, Finland's right-wing government has introduced drastic budget cuts on universities, leading to over 500 lay-offs at the country's leading institution, The University of Helsinki, in 2016. It is clear that those highest standards referred to by Chomsky are quickly being evaporated in favour of the US-style neoliberalisation of academia including higher tuition fees – and, as the results suggest, lower standards. What is most worrying in this process, we have observed, is the growing sense of disempowerment experienced by academics themselves in the face of these changes introduced from above and outside our own realms of control and influence. The question we would like to pose in the midst of these concerns is what and how to *feel* as a labouring subject in the global academy and its affective infrastructures?

Our experience on academic work is located in Finland; nevertheless, the political and cultural landscape of the political economy of academic work is global. We are certainly not alone: recent research on academic work focusses mostly on the emotional injuries caused by the competitive and individualised work culture in the midst of the fast temporalities of neoliberalism (Cannizzo, 2018; do Mar Pereira, 2017; Gill, 2018a, 2018b; Gill & Donaghue, 2016; Mannevuo, 2016). Despite all the breeze shot, ink spilt, and the number of affects circulated in these discussions, the competition, pace and stress in academia seem to accelerate. This discrepancy between critical theory and reality has led us to ponder, whether there is something we have missed when analysing the agency of academic labourers. It might be possible that our discussions reify binary power relations when we lament the aspirational attachments that we, as pure-hearted scholars, feel towards our work in the cruel neoliberal academy. In doing so, we might overlook the fact that subjects also shape and modulate the social structures and affective atmospheres where they move with their actions and inactions. These guiding tenets focus our consideration of the transformative possibilities at our disposal as mid-level actors in global academia.

As members of the so-called middle constituency in the academic world, we (a senior lecturer and a post-doc) represent the most ordinary of academic workers: not yet full professors, no longer students. We are right in the middle. What options do we have to *feel* a sense of empowerment in an environment that denies us affective and other sorts of agency? While we agree that the contemporary academic subjectivity is a crisis-based subjectivity based on a feeling of ontological insecurity at least to us in the middle, we also want to stress, paraphrasing Raymond Williams (1977, p. 132), that this subjectivity is a subjectivity-in-formation. The progressive nature of subjectivity prevents us from fully ossifying it into a sinister truism, wherein lies an opportunity for envisioning more liberated futures, as well.

In what follows, we suggest that affect theory provides tools for rethinking the hierarchical separation between the spheres of affective intimacy and the political economy of global academia. This chapter develops previous critical work on the psychosocial life, political economies and micropolitics of universities. It begins with an overview of the field by mapping the affective cartographies of global academia in Finland. Drawing connections between various affective trajectories, the second half of this chapter focusses on loving the job and 'the complaint genres' (Berlant, 2008) and 'reluctant individualism' (Gill & Donaghue, 2016) in academia. In what follows, we locate these sentimental accounts of academic injuries as orientation towards agency that is focussed on ongoing adaptation and improvisation. This partly explains the growing popularity of resilience training and 'brain gyms', where the individual mind is a muscle to be developed into a desired capacity that best serves neoliberal pursuits. In the final part of the chapter we weave all this together with Sedgwick's notion of the middle ranges of agency, thereby offering a suggestion for understanding the affective and social structures of global academia as creative and changing as well as in need of creative change.

Locating Finland on the political map of global academia

As Jamie Peck and Nik Theodore describe in their *Fast Policy* (2015), neoliberal reforms are transnational and they travel fast, but 'best practices' take different forms in different socio-economic environments. Nonetheless, 'local' reforms can be seen as a window to larger political-economic geography, including the political economies of global academia. In higher education, the recent large-scale neoliberal reforms, be they legal, organisational or managerial – are each their own particular case, but what they have in common is an amalgamation of geography and epistemology, when knowledge produced in English-speaking top universities is considered more advanced and 'exportable' than knowledge produced elsewhere. In her analysis on the local and global geopolitics which have served to construct the epistemic status of feminist theory, Maria do Mar Pereira (2017) defines these negotiations as entanglements where *geo*politics meets *chrono*politics (p. 150) in a way that geographical location frames chronological difference through highlighting the differences between peripheral 'backwardness' vis-à-vis the 'foreign' and 'modern'.

do Mar Pereira's analysis focusses on Portugal, but her geopolitics of academia is useful to analyse Finland and its position on the global academic map. The two countries are – despite their differences – quite comparable in terms of academic marginality: both are physically peripheral countries on the Western- (Portugal) and Eastern-most (Finland) edges of Europe, and their languages are spoken in small numbers on the continent (some ten million speak Portuguese and 5.5. million speak Finnish). Both countries are eager to embrace Anglo-American-derived academic reforms at the expense of their own, more insular yet perhaps worthwhile academic practices. As do Mar Pereira details the Portuguese context, herewith we focus on Finland's place on the geopolitical map, where reforms emanating from the centre to the margin take peculiar shapes and sizes which then again modulate our scholarly practices and our understanding about ourselves as global-yet-always-merely Finnish scholars.

What makes the case of Finland particularly interesting, we claim, is its reputation as a top country in terms of both education and happiness, curiously fusing two fields at stake in our endeavour to map the affective cartographies of global academia. Finland's fame as a top educator heralded by Noam Chomsky derives from its consistently high placement in the international PISA rankings, spawning newspaper headlines comparing education systems between the United States and the United Kingdom citing PISA results as evidence of Finland's superiority.[1] These headlines coincide with Finland and the rest of the Nordic countries frequently perceived as 'happy' countries in various happiness assessment exercises. To wit, Finland took the first place in The World Happiness Report in 2018, prompting the *New York Times* to headline its piece on the topic 'Want to Be Happy? Try Moving to Finland' (March 14, 2018). Finland, happiness and education thus seem to go together in Anglophone media, which sets us up for a juicy discussion on their convergence in the context of global academia – especially when these stories about happiness find little resonance with our own experiences on the shop-floor.

Recent reforms in the Finnish institutions of higher education mentioned in our introduction partly explain the discrepancies we feel between stories about happiness and our lived reality in academia. In Finland, institutions of higher education are legislated by the Finnish Universities Act, whose major overhaul in 2010 expedited the process of neoliberalisation within Finnish universities. Previously state offices with no mission to garner profit or operate in corporate terms, universities are now independent legal persons and 'autonomous' in the sense that besides (diminishing) state funding, they are expected to acquire external (mostly corporate-sponsored) funding and operate as businesses. Perversely, corporate funding (mostly by the technology industry) is seen as a sign of independence, whereas self-government without outside influence is seen as compromising academic integrity, whose primary goal now is to directly benefit society's need for economic growth. For the purposes of this paper, one of the most tangible changes in this new legal scenario was the centralising of power to the rector and the university board (oftentimes mostly comprising members from the third sector). Gone was the democratically operating tripartite representation system of university-level decision-making, dictating that all governing bodies (such as the faculty council, school council or the university board) contain a three-tier representation from the constituencies active in the university: degree students, full professors and the so-called middle constituency: lecturers, post-docs and other members of the teaching and research staff not belonging to the two previous groups. While full professors maintained some or most of their leverage in the face of this sea change, and students have always been well organised and included by necessity in decision-making, it seems now, after eight years of the new regime behind us, that it is the middle constituency who bears the main brunt of the changing affective infrastructure of Finnish academia brought upon by the new legislation. The question we would like to pose to counter the situation which strains the mid-level actors in the university (like us, the authors of this piece) is what kinds of affective resources can we draw upon to maintain a sense of autonomy despite a legislative system that boasts autonomy but *feels* like something quite different?

For the middle constituency, our expulsion from the previously sacred tripartite decision-making structure poses a great deal of challenges; we no longer know what is going on and who decides what. We are almost like the 'organization man' in the grey suit (Whyte, 1956/2002), the people who work for the organisation driven by Protestant Ethics, but nevertheless have no idea what is expected from them. Instead, we drift from one reform to another in the middle of evaluation processes, faceless bureaucracy and resilience training which are supposed to strengthen our 'muscles for change'. There are cosmetic inclusions of the mid-level employees in some administrative bodies (which have largely lost their significance and stripped of their previous functions), but the overall shared agony is the same; meeting with our colleagues formally or informally the discussion turns almost immediately to the problems, confusion and nervousness people face in contemporary academia. The process of these reforms is a topic for another full-length paper, but generally speaking, Finns have a reputation of being ridiculously law-abiding; speeding, jaywalking and littering are frowned upon and law is seldom questioned but rather taken as a given. This tendency to rely on legislation is partly to explain why the Universities Act began to take effect instantly; historically speaking, Finns regard laws and reforms as a good thing. For example, the Nordic welfare state is an offspring of a highly legislative people, who in the aftermath of the Second World War placed its hopes for a better society on government and laws guaranteeing social and health services (Valovirta & Kuortti, 2015, p. 249). Despite protests in the year leading up to the reform, the Universities Act was passed and is adhered to in a typically Finnish fashion, where the highly secular people places its faith in the law and not the church. The somewhat reluctant, but ever-dutiful observance of the new legislative situation, however, has proven quite taxing on the academic workforce.

The exhaustion felt by academics today in Finland is also connected to the means through which Finnish universities have decided to conquer their position on the map of global academia. These means are mostly adapted from the business culture (followed by the success story of Nokia – despite its downfall, one might add) whose contemporary forms of strategic management are mostly lessons from the United States and Great Britain. However, these imported lessons are not solely used to secure our national position in global competition. Instead, they are also used to create local hierarchies and rankings from top to bottom; from universities to schools and from schools to fields of study and individual scholars. The most often used category of distinction in the universities now is the designation, 'international', which means that the entanglement between geopolitics and chronopolitics forms the basis of the political economies of Finnish universities. For instance, the major Finnish academic funding instrument, the Academy of Finland, has intensively focussed on 'internationalising' Finnish scholarship and science. This aim is, naturally, supported by legislation; the Finnish Act on the Academy of Finland (2009) ensures that Finnish researchers are required to engage in high-standard international research collaborations and that they visit top-level research centres around the world (while the possibility that these visits amount to nothing is overlooked). Thus, only the 'right' connections and evidence of mobility (e.g. in the form of signed invitation letters from academics outside Finland) make it even possible to apply for funding. In other words, we have to self-fashion ourselves after top universities, and present that our systems of knowledge production, allocation of resources and also modes of local management and evaluation of performance are – not merely Finnish and thus inferior – but *international*, and therefore automatically of high quality. These changes in national science policies is in line with do Mar Pereira's analysis on Portugal as well as Tereza Stöckelová's

(2012) analysis on Czech Republic and Eve Cherniavsky's (2017) analysis on the rise of American Studies in the former Soviet bloc to reorganise the relationship between the state and academia.

The imposed internationalisation does not only affect knowledge production but also reconfigures our subjectivity as Finnish academics. As we cannot escape our 'peripheral' and 'backward' status as academics from outside the centre, we have to continuously present our (international) activity and demonstrate that we *strive* to be something other than a domestic scholar and that we have the *potential* to overcome our handicap, Finnishness. This forced internationalisation signals to us that being 'merely Finnish' equals to a crisis condition, and, as crisis often does, this leads us to increased vigilance and frantic calculation of the possibilities of survival in highly competitive surroundings. Consequently, Finns have their role in the 'psychosocial and somatic catastrophe' (Gill & Donaghue, 2016, p. 91) that has emerged in the fast and performative neoliberal academia, but the experience of the crisis looks slightly different from a 'peripheral' point of view. The Finnish crisis-shaped collective academic subjectivity is based on the awareness that we join the competition as an underdog, as someone who must win the world *over* yet is unlikely to *win*. Simultaneously with the quest for internationalisation, the persistent discourse about 'top universities' and 'top scholars' is filled with national fantasies ('yes we can'), paranoia ('what people think about us') and self-loathing ('oh no, we did not make it to the top 100'). These entanglements between aspiration and shame offer a possibility to analyse the 'double movement shame makes' (Sedgwick, 2003, p. 37) when it leads towards painful individuation and uncontrollable relationality when shame arises from our failed internationalisation as *the* affect of our failed globality. We are shameful, as we are not international, but we are also shameful, as by way of our peripheral place as Finns, we always fail to be international *enough*.

Love and cruel optimism as mess-making forces in academia

If shame is *the* academic affect which defines our scholarly identity, we cannot help but wonder how it is possible to work on it in a competitive environment under constant evaluation. We suggest, somewhat provocatively, that a partial answer is love, the powerful yet ambivalent affect and the partner in crime in the construction of excessively self-exploitative work cultures. In her analysis of autobiographical narratives of Finnish researcher-mothers, Mannevuo (2016) has previously argued that a romantic relationship to academia is not just a difficult relationship but it is a bad relationship, one profoundly based on utilisation of love and individual attachments and desires (see also Gill, 2018b). Drawing on Berlant's (2011a) analysis of love, love nurtures the tendency we have to exercise patience towards structures that are not actually working, and love gives us patience to be flexible even in psychologically damaging labour conditions. This is not to say that loving one's work is 'wrong', but rather that it offers a basis to an affective infrastructure that normalises the repetition of exhaustive patterns. Furthermore, academics do not always chase their individual dreams, but they also – feminists in particular – work like driven maniacs as they consider their job a vocation and a political and moral project which has to be done despite its labour conditions (Skeggs, 2008, p. 680). Thus, it is justifiable to question the consequences of our own actions and inactions and how they fuel the cycles of fast academia and national fantasies of academic success.

As do Mar Pereira (2017, p. 74) brilliantly puts it in her analysis of the performative academy, the subjectivity of the top scholar is filled with Butlerian 'stylized repetition of acts' based on displaying (international) productivity and future potentiality. Meanwhile, these repetitions of acts are sensed and felt as overwhelming and exhaustive globally and locally. To wit, after writing an essay on hidden injuries in neoliberal academia in 2010, Rosalind Gill received over 2000 emails in the following years about the correspondents' toxic experiences within academia (2018b, p. 103). Despite this global psychosocial catastrophe, academics appear to have accepted the managerial imperatives by accelerating productivity as if it were the solution to the growing demands. Similarly, Fabian Cannizzo (2018) noticed when he interviewed academics that they tend to explain their actions and motivations through hierarchical distinction between the pleasurable love towards academia and forced competition within it. Cannizzo's analysis matches our own observations: performative university is often described as a scene from which academics distance themselves by hierarchical distinctions between intrinsic (pleasurable) motivations and extrinsic (competitional) motivations. This could be seen as an example of 'modern alienation' (Liu, 2004, p. 103) in corporatised work culture, where employees think that the structure is 'just' an environment which actually has nothing to do with 'me'.

Academia, however, is a different environment than a corporation. Sometimes it is difficult to make distinctions between these two, especially when the intrinsic pleasures of academic work are put to work in marketing campaigns and mission statements. Our own university, The University of Turku, for instance, markets itself in an ad campaign as the 'campus that never sleeps' because it is filled with productive teams and top scholars pursuing excellence 24/7 (Luhtala, 2012). As residents of such a sleepless hotbed of action that is our campus, we wonder how academics are able to explain to themselves their autonomy in an organisation filled with the language of business opportunism. This twisted relationship to work might best be explained by Lauren Berlant's (2011b) notion of cruel optimism because it is a description of *an attachment* that allows us to encounter and accept what is enigmatic and even irrational in our attachments. As Berlant writes, cruel optimism is 'a relation of attachment to compromised conditions of possibility whose realisation is discovered either to be *im*possible, sheer fantasy, or *too* possible, and toxic' (2011b, p. 24). In other words, cruel optimism is not solely a description of something we would like to have – a permanent job, a decent salary or a long-lasting relationship – and that we know is difficult to find, keep and maintain. Instead, cruel optimism is a way to explain the continuity of the subject's sense of what it means to live in this academic world 'that never sleeps'. Therefore, cruel optimism is not just a description of impossible dreams and hopeless hopes, but it explains practices of self-suspension and self-abeyance. In addition, what is important in the analysis of global academia is that cruel optimism is a relation that allows us to mirror ourselves to the impossible and toxic ideals of performative university without losing our sense of endurance as we work 24/7 on the campus that never sleeps.

Examples of these stubborn attachments to disaffirming scenarios are the growing numbers of books and articles that diagnose the crisis of contemporary academia. Although these academic complaints can be seen as 'archives of tactics of not being defeated' (Berlant, 2008, p. 273), they also share similarities with the female complaint as a sentimental genre. The problem of this genre is that it may create a public space where academics blame flawed ideologies for individual sufferings while 'at the same time maintaining some fidelity to the world of distinction and desire that produced such disappointment in the first place' (Berlant, 2008, p. 2). This is not to say that academics suffer from self-alienation, but rather that they struggle with a 'poetics of misrecognition' (Berlant, 2011b, p. 122) in impossible conditions of possibilities where they project desired qualities towards their work depending on their present need to sustain their desires and attachments. As Berlant explains, cruel optimism and the complaint genres related to it are not examples of alienation, but they are ways to sustain a subject's coherence so that the subject can mirror itself as a full and uncompromised person while feeling vulnerable and disorganised (see also Berlant, 2008, p. 196). This is perhaps the most repeated survival scenario in the performative academy, where academics need to present themselves as self-confident and rational although they are confused and overly anxious to the point of paranoia.

The flipside of our love projected towards academic work is present on an almost daily basis in our formal and informal discussions with our colleagues. Despite injuries and constant shame of not being the top scholar, academics are masters of creating survival strategies and affective bargains to secure their object of desire. Although most of us manage somehow, we cannot turn our gaze away from the emotional costs of the operations of cruel optimism, especially when this psychic process accelerates the exhaustive work rhythms and over-productivity inscribed in academic labour. Academics are often overly critical and self-reflective, but, as often happens in unfortunate love plots, they (including ourselves) drop out the structural and political analysis when they evaluate themselves. Seeing themselves as victims who are not able to change the structures, they think it is *I* whose behaviour is susceptible to radical change. This is the momentum for new managerial solutions, such as resilience training, that the university offers to overworked academics. Whether these individualised solutions are helpful, or just momentary reliefs to driven maniacs and exhausted workaholics, will be the topic of the next section.

Resilience training for exhausted workaholics

Rosalind Gill and Ngaire Donaghue (2016) have observed that the hidden injuries of neoliberal academia are no longer concealed, but rather, universities today operate in full crisis mode tackling the psychosocial and somatic catastrophes that afflict their employees. To make sure that their employees are able to operate in this crisis mode, the infrastructures of global academia are now filled with consultants that offer resilience training, well-being services and programmes for stress and time-management. What is typical of these courses and programmes is that they all place the responsibility firmly on the shoulders of the individual worker who dutifully tries to improve one's inadequate self to become more productive (Gill & Donaghue, 2016, p. 97). Thus, instead of solving the underlying structural problems, the university as an employer uses elements of therapeutic management to make sure that their employees are able to secure their twisted relationship towards their work.

In the uses of therapeutic management, academia follows recent management trends rooted in positive psychology and resilience training. These managerial trends have a long history; from dealing with early-twentieth-century industrial fatigue and labour turnover to the recent demands of aspirational and entrepreneurial relationship towards work (e.g. Davies, 2016; Gregg, 2017; Mannevuo, 2018). But what is new in these recent managerial developments is their focus on the brain and cognitive processes to produce optimism and optimisation in the workplace via adapting lessons from neurosciences. As Jessica Pykett (2015) has noticed, these neuro-inspired behaviouristic trends have emerged after the financial crisis of 2007–2009, after which workers needed to do more with less and thus managers needed to invent happiness-based management solutions in times of austerity. Similar to Gill and Donaghue, Pykett suggests that the so-called resilience training is a technology of the self aimed at optimising workers for a life in the precarious workplace through developing individual character virtues (p. 163). Furthermore, Nikolas Rose and Joelle M. Abi-Rached's (2013) Foucauldian analysis of brain-focussed resilience training and mindfulness suggests that it is a technology designed to improve oneself with brain awareness and brain education. These intersections between neuroscience, Buddhism and management do not expect that you are identical with your brain, but that you can act on your brain, 'and so acting you can improve yourself – not as a brain, but as a person' (Rose & Abi-Rached, 2013, p. 222). Our experience of brain-focussed resilience training likewise reeks of old-fashioned behaviourism, which suggests that productivity can be increased by fixing character flaws in certain individuals. By focussing only on our individual abilities for time-management, healthy diet and sleep rhythm, it also alleges that exhaustion is caused by our individual, unhealthy lifestyle choices and personal workaholism, which then cause stress and diminish our cognitive capacities. In other words, we only have ourselves to blame for our shortcomings in workplace well-being.

But there is also another feature in neuro-inspired management interventions that is worth noting: its similarities with Taylorism and scientific management. Scientific management is often understood solely as a time-management scheme, but it also includes a depersonalised technological system that absorbs worker frustration and fatigue into technical rules, procedures and instructions that include features from ergonomics to well-being. While doing so the system not only diminishes worker autonomy, but it also increases risks of work-related mental and physical pathologies when workers feel that they are treated as machines who are optimised and synchronised to work in a same rhythm despite their personal differences (e.g. Sampson, 2017, pp. 63–64). In the performative university these Tayloristic protocols replace natural rhythms, seasons and personal working patterns into continuous frenetic production coordinated by personnel departments, evaluation panels and other depersonalised forms of management. Furthermore, although there is clearly an epidemic of emotional injuries, no one actually knows where one should complain and which form one should fill to protest and mourn (obviously no one has time or energy to co-ordinate collective demonstrations). With these Tayloristic systemic models, the managerial focus turns from the individual working subject to a preconstituted and worked object in a way that rather creates than relies on docile subjects (Salzinger, 2003, pp. 17–18). In academia, this means that the evaluation of one's productivity is focussed not solely on the actual individual work but also on one's future potentiality and docility to work in a same rhythm with imaginary 'international top scholars' which is presented through a series of performative acts that 'do and re-do epistemic status every day' (do Mar Pereira, 2017, p. 73). Consequently, employees' personal values and capacities merge with neuro-inspired managerial norms that morph into the political economies of the performative and performance-driven university.

These intersections of Taylorism, individualised performativity, exhaustion and resilience training are a strange mixture for labour politics. As Melissa Gregg notes, whereas 'labor politics was once premised on the idea of placing limits on work – reducing hours, resisting speed-up, guarding rights and benefits – in today's industrial settings the challenge is to adopt this politics to an environment which fails to recognize work as laborious' (Gregg, 2017, p. 111). It is indeed difficult to argue against individual choices regarding stress management, like a healthy lifestyle, yoga, mindfulness and meditation; one hardly finds fault in those. It is also useless to criticise individual psychologists and consultants for offering momentary neuro-reliefs. It even seems that psychiatrists and clinical psychologists know that the problems they are paid to deal with do not start with the mind or body of one individual. Even Robert Spinzer, the chief architect of the Diagnostic and Statistical Manual of Mental Disorders, Third Edition (DSM-III) in 1980, has argued that the extension of medical diagnosis has gone too far and the solution is to build alternative social and economic institutions (Davies, 2016, p. 271). But how is it possible to see stress and exhaustion as a collective issue in the political economies of global academia which are built on the impossible requirements of performativity and continuous self-blame and shame of not being able to reach those requirements? Indeed, to consider stress and exhaustion as a political issue rather than an individual and medical one, workers should be able to be critical and angry '*about* something which is external to themselves' (Davies, 2016, p. 270). But as previous research and our own experience about academic work show, academics tend to turn their complaints inwards and turn to resilience trainings to optimise their brains to become *more* productive. Thus, it is easy to see how neuro-inspired resilience training is welcomed as the heroin/e, which academia offers for struggling workaholics.

Little Machiavellians getting through by middle ranges of agency

As we have presented, individual academics rarely have the resources to change the structures of feelings in global academia. Nevertheless, as critical scholars, academics themselves cannot overcome the fact that everyone – especially in such a privileged position – has to have some form of agency to turn oneself from a worked object to a working subject. The question of agency worries us – as members of the middle constituency – in the midst of the ongoing neoliberal reforms in Finnish academia. We are right in the middle, but what does that tell about our agency? We are certainly not the first ones to wonder about this: the first and perhaps most famous description about powerless white collars was written in the 1950s by C. Wright Mills, who claimed that the white-collar eminence is a morally defenceless, self-alienated and politically impotent group whose work often clashes with forces they can neither influence nor understand. Therefore, as Mills ruthlessly writes, this middle constituency is filled with standardised losers and potential little Machiavellians (1951/2002, p. xvii). And indeed, the white collars are often depicted as tragi-comic figures, most famously in the television show, *The Office*, where the workers learn to live with their frustrated desires amidst absurd managerial interventions that let them know every day that they are worth nothing (Moran, 2005, pp. 41–48). It is easy to laugh at these distorted yet familiar caricatures, but perhaps we should also take these disappointed and frustrated figures seriously when we analyse the actions and inactions that are possible for the members of the middle constituency.

As trained feminist scholars, we suggest that our existence in the middle echelons of the academic social order begs comparison to the idea of mid-level agencies as formulated by Eve Kosofsky Sedgwick, our go-to feminist theorist. In her influential and much-cited notions of paranoid and reparative reading stances as emblematic of feminist, queer and other critical knowledge-production modes, she mentions how 'the middle ranges of agency' (Sedgwick, 2003, p. 13) are in fact productive of creativity and change. By the notion, Sedgwick comments on the tendency in Gramscian-Foucauldian thinking to focus on either the hegemonic or the subversive, which is done at the expense of that which lies between and beside them. Rosalind Gill's (2018b) consideration of the academic work of Les Back and his gentle and subtle actions resonates with Sedgwick's ideas: Back's work may be considered more gentle and soft than, for instance, the autonomist Marxist 'refusal of work' (Tronti, 1980), but perhaps his methods are even more subversive. How might we, as the mid-range agents and the most ordinary of academic labouring subjects, then, effect change?

Sedgwick had queer relationships and literary criticism in mind when thinking about the rewards of new types of agencies located between hegemony and emancipation. Yet the overall goal of developing agential space for middle-dwellers is very lucrative to think about in the context of academia – a playground Sedgwick herself knew so well. It is possible, we allege, that more subtle becomings, affective formations and experiences become possible outside the extremes of 'top research' or 'academic loser', when we embrace the seemingly modest idea of the middle ranges of agency, here seen as something produced in affective and experiential engagements with the self and the other. The notion of full human agency is obviously a myth – particularly in the academic machinery – so why not embrace the idea of making the middle and the mundane recognisable and, thus, potentially recalcitrant? What if, as also Gill (2018b, p. 98) suggests, instead of self-obsessed resilience trainings, we focussed on things that are *collectively* regarded as worth valuing?

One example of our own mundane, collective, potentially recalcitrant forging of agency was born in 2010, when a group of academics began convening every Wednesday for a pub quiz. Coincidentally, this was the same year that the Finnish Universities Act was reformed and we began to witness government-led infrastructuring of research funds to innovation-producing research ventures instead of 'basic' research, which most of us do in the humanities. The quiz team consists of a roster of members, all academics, keen to let off steam and excel in a competitive environment that does not threaten but offers sustenance. Winning is a rare luxury and in no way the goal (although it does feel nice when it happens); quizzing is no fun if one team always dominates. The important thing for all of us is to get away from it all, use our collective knowledge for the team and have fun.

One great lesson learned from the pub quiz experience has been – contrary to what the individualism of neoliberal academia leads us to believe – that collectively, we can excel. When one is missing from the five-member team, we do not fare as well as normally. The harnessing of collective intelligence, where one's vague inkling of knowledge put on the table feeds the others to together work out the right answer, is a powerfully exhilarating experience. In the eight years quizzing together, we have learned to know each other's strengths and weaknesses and use them to the team's benefit. This collective infrastructure of positive affect has had a surprising side effect: when we focus on something completely different and succeed, those successes feed into academic success. It was never explicitly meant to happen, but it did. In a similar vein, Maria do Mar Pereira explains that her strategy to endure in the ruthless competition is the meaningful conversations she has had with their colleagues within and feminist activists beyond academia (pp. 195–196). These encounters and conversations may, as we all know, have more transformative effects than acting like a solitary genius, the international top scholar filled with business opportunism.

Certainly, we are well aware that fusing private and working lives in this way can be understood as yet another example of academics living and breathing academia, but in pub quizzing, hedonism is a bigger incentive than opportunism. We did not come together to win in academia, we came together to drink beer, play and occasionally win the quiz. The rest – project funding and joint articles – grew organically from conversations had during the decompressing. For example, the decision to co-author this piece grew from a night at the quiz and is the reason why we wanted to incorporate it as an example of creative mid-range agencies, who rely on collectivity, which Gill (2018a, p. 209) calls for as a 'consciousness and action to bring about change' in her discussion on neoliberal academia.

However, more than playing and winning, these types of informal gatherings among academics such as the pub quiz Wednesday – located nicely in the middle of the working week – serve the purpose of dealing with our inevitable failures. After all, it is not like any of us has achieved world domination as 'top researchers'. We have collectively done reasonably well. Most importantly, however, consolation and laughter in the face of yet another absurdity or injury is the best that we can give one another as a collective. In the context of coping with rejection, it becomes clear that reaching the top as a researcher is not so much about how many wins you achieve, but rather, how you cope with the losses. We may not be able to help each other get on *top*, but we are able to help each other get *through*. From one perspective, our rants in the pub could be seen as yet another 'complaint genre' focussing on adaptation rather than revolution. Nonetheless, we want to stress that this intimate form of affective publics has also encouraged us to reconfigure a realistic political subjectivity in the global academy. This may contain elements of adaptation to the performative university, but it also contains collegial friendship based on ethics, co-work and sharing.

For us the potential of the middle-range existence lies in our collectivity and informality, and in the way in which we, to quote Sedgwick 'succeed in extracting sustenance from the objects of a culture – even of a culture whose avowed desire has often been not to sustain them' (2003, p. 151). Banter, irony, laughter and release emerge from meetings in the middle, when we exercise our 'academic birthright', complaining (Sylvia, 2007). We ironise, play with and joke about our object of desire while dramatising possession and loss at the same time (Berlant, 2008, p. 212). Like the hundreds of letters Gill received as a result of her article on flawed 'practices of power in academia' (2018a, p. 193), our nights at the pub form a similar 'catalogue of tales of toxic experiences within the neoliberal University' (Gill, 2018a, p. 196). The trick, of course, is to avoid falling into collective misery, a danger always looming behind every shared article rejection, unfunded grant application or experience of unjust decisions made on a higher level with little to no understanding about the effects of those decisions on overworked labourers trying to survive. But as Gill comments, these stories – and those who listen to them – are not just laments, they are in fact 'gifts' (Gill, 2018a, p. 196) that we collectively reward each other with in those infinitely reparative moments that we share in order to cope. In those reparative moments, the gifts of listening, 'being interested and curious' (Gill, 2018b, p. 100) and, most importantly, giving each other the gift of time are exchanged lavishly. To put it in Randall Collins' terms (1993, p. 208), interaction rituals such as the weekly quiz (including the occasional shared victory), replenish one's emotional energy in a way that is highly contagious in the positive sense. These kinds of interactions, entailing solidarity and a common goal, are experienced as 'extremely rewarding' and often 'regarded by most people as the most significant events of their lives' (Collins, 1993, p. 209). To be sure, there is hardly a bigger luxury in the life of an academic than having – and taking – time to spend together in good company and in peace.

These collective experiences are important also because individually it is hard to balance the narrow ridge of being sufficiently overworked, excessively dynamic and productive but not too much as to burn out, that is, fail. In the same way, sharing your feelings of injury or injustice is risky, as 'the little Machiavellian' may come across as self-indulgent or whiny when you know how fortunate you are to work in a field you love. Gill (2018a, p. 195) writes that she was initially reluctant to share her feelings in the article which was ultimately welcomed with massive feedback from scholars comforted by her experiences. Tellingly, she acknowledges a hesitance to speak up in two other articles, as there are 'those who we know have it worse' (Gill & Donaghue, 2016, p. 96) so one must be careful not 'to engage in some narcissistic project of self-indulgence' (Gill, 2018b, p. 103). Having qualms about sharing your injuries is understandable because, after all, as critical thinkers we are always extremely conscious of our privilege, yet the hurt feelings all of us experience in the face of a flawed system are very real. The academic confessional is therefore always affectively ambivalent.

Conclusion

As we have presented, the political economy of global academia has created an affective infrastructure where working on the verge of a breakdown is normal and it means you are productive, active and have different (preferably international) projects brewing. These entanglements of productivity and geopolitics create a rhetorical space where there is no place for an average scholar even in a local, national scene. As our experiences and our formal and informal discussions with our colleagues show, this causes a lot of stress – and also awkwardness – especially for the members of the so-called middle constituency in the academic world who themselves consider a proper academic to be ethical, collegial and productive not based on numbers but on quality and productive sharing of their ideas. This applies also to internationality: previously it has been an important feature of the job – depending on the subject – to travel and exchange ideas, but in the performative university it has become more of a strategy for presenting activity and productivity than a helpful chance to develop new ideas.

Instead of only diagnosing the problems of neoliberal globalised university from our inevitably peripheral, Finnish, point of view, we have also wanted to think about how our own actions and inactions as middle-range scholars affect to social structures and political economies of global academia. In doing so we have elaborated on Berlant's notion of cruel optimism and pondered how cruel optimism may offer a productive tool to analyse the problems in the academic complaint as well as in resilience training. After this, we have also turned to Sedgwick's writings where she searches for ways to find nourishment and kinship in a hostile world. We have translated this to the academic setting which has helped us question the conditions on which emancipation and oppression or success and failure are based. While academics as a rule tend to lead lives more privileged than the ones Sedgwick discusses, her interrogation enables us to regard other types of agencies than just the winners as valuable, even desirable. Being able to support oneself as a working academic cannot be considered a life of failure, yet we oftentimes *feel* like failures.

Embracing the Sedgwickian middle ranges of agency makes us pay attention to types of micro-emancipations offered by the collectivity of the complaint choir in the pub quiz, which helps put our lives in perspective:

we may fail, but we are not failures. Similarly, we may experience successes and wins, but we are not always winners. In fact, it would be an unrealistic – even self-harming – specimen of cruel optimism to cling to the neoliberalist idea of the top as the only worthwhile place to aspire or winning as a rule possible to attain. After all, if we keep evaluating ourselves vis-à-vis the constructed managerial ideals of top scholars, we may forget that our academic subjectivity is also a subjectivity in transformation, and thus it also depends on who we are and what we may become in the future. This does not mean that we should distance ourselves from competitive and performative work cultures, but that we can collectively affect the ways we adapt to the work cultures. In doing so we may reconfigure our political subjectivity in academia by turning the gaze from ourselves to the affective structures working against us. This way, we might become more cognisant of how our own actions and inactions mould these very structures, including the persistent idea put forth by academic decision-makers that one's Finnishness is a congenital impairment in need of rehabilitation by the panacea of 'internationalisation'. Our present condition in academia may be an unfortunate love plot, but we can try to rearticulate the sob story into a more compassionate one, turning cruel optimism into modest, collective optimism.

Note

1 Headlines over the past few years in various English-language newspapers in the United States and the United Kingdom include the following: *The New York Times*: 'I have seen the school of tomorrow. It is here today, in Finland' (2016); 'For generous parental leave and great schools, move to Finland' (2016); *Independent*: 'Eight reasons Finland's education system puts the US model to shame' (2018); *Washington Post*: 'What if Finland's great teachers taught in U.S. schools?' (2013).

References

Astor, M. (2018, March 14). Want to be happy? Try moving to Finland. *The New York Times.* Retrieved from https://www.nytimes.com/2018/03/14/world/europe/worlds-happiest-countries.html. Accessed May 18, 2018.

Berlant, L. (2008). *The female complaint: The unfinished business of sentimentality in American culture.* Durham: Duke University Press.

Berlant, L. (2011a). A properly political concept of love: Three approaches in ten pages. *Cultural Anthropology, 26*(4), 683–691.

Berlant, L. (2011b). *Cruel optimism.* Durham: Duke University Press.

Cannizzo, F. (2018). 'You've got to love what you do': Academic labour in a culture of authenticity. *The Sociological Review, 66*(1), 91–106.

Cherniavsky, E. (2017). *Neocitizenship: Political culture after democracy.* New York, NY: New York University Press.

Chomsky, N., & Spooner, M. (2018). An interview with Dr. Noam Chomsky on neoliberalism, society, and higher education. In M. Spooner & J. McNinch (Eds.), *Dissident knowledge in higher education* (pp. 55–62). Regina, SK: University of Regina Press.

Collins, R. (1993). Emotional energy as the common denominator of rational action. *Rationality and Society, 5*(2), 203–230.

Davies, W. (2016). *The happiness industry: How the government and big business sold us well-being.* London: Verso.

Dean, M. (2016, July 19). For generous parental leave and great schools, move to Finland. *The New York Times.* Retrieved from: https://www.nytimes.com/2016/07/24/books/review/nordic-theory-of-everything-anu-partanen.html?rref=collection%2Ftimestopic%2FFinland. Accessed May 18, 2018.

Finnish Act on the Academy of Finland. (2009). Translation in English available: https://www.finlex.fi/fi/laki/kaannokset/2009/en20090922.pdf

Gill, R. (2018a). Beyond individualism: The psychosocial life of the neoliberal university. In M. Spooner & J. McNinch (Eds.), *Dissident knowledge in higher education* (pp. 193–216). Regina, SKA: University of Regina Press.

Gill, R. (2018b). What would Les back do? If generosity could save us. *International Journal of Politics, Culture and Society, 31*, 95–109.

Gill, R., & Donaghue, N. (2016). Resilience, Apps and Reluctant Individualism: Technologies of Self in the Neoliberal Academy. *Women's Studies International Forum, 54*, 91–99.

Gregg, M. (2017). The athleticism of accomplishment: Speed in the workplace. In J. Wajcman, & N. Dodd (Eds.), *The sociology of speed: Digital, organizational, and social temporalities* (pp. 102–114). New York, NY: Oxford University Press.

Heim, J. (2016, December 8). Finland's schools were once the envy of the world. Now, they're slipping. *The Washington Post.* Retrieved from https://www.washingtonpost.com/local/education/finlands-schools-were-once-the-envy-of-the-world-now-theyre-slipping/2016/12/08/dcfd0f56-bd60-11e6-91ee-1adddfe36cbe_story.html?utm_term=.d9afa00b7c8a. Accessed May 18, 2018.

Liu, A. (2004). *The laws of cool: Knowledge work and the culture of information.* Chicago, IL: University of Chicago Press.

Luhtala, J. (2012, October 16). The film campus that never sleeps has been released. *University of Turku* (www.utu.fi). Retrieved from http://www.utu.fi/en/news/news/Pages/The-Film-Campus-That-Never-Sleeps-Has-Been-Released.aspx. Accessed May 20, 2018.

Mannevuo, M. (2016). Caught in a bad romance? Affective attachments in contemporary academia. In L. Adkins & M. Dever (Eds.), *The post-Fordist sexual contract* (pp. 71–88). Houndmills and New York, NY: Palgrave Macmillan.

Mannevuo, M. (2018). The riddle of adaptation: Revisiting the Hawthorne studies. *The Sociological Review, 66*(6), 1242–1257.

Mills, C. W. (1951/2002). *White collar: The American middle classes.* New York, NY: Oxford University Press.

Moran, J. (2005). *Reading the everyday.* London: Routledge.

Peck, J., & Theodore, N. (2015). *Fast policy: Experimental statecraft at the thresholds of neoliberalism.* Minneapolis, MN: Minnesota University Press.

Pereira, M. (2017). *Power, knowledge and feminist scholarship: An ethnography of academia.* London: Routledge.

Pykett, J. (2015). *Brain culture: Shaping policy through neuroscience.* Bristol: Policy Press.

Rose, N., & Abi-Rached, J. M. (2013). *Neuro: The new brain sciences and the management of the mind.* Princeton, NJ: Princeton University Press.

Salzinger, L. (2003). *Genders in production: Making workers in Mexico's global factories.* Berkeley, CA: University of California Press.

Sampson, T. D. (2017). *The assemblage brain: Sense making in neuroculture.* Minneapolis, MN: Minnesota University Press.

Sedgwick, E. K. (2003). *Touching feeling: Affect, pedagogy, performativity.* Durham: Duke University Press.

Skeggs, B. (2008). The dirty history of feminism and sociology: Or the war of conceptual attrition. *The Sociological Review, 56*(4), 670–690.

Strauss, V. (2013, May 15). What if Finland's great teachers taught in U.S. schools? *The Washington Post.* Retrieved from https://www.washingtonpost.com/news/answer-sheet/wp/2013/05/15/what-if-finlands-great-teachers-taught-in-u-s-schools-not-what-you-think/?utm_term=.603ea85a011c. Accessed May 18, 2018.

Strauss, V. (2016, May 7). I have seen the school of tomorrow. It is here today, in Finland. *The Washington Post.* Retrieved from https://www.washingtonpost.com/news/answer-sheet/wp/2016/05/07/i-have-seen-the-school-of-tomorrow-it-is-here-today-in-finland/?noredirect=on&utm_term=.dde09065a6ef. Accessed May 18, 2018.

Stöckelová, T. (2012). Immutable mobiles derailed: STS, geopolitics, and research assessment. *Science, Technology & Human Values, 37*(2), 286–311.

Sylvia, P. (2007). *How to write a lot: A practical guide to productive academic writing.* Washington, DC: American Psychological Association.

Tronti, M. (1980). The strategy of refusal. *Semiotext(e), 3*(3), 28–34.

Valovirta, E., & Kuortti, J. (2015). Moderate Finnish feminism: From a struggle for equality in the welfare state to diverse and established Gender Studies. In R. Haas (Ed.), *Rewriting academia: The development of the Anglicist women's and gender studies of continental Europe* (pp. 247–276). Frankfurt am Main: Peter Lang.

Weller, C. (2018). Eight reasons Finland's education system puts the US model to shame. *Telegraph.* Online. 8 January 2018. Retrieved from: www.independent.co.uk/news/education/education-news/finland-education-system-schools-model-superior-us-helsinki-children-a8147426.html. Accessed May 18, 2018.

Whyte, W. H. (1956/2002). *The organization man.* Philadelphia, PA: University of Pennsylvania Press. (Original work published 1956).

Williams, R. (1977). *Marxism and literature.* Oxford: Oxford University Press.

Chapter 6

Academic craftwork

On authenticity and value in academia

Fabian Cannizzo

Academic work as craft and commerce

In this era of mass higher education, academic careers are assembled from diverse and potentially conflicting motivations. Blackmore and Kandiko (2011) helpfully describe academic life as an intersection between the intrinsic value of scholarship, monetary economies and prestige economies. Both monetary and prestige economies imply that academic labour and career planning can be motivated by external reward systems – whether in the form of financial gains or through 'prestige rewards', which may materialise in the form of a spacious corner office, for example (Blackmore & Kandiko, 2011, p. 404). The values associated with doing academic and scientific work are often presented as opposed to the pursuit of external rewards. Davies and Horst (2015), for example, describe the craftwork of group leaders and principle investigators in bio-technology laboratories, which is invested with a great deal of care and careful work. The performance of craftwork 'brings together skill, a focus on utility or purpose and a particular emotional orientation (care, passion, commitment)' (Davies & Horst, 2015, p. 376). This craftwork requires an appropriate ethical disposition: to do careful work is to reflect on 'good' means and ends. Instrumentalising academic craftwork, on the other hand, runs the risk of corrupting its intrinsic value. In the appendix to *The Sociological Imagination*, C. Wright Mills (1959) describes academic labour as 'the practice of a craft', arguing that the work of a social scientist as inseparable from their personal life. He claims that:

> the most admirable thinkers within the scholarly community you have chosen to join do not split their work from their lives. They seem to take both too seriously to allow such dissociation, and they want to use each for the enrichment of the other... Scholarship is a choice of how to live as well as a choice of career; whether he (*sic*) knows it or not, the intellectual workman forms his own self as he works toward the perfection of his craft; to realise his own potentialities, and any opportunities that come his way, he constructs a character which has as its core the qualities of the good workman.
>
> (Mills, 1959, pp. 195–196)

The form of labour control most appropriate to craftwork is one in which the skilled craftsperson 'establishes their own working conditions, protected by the quality of their products, and limited access to their industry' (Edwards, in Tancred-Sheriff, 1985, p. 380). Tancred-Sheriff (1985, p. 371) notes that craftwork often allows for the development of a kind of 'personal style' in how work is carried out. That is, 'thinking and feeling are [both] contained within the process of making' (Sennett, 2008, p. 7). However, the personal investment in craftwork jars against the monetary and prestige economies associated with it in academic labour, or as Richard Sennett (2008, p. 9) claims, 'the craftsman (*sic*) often faces conflicting objective standards of excellence' that include 'competitive pressure'. Tancred-Sheriff describes this tension in terms of the university's role in academic craftwork: while academics retain control of their work tasks, 'the rewarding the disciplining of craftspeople becomes the partial responsibility of outsiders' (1985, p. 380). Performance metrics and other means of representing the relative value of academic work are hence central to the disciplining of craft, investing it with external incentives.

Motivations are important to craftwork because craftspersonship requires a special space and time to allow a worker to become immersed in craftwork. The call to slow down the pace of personal and work life in the slow scholarship movement can be seen as one expression of the desire for a temporality conducive to craftwork. In their book, *The Slow Professor*, Berg and Seeber (2016, p. 17) claim that increased time pressures in the university are 'detrimental to intellectual work, interfering with our ability to think critically and creatively'. What is often overlooked in calls to slow down higher education and research is that craftwork is not only a practice but also an ideal that is shaped by gender and class norms. Craftwork is not only seen as limited by the corrupting forces of external motivations (i.e. performance metrics) but also by distraction (Sennett, 2008). Both domestic caring responsibilities and concern for one's (perhaps vital) salary may hence produce inauthenticating experiences of academic work. Inequality is reproduced through the use of casual academic labour here. Several studies have traced what May et al. (2013, p. 264) describe in their Work and Careers in Australian Universities study as the segmentation of the academic labour market, which stems from the use of informal recruitment methods for casual academic staff in internal labour markets. Kimber (2003) similarly claims that casual teaching work is bought in secondary labour markets, identifying a division between the tenured core of ongoing academics and a tenuous periphery of casual teachers. Looking at this so-called periphery through the lens of craftwork suggests that workplace marginalisation is enacted through the marginalisation of teachers and carers with temporal experiences that diverge from the model of the craftworker.

The invisibility of casual workers, due to their absence in routine workplace forums, offices and breakrooms, for example (Tweedie, 2013, p. 305), lessens their opportunities for having input into organisational planning. This tenuous periphery of casual workers experiences class subordination to higher education managers to the extent that they are locked out of organisational planning and decision-making (Brown et al., 2010) and professional development that would make them suitable for higher status positions (Ryan & Bhattacharyya, 2012; Ryan et al., 2013). Disempowering contingent academic staff through withholding opportunities for professional advancement is a form of opportunity hoarding, which Wright (2015, p. 8) notes is a key strategy of middle-class exclusion. However, an additional effect of this disempowerment is that casual staff are restricted in where they may exercise 'care' in their work. Craftwork requires autonomy to ethically reflect on scholarly practice and enact decisions. The development of a careful work ethic may be stunted where casual staff feel that the responsibility for the quality of their work rests with senior members of staff. Gottschalk and McEachern's (2010, p. 40) study highlighted that while a growing number of academics use casual employment as a career strategy for seeking more permanent work, this option can become a career trap when aspiring academics comes to be seen as a 'casual workers' and less attractive as a prospective permanent staff member. Being seen as piecemeal workers rather than craftworkers may contribute to their marginalisation, although as of yet there have been no empirical studies exploring this possibility. Most casuals in Gottschalk and McEachern's study desired to progress to more permanent work, but found only 'frustrated careers' as they came to recognise that their relationship with the university was 'largely functional'; disillusioned, they internalised their status as casual workers (Gottschalk & McEachern, 2010, p. 48). The ideal that academic work is a kind of craft needs to be taken seriously to better elaborate the cultural reproduction of these class relations.

Craftwork is also a gendered practice. Studies of the academic profession have identified a number of gendered differences in both academic careers and beliefs about careers. Probert (2005) notes in her study of the University of New South Wales (UNSW) that women did not apply as often for promotion as their male counterparts, so despite roughly even odds of being successfully promoted and were also more likely to be the primary carer for children or elderly parents (p. 62). Using interview data, Probert determined that the organisation of the division of household labour was perceived as a significant career barrier for female academics, as participants had developed an 'internalized understanding of what senior academics should be doing'; that is, publishing, which often occurs outside of workplace hours where it may encroach on other obligations (Probert, 2005, p. 69). Further to this, not all academic work is rewarded equally. In a large study of Australian and British academics, Brew et al. (2018, p. 117) found that a large amount of academic work goes 'unnoticed and unrewarded', often misrepresented as 'service' in institutional workload and promotion practices. They have coined the term 'academic artisanal work' to describe the careful labour necessary to sustain the university, such as coordination responsibilities, curriculum development, student administration, professional development, outreach activities and industry-oriented work (Brew et al., 2018, p. 121). Academic artisanal work is vital to the smooth operation of universities, yet is often overlooked because it is not captured by research and teaching productivity metrics. Recent international quantitative studies have suggested that women take on more unrecognised labour than their male counterparts (Aiston & Jung, 2015; Guarino & Borden, 2017), making artisanal work an issue of gender equity issue for academics. Although this artisanal work contains all the characteristics of craftwork (caring work, a personal style, standards of quality), its lower status in comparison to other forms of work (and outputs) marginalises recognition of its value.

Institutionalised assumptions about how 'real' academics approach work may also devalue those with domestic and caring labour responsibilities. The barriers to gender parity in professions have a normative dimension, making the provision of flexible workplace policies a necessary but inadequate condition for addressing gender inequalities. If binary gender norms still determine much household labour, then flexible work practices may enable these norms to feed back into the organisation of workplace and household labour. Or, as Bailyn (2003, p. 141) claimed in her study of MIT, if the 'ideal worker' continues to be seen as having 'no interests or responsibilities outside of work', then practice will 'continue to disadvantage women', thus promoting a male model of the ideal academic (see also Coate & Kandiko Howson, 2016). The risks of a masculine model for academic and scientific careers are reflected in the empirically documented 'tipping point' around the age of 35, where the average career trajectories of men and women diverge (Bell & Yates, 2014, p. 13). The idealisation of academic work as a deeply personal and consuming practice hence has implications for the classed and gendered reproduction of academic practice.

Having elaborated the gendered and classed features of academic craftwork in a very broad sense, this chapter will now explore the role that assumptions about 'real' academic work play in how academics recognise value. I use discourse analysis to explore conversations with academics about career and life planning. While managerialism is often blamed for perverting collegiality and scholarly values, I aim to demonstrate here that when planning for their futures, academics already circumscribe what academics can and should be. Idealisations of 'real' academic work and lives already make reference to status hierarchies that privilege individuals with particular temporal experiences, marginalising those who work between qualitatively different timescapes, such as individuals with caring duties and academics employed on short-term (and casual) contracts. But what are the characteristics of authentic academic work?

Authenticity in the social and biological sciences

The idea of 'real' or authentic academic work is useful in identifying the norms associated with the academic role. 'Real' academic work is distinguishable from the subjective experience of *feeling* authentic in a work role, which is sometimes discursively constructed as being 'passionate' about work (James, 2015). While research participants did express authenticating and inauthenticating feelings in relation to their work (see Cannizzo, 2018), a second, more normative, authenticity emerged in talk. As discussed later, interviews with academics elicited a variety of assumptions about what *should* be seen as legitimate academic work, what is valued about scholarly work and what academics value in their colleagues. These data were generated from interviews, lasting from approximately 45 to 90 minutes, with academics in eight Australian universities in 2014. Interviewees were invited to participate from a range of university types, including the research-intensive Group of Eight (three universities), the Australian Technology Network (two universities), the Regional University's Network (one university) and unaffiliated universities that were located in regional/rural areas (two universities). Participants were purposively sampled to achieve diversity across university types, career stages, gender and working environments (both monastic social scientists and laboratory-based biological scientists were sampled) (Table 6.1).

In interviews, academics were asked about their entry into an academic role and scholarship more generally, their roles in the university, their career goals, their approaches to publishing and grant applications, goals related to teaching and research innovation, their professional networks, their reflections on career planning activities, and their sense of a future in

Table 6.1 Research participants (Total n=29)

Career stage	Early-career	8
	Mid-career	17
	Late-career	4
Disciplinary grouping	Biological sciences	11
	Social sciences	18
University type	Group of eight	8
	ATN	9
	Regional	12
Duties focus	Research	4
	Teaching	1
	Mixed	24
Contract type	Continuing	21
	Fixed-term	8
Gender	Male	16
	Female	13

academia. Participants were interviewed at a venue of their choosing and efforts were made to establish a collegial rapport and respectful atmosphere for the interviews. Perhaps because of the interviewer's social status among employed academics, as a doctoral student and casually employed teacher, interviewees tended to offer career advice as well as recount personal experiences. These interviews were conducted by a participant-researcher with an 'insider' status (Corbin Dwyer & Buckle, 2009), affording access to situated, *in situ*, talk about academic career planning and life between scholarly group members.

Interviews were transcribed verbatim and a combination of open and closed coding (Strauss & Corbin, 1998) was used to isolate instances where academics used both explicit and implicit ideas about what constituted a 'real' academic or 'real' academic work. Open coding consisted of coding explicit statements and implicit schemas that academics used to describe their careers and future planning. Closed coding was subsequently used to develop sub-categories and to collate similar assumptions framing academics' use of the concept of 'authentic' or 'real' academic work and careers. Closed codes were constructed for both explicit and implicit uses of the concept of authenticity, distinguishing where the idea of 'real' work was used intentionally in discourse from the habitual use of ideas about the 'real' that may occur in talk as an assumption that structures communication. Vaisey (2009, p. 1687) discusses the distinction between discursive and practical uses of culture, arguing that theorists who rely on the view that culture can only be used consciously, as interpretive repertoires or discourses, 'cannot rule out the possibility that deeply internalized moral attractions and repulsions... are patterned in motivationally important ways'. The possibility that cultural norms may come to structure behaviour and motivations outside of discourse invites analysis of the assumptions that structure interaction, which may never enter into conscious discourse. The appearance of assumptions about 'real' work shaping talk was coded to contribute to an exploration of how such assumptions may structure interaction. The discussion of 'real' academic work and careers below hence presents an account of how academics can think about, talk about and act on their work and lives while acknowledging that other stories, models and plans of action are possible. These discourses and schemes are common, but not necessarily hegemonic.

What is a 'real' academic?

When talking about careers, Australian academics often described their ambitions and expectations through reference to authentic work experiences. In total, 22 of the 29 academics interviewed expressed assumptions about what constituted 'real' or authentic experiences of academic work and life. These assumptions were categorised into six groups, each a distinct perspective through which academic work and life are spoken about.

The most common assumption of a 'real' academic is a concern with status: a real academic is recognised as such among members of a peer group. Some participants in the present study described status-seeking as a kind of 'elitism' that disadvantaged those marked as outside the group. A number of categories were 'marked' by the in-group, such as persons who were on part-time or fixed-term contacts, had not completed a doctorate, were parents or carers for older relatives, were in teaching-focussed roles, did not desire promotion to professor, were not vocal in lab meetings and were not praised by colleagues. The most common group to express the status-based definition of 'real' academic were early-career women. Status anxiety often intersected with managing non-academic commitments, such as maternity, as the following early career academic (ECA) describes:

> Since I've had a baby I've come back 0.6 [of full-time equivalent work hours] but that's been a bad experience to be honest. So I'm actually negotiating. My partner wants to go back to study, so what we're thinking is that I'll go back full-time next year and he'll study and be the primary carer of our little girl because there's still that sense of elitism that an academic is a certain thing. That it's not something that you can treat as a job and therefor do 0.6 of. The idea is that *it has to be who you are and it has to be your whole life* therefor if your 0.6, you're just a waste of space. You're just wasting that a position that *a whole academic* could be taking... There's just this complete illegitimacy about the concept of being a part time academic. Legally, it's fine. Like if you look at the enterprise bargain, it's set up to be doable. But because of how the culture and how people think about what an academic is, it's not actually possible to do it in my experience.
>
> (Belinda, emphasis added)

Being 'a whole academic' is conflated here with expressing 'total commitment' to the academic role (Rafnsdóttir & Heijstra, 2013, p. 286), as if the labour of part-time scholars is of less value than a full-time counterpart. Kandiko Howson et al. (2017) note that their participants expressed anxieties about pursuing status recognition as female academics. Some of their participants reported an ambivalence about status-seeking activities, which were framed as both expected in an academic career but also in conflict with aspects of their professional and gender identities (Kandiko Howson et al., 2017, p. 7). In a previous analysis (Cannizzo, 2017), I documented a range of different career aspirations held by members of this sample group. While not every participant aspires to the same career goals, there is a wide-spread recognition of the value of being seen *as if* professorhood is the underlying objective.

The second most common assumption about 'real' academics is that they live, and learn how to live, with precarity. ECAs and especially contingent workers lack several of the forms of labour security described by Guy Standing in *The Precariat* (2011). Mid-career academics more often implied that academic authenticity was developed through learning to manage the precarious aspects of their employment, most commonly labour market insecurity, employment insecurity and representation insecurity (Standing, 2011, p. 10). For example, Harold describes a tension of feeling that his work contract has prevented him from realising employment security:

> Something that's probably pretty important to talk about is my employment status, which is still contractual. I am on a contract... prior to that, I've had a number of short-term contracts. I had a full-time contract... and that was when I first coordinated units and had the responsibility of teaching full semesters, whereas prior to that, I was just doing tutoring and the occasional guest lectures. So that year helped formalise my academic identity, but I was still doing my PhD... Yeah, so, that's – there's probably more questions that pertain to this more closely down the track – that obviously *impacts upon your sense of identity*: when you're work is not permanent. You feel like there's that until further notice quality and that sense of *being here, but not being here*.
>
> (Harold, emphasis added)

By contrast, another mid-career academic who expressed greater confidence in his status claimed that becoming an authentic academic was 'about the flexibility'; that in career planning one should 'be flexible, be pragmatic... be Machiavellian: be strategic in your approach' (Thomas). Another manifestation of this approach is appeals to developing 'resilience': 'I bounce back a lot, when I need to or even when there's uncertainty in the future' (Whitney).

Mid-career academics exclusively expressed assumptions about the degree of competition that was expected of real academics (the third theme) as they spoke most about negotiating the expectations of upper management – some describing themselves as 'go-getting' (Lachlan) or, perhaps more critically, as 'a good neoliberal subject' (Harold) and 'box-ticking' (Whitney). Less common than the themes described so far were the latter three themes: that being a 'real' academic is about the expression of certain values (n=4), that it is about establishing an identity (n=3) and that it is about recognition within a community of peers (n=3). The low rate of mention of these themes is interesting, given that they are among the most prominent descriptions that academics use to describe academic work and life when asked explicitly about authentic academic experiences and managerialism within universities (Cannizzo, 2018). In interviews, curiosity, passion, justice and professionalism were named as key values of 'real' academics; authentic academic identities were linked to discipline, research programme, institution and celebrity status; and valued communities of authentic academics included professional associations (such as The Australian Sociological Association), the laboratory group and mentorships. Overall, anchors of support and belonging (values, identity and community) were less common than phenomena associated with difficulties in performing academic work (status, precarity and performance). For many, these challenges, and strategies for overcoming them, have come to define authentic experiences of academic careers.

The gendered limits of 'real' academic careers

Also present in academics' talk about their careers are ideas about what might enable or be a barrier to an authentic academic career. Enablers and barriers were described in terms of real experiences that academics reported but also from talk with colleagues and mentors, from rumours and second-hand narratives, and less frequently from peer-reviewed research. The truth-value of such statements was derived from their presentation as personal testimony; the authority of personal experience. After coding every instance where an academic described a phenomenon that disrupted the realisation of authentic academic work, the three most common themes to emerge from this testimony were sponsorship, maternity and competition.

Ten of the 29 academics interviewed identified forms of sponsorship – a person's social networks, friendships, mentorships and other informal relationships – as being an important factor in experiencing an authentic academic career. The most common type of statement here is that real academics need advocates in the current higher education system, to assist in workplace socialisation, to put their names forward for opportunities and to introduce them to the academic community. The following ECA, who expressed confidence in progressing within an academic career, describes mentorship in the following terms:

> even if you don't know it at the time, they are giving you advice that will have those long-term implications that it is difficult to perceive. I didn't think much about career early on in my PhD... So, I taught a lot, textbook, like three journal articles, and good progress on the book that's coming out this year. So, all that sort of stuff happened that has worked out well for me now. But it is weird, thinking back on it: if I'd made different decisions, would I be in a position, or would I still be in that [non-academic] professional job... I don't know. You just got to choose your mentors and trust them.
>
> (Iain)

Homophily may play a significant role in the informal academic labour market as in the formation of social networks. Bagilhole (2007, p. 41) argues that where men dominate departments or universities, they are more often tutored by other men and 'have more natural access to these support systems than women'. Such sponsorship can both allow majority groups greater access to tacit knowledge within an organisation, such as the taste of a group, its taken-for-granted worldviews and socialised competencies – and consequently have positive effects on their self-esteem (Bagilhole, 2007, p. 41). To the extent that 'real' academic work relies on sponsorship, it is open to being shaped by the tastes of dominant groups.

The second most common theme was the perception that maternity and domestic care labour formed a barrier to experiencing an authentic academic career. Respondents from this category were nearly exclusively female and mid-career, suggesting an intersection between the life course of many women and perceptions of career difficulties. The work/life issues that participants identified here concerned their use of non-work time for academic labour. Gail, a mid-career academic, describes a well-documented conflict time pressure that particularly impacts academic mothers (Evans, 2010; Ramsay, 2007):

> But I think it doesn't matter how much you publish, you always want to be publishing more. Things that have held that back a bit: obviously, starting teaching – it takes a huge amount of time. And having kids, you know, time out with maternity leave and just being continually tired and instead of working on weekends and working until late at night, you actually go home and play with your kids on weekends and everything like that. It's a reduction in the number of hours available to dedicate to work, at the end of the day. If you've got kids, you have kids.
>
> (Gail)

Although most participants described publication metrics as a poor representation of the value of academic work, ignorance of these measures was described as an existential career risk. For example, for one early-career microbiologist, if she could not publish at a high enough rate, 'the plan is to leave academia' (Danielle). Another academic with a large teaching responsibility reported that she was leaving her ongoing position to care for a parent who had developed a debilitating illness, abandoning what she perceived to be a lifelong role. Agnes Bosanquet (2017) notes that the idea of an 'early-career' researcher is not only a policy construct but also a normative one: it assumes 'steady employment and continuous research and professional development', which contradicts the experiences of many ECAs (Bosanquet, 2017, p. 73). The use of extensive work hours from the career development phase is part of an individualistic career strategy identified by Acker and Armenti (2004), that is, working harder and sleeping less – or what Clarke and Knights (2015) have termed 'careering'. The conceptualisation of care labour and maternity as an individual choice, rather than a policy issue, both responsibilises mothers and carers for their 'performance' in evaluations, and is in tension with the ideal of the academic labourer as a craftsperson, consumed by their work. In discussing their careers, academics in this study drew on assumptions about what constitutes 'real' academic work and described gendered barriers to engaging in that work. 'Real' work here is not simply about high citation counts or grant money, but about presenting oneself to others as a certain kind of worker with particular kind of temporal autonomy and experiences.

Authentic work and the value of time

The impact of higher education policy changes to the academic profession cannot be understood without considering how academics make sense of their careers and lives. When seen as a kind of craftwork, academic labour is irreducible to measurement, quantification and 'athleticism' associated with Taylorism (Gregg, 2017). However the swelling metric tide (Wilsdon et al., 2015) of performance metrics that direct the comparison of academic productivity in the United Kingdom and other countries would *seem* to attest to the contrary. The measurement of academic productivity has been central to attempts to transform the higher education landscape into a customer and end-user centred economic model. However, Rob Watts (2017, p. 147) argues that just because policymakers from the 1980s onwards have claimed to transform higher education into marketable good doesn't necessarily make it so. He claims that their assertions entertain a category mistake: 'Higher education is an "experience good": its value, point, and purpose to say nothing of that evanescent idea of its quality, will only be revealed once the student fully engages in the educational experience' (Watts, 2017, p. 159). Knowledge and its use in education have been framed in policy as market goods, being described as a 'demand-driven system' guided by student 'choice' (Department of Education and Training, 2016, p. 2), but do not resemble markets in practice. The managerial and policy solution to the disjuncture between policy discourse and the reality of education and knowledge has been to create proxy measures. What Watts describes as the 'market-crazed governance' in higher education tends to 'evaluate procedures rather than real consequence or to measure "customer satisfaction" with "imaginary penalties" issued so that regulators can appear "tough" on public issues' (2017, p. 118). Knowledge production is also measured through proxies such as journal publications, citation counts, h-indices, grant income and other measurements of productivity associated with an audit culture (Burrows, 2012).

Because the economic rationalisation of academic work is limited to what can be measured, and what is measured depends on measurement procedures and devices, this rationalism depends on the will of academics themselves. Descriptions of early- and mid-career transitions in academia in terms of temporal metaphors – that is, the tenure clock, the publication treadmill – suggests the psychological internalisation of the productivity imperative of technologies of performance. However, Vostal (2015) has noted that the pace-setting activities of university management – notably the institutional drive to attain 'excellence' in international performance comparisons – can produce a range of experiences for staff. Time pressure is only part of the range of temporal experiences that shape academic life. Vostal claims that academics experience 'oppressive acceleration' of work when there is an involuntary increase in the pace of work activities, perhaps driven by 'the net of technologies, which monitor, measure and regulate late modern work' (Vostal, 2015, p. 78). The experience of being harassed and harried that may result from performance monitoring is not a problem of pace *per se*; indeed, Vostal (2015, p. 85) demonstrates that information communication technologies have allowed for positive experiences of the speeding up of scholarship. Pace is not as important as the experience of control of rhythm and congruence or conflict between different temporalities (Vostal, 2015, p. 86). Gail, above, described the pace of publishing as beyond satisfactory control ('you always want to be publishing more') and therefore a double disadvantage for a primary carer ('If you've got kids, you have kids'). To cope with the demands of academic publishing quotas and competition, extended, unpaid, work outside of the university is widely assumed to be both normal and necessary amongst Australian ECAs (Cannizzo et al., 2018). This unremunerated work may be described as motivated by the hope that future employment opportunities may follow – a kind of 'hope labour' (Kuehn & Corrigan, 2013). The perseverance of traditional gender roles in the family lives of academics hence reproduce gendered assumptions about the ideal aspiring academic and their motivations.

While slow scholarship advocates such as Berg and Seeber (2016) have pointed to 'the corporatisation of universities' as producing 'a sense of urgency' in academic life, Vostal's (2015) critique of scholarship's heavy focus on 'oppressive acceleration' raises the question: What assumptions are being made about academic work here? If acceleration can be a 'thrilling' experience as well as an oppressive one, what temporalities facilitate 'real' academic work? For the Australian academics who participated in this study, authentic academic work is committed work, it is felt to be insecure work (especially for contingent staff), it is sponsored work and it is time-consuming. It is not the kind of work that can be readily recognised in productivity performance measurement, but rather through the development of a craft. Craftspeople are 'dedicated to good work for its own sake… their labor is not simply a means to another end' for Sennett (2008, p. 20). The 'real' academic work described by participants has the qualities of craftwork: it's temporality coincides with the life course ('it has to be who you are and it has to be your whole life' – Belinda), meaning that a lack of temporal autonomy is felt to be a threat to self-identity (insecurity 'impacts upon your sense of identity' – Harold). Set in our contemporary political economy, this craftwork is faced with common challenges: to find sponsorship that enables an apprenticeship in the craft ('you just got to choose your mentors and trust them' – Iain) and time amid other responsibilities (that might influence 'the number of hours available to dedicate to work' – Gail). Craftwork has its own values that are distinguishable from the metric evaluation of its products. Although a piece of research or educational course may produce, for example, patents, publications or student satisfaction scores, the craftsperson values doing the work well for its own sake; consequently improving science, making a more convincing argument, imparting knowledge or skills, helping other people and so on. The mastery of an academic craft implies a different system of values to those expressed in the production of measurable 'goods' for utilitarian exchange as well as the temporal autonomy to enact craft practices.

Treating academic work as craftwork and as a means to some other end have different logics of value. Craftwork thrives in the presence of a community of craftspeople and practices of apprenticeship (Sennett, 2008). Value in craft is produced through contributing to and mastering the activity itself. Performing work for its utility towards some other end may incentivise compromises in the quality of work where the quality of work and attaining the other end come into conflict. Academics contracted to provide consultancy for firms, for example, may find their time constrained or their methods unsuitable for the service that the firm has purchased. This distinction is part of the reproduction of both classed and gendered divisions within academic communities and the privileging of those with autonomy over the rhythms of their daily lives. The experience of autonomy over work pace and rhythms has become central to whether faster paces have come to be experienced as career barriers or opportunities to experiment with temporalities. Ylijoki (2005) notes in her narrative analysis of Finnish academics that a sense of nostalgia was connected to a felt loss of 'freedom'. In analysing the meaning of the discourses of freedom and loss used by participants, Ylijoki finds several very similar ideas of how freedom is expressed: as 'the academic characteristics in research work' (p. 565), 'the overall quality of research' (p. 566) and 'contributing to the advancement of [the participant's] discipline' (p. 569). The sense of a loss of 'home' expressed in Ylijoki's study is for the freedom to immerse oneself in meaningful work through focus on one's craft; that is, to pace oneself. For academics who have only ever worked on contingent contracts (casual, sessional, short-term and probationary), and for those with care labour responsibilities outside of the university, there has perhaps never been a sense of temporal autonomy to mourn, but rather only a lingering sense of inauthenticity – an imposter syndrome.

Conclusion

The political implications of academic craftwork have long been acknowledged, but only in a limited way. A long-touted discourse of the loss of academic freedom or a nostalgia for a by-gone 'golden age' of scholarship has been circulated among an international professoriate (Cannizzo, 2018; Ylijoki, 2005). However, transformations in the demographic composition of the academic workforce, the massification of higher education and managerialism in universities have also seen some very old forms of social division reconfigured. Although not excluded by policy or official rhetoric, women academics face higher rates of attrition or career interruptions due to maternity and care labour obligations (Bell & Yates, 2014). Additionally, the growing use of contingent labour for both project-based research and regular teaching in universities since the 1980s has produced a pool of labourers who feel and often are detached from their employing organisations. Calls by advocates of slow scholarship, such as Berg and Seeber (2016, p. 89) to promote 'the conviviality of thinking together' already assumes a close comradery and friendship between participants. However, the persistence of an ideal that academic work entails a lifestyle – that there is 'real' academic work – contributes to experiences of inauthenticity, or what is sometimes described as imposter syndrome or 'toxic shame' (Gill, 2010). Those seeking to build greater solidarity, community and collegiality between academics from across disciplines may benefit from exploring how value is expressed in academic everyday life. While all academic staff share experiences of organisational transformation and narratives about the influence that corporatisation has had for scholarly freedom, the working conditions of academics have not been affected equally. The status distinction of 'real' academic work is shown here to occupy a place in how academics interpret and plan their careers through academia. A frank discussion of what ideals are promoted in career planning *in situ* and in workforce plannings is needed to produce a more inclusive and secure workforce.

References

Acker, S., & Armenti, C. (2004). Sleepless in academia. *Gender and Education, 16*(1), 3–24.

Aiston, S. J., & Jung, J. (2015). Women academics and research productivity: An international comparison. *Gender and Education, 27*(3), 205–220.

Bagilhole, B. (2007). Challenging women in the male academy: Think about draining the swamp. In P. Cotterill, S. Jackson, & G. Letherby (Eds.), *Challenges and negotiations for women in higher education* (pp. 21–32). Dordrecht: Springer.

Bailyn, L. (2003). Academic careers and gender equity: Lessons learned from MIT. *Gender, Work and Organization, 10*(2), 137–153.

Bell, S., & Yates, L. (2014). *Women in the science research workforce: Identifying and sustaining the diversity advantage.* Melbourne, VIC: University of Melbourne. Retrieved from http://www.womeninscienceresearch.org.au/

Berg, M., & Seeber, B. K. (2016). *The slow professor: Challenging the culture of speed in the academy.* Toronto, ON: University of Toronto Press.

Blackmore, P., & Kandiko, C. B. (2011). Motivation in academic life: A prestige economy. *Research in Post-Compulsory Education, 16*(4), 399–411.

Bosanquet, A. (2017). Academic, women, mother: Negotiating multiple subjectivities during early career. In R. Thwaites & A. Pressland (Eds.), *Being an early career feminist academic: Global perspectives, experiences, and challenges* (pp. 73–92). London: Palgrave Macmillan.
Brew, A., Boud, D., Lucas, L., & Crawford, K. (2017). Academic artisans in the research university. *Higher Education*, *76*(1), 115–127.
Brown, T., Goodman, J., & Yasukawa, K. (2010). Academic casualization in Australia: Class divisions in the university. *Journal of Industrial Relations*, *52*(2), 169–182.
Burrows, R. (2012). Living with the h-index? Metric assemblages in the contemporary academy. *The Sociological Review*, *60*(2), 355–372.
Cannizzo, F. (2017). *Governing Australian academics: An analysis of governance and subjectivity in Australian universities* (Doctoral dissertation). Retrieved from https://figshare.com/
Cannizzo, F. (2018). 'You've got to love what you do': Academic labour in a culture of authenticity. *The Sociological Review*, *66*(1), 91–106.
Cannizzo, F., Mauri, C., & Osbaldiston, N. (2018). *Moral barriers between work/life balance policy and practice in academia.* Manuscript submitted for publication.
Clarke, C. A., & Knights, D. (2015). Careering through academia: Securing identities or engaging ethical subjectivities? *Human Relations*, *68*(12), 1865–1888.
Coate, K., & Kandiko Howson, C. (2016). Indicators of esteem: Gender and prestige in academic work. *British Journal of Sociology of Education*, *37*(4), 567–585.
Corbin Dwyer, S., & Buckle, J. L. (2009). The space between: On being an insider-outsider in qualitative research. *International Journal of Qualitative Methods*, *8*(1), 54–63.
Davies, S. R., & Horst, M. (2015). Crafting the group: Care in research management. *Social Studies of Science*, *45*(3), 371–393.
Department of Education and Training. (2016). *Driving innovation, fairness and excellence in Australian education* (Report No. ED16/000060). Retrieved from Department of Education and Training website: https://docs.education.gov.au/documents/driving-innovation-fairness-and-excellence-australian-education
Evans, M. (2010). For us or against us: Coercion and consensus in higher education. *Learning and Teaching*, *3*(2), 39–54.
Gill, R. (2010). Breaking the silence: The hidden injuries of the neoliberal university. In R. Ryan Flood & R. Gill (Eds.), *Secrecy and silence in the research process: Feminist reflections* (pp. 228–244). Abingdon: Routledge.
Gottschalk, L., & McEachern, S. (2010). The frustrated career: Casual employment in higher education. *Australian Universities' Review*, *52*(1), 37–50.
Gregg, M. (2017). The athleticism of accomplishment. In J. Wajcman & N. Dodd (Eds.), *The sociology of speed: Digital, organizational, and social temporalities* (pp. 102–116). Oxford: Oxford University Press.
Guarino, C. M., & Borden, V. M. H. (2017). Faculty service loads and gender: Are women taking care of the academic family? *Research in Higher Education*, *58*(6), 672–694.
James, S. (2015). Finding your passion: Work and the authentic self. *M/C Journal: A Journal of Media and Culture*, *18*(1). Online publication. Retrieved from http://journal.media-culture.org.au/index.php/mcjournal
Kandiko Howson, C., Coate, K., & de St Croix, T. (2017). Mid-career academic women and the prestige economy. *Higher Education Research and Development*. Advance online publication. doi:10.1080/07294360.2017.1411337

Kimber, M. (2003). The tenured 'core' and the tenuous 'periphery': The casualisation of academic work in Australian universities. *Journal of Higher Education Policy and Management*, *25*(1), 41–49.
Kuehn, K., & Corrigan, T. F. (2013). Hope labor: The role of employment prospects in online social production. *The Political Economy of Communication*, *1*(1), 9–25.
May, R., Peetz, D., & Strachan, G. (2013). The casual academic workforce and labour market segmentation in Australia. *Labour and Industry*, *23*(3), 258–275.
Mills, C. W, (1959). *The sociological imagination*. Oxford: Oxford University Press.
Probert, B. (2005). 'I just couldn't fit it in': Gender and unequal outcomes in academic careers. *Gender, Work and Organization*, *12*(1), 50–72.
Rafnsdóttir, G. L., & Heijstra, T. M. (2013). Balancing work-family life in academia: The power of time. *Gender, Work and Organization*, *20*(3), 283–296.
Ramsay, K. (2007). Women: Mothers and others. In P. Cotterill, S. Jackson, & G. Letherby (Eds.), *Challenges and negotiations for women in higher education* (pp. 33–52). Dordrecht: Springer.
Ryan, S., & Bhattacharyya, A. (2012). Barriers to professional development among contingent academic employees: An Australian case study. *The International Journal of Learning*, *18*(4), 247–261.
Ryan, S., Burgess, J., Connell, J., & Groen, E. (2013). Casual academic staff in an Australian university: Marginalised and excluded. *Tertiary Education and Management*, *19*(2), 161–175.
Sennett, R. (2008). *The craftsman*. New Haven, CT: Yale University Press.
Standing, G. (2011). *The precariat: The new dangerous class*. London: Bloomsbury Academic.
Strauss, A., & Corbin, J. (1998). *Basics of qualitative research: Techniques and procedures for developing grounded theory*. Thousand Oaks, CA: Sage.
Tancred-Sheriff, P. (1985). Craft, hierarchy and bureaucracy: Modes of control of the academic labour process. *Canadian Journal of Sociology*, *10*(4), 369–390.
Tweedie, D. (2013). Precarious work and Australian labour norms. *The Economic and Labour Relations Review*, *24*(3), 297–315.
Vaisey, S. (2009). Motivation and justification: A dual-process model of culture in action. *American Journal of Sociology*, *114*(6), 1675–1715.
Vostal, F. (2015). Academic life in the fast lane: The experience of time and speed in British academia. *Time and Society*, *24*(1), 71–95.
Watts, R. (2017). *Public universities, managerialism and the value of higher education*. London: Palgrave Macmillan.
Wilsdon, J., Allen, L., Beliore, E., Campbell, P., Curry, S., Hill, S., ... Johnson, B. (2015). *The metric tide: Report of the independent review of the role of metrics in research assessment and management*. Retrieved from http://www.hefce.ac.uk/pubs/rereports/year/2015/metrictide/
Wright, E. O. (2015). *Understanding class*. London: Verso.
Ylijoki, O.-H. (2005). Academic nostalgia: A narrative approach to academic work. *Human Relations*, *58*(5), 555–576.

Chapter 7

Happy in academia

The perspective of the academic elite

Oili-Helena Ylijoki

Introduction

Over the last decades, universities have turned into increasingly managerial and entrepreneurial institutions. The implementation of the New Public Management doctrine in various countries has brought private sector practices and values into universities, emphasising such virtues as accountability, efficiency, productivity and impact. Likewise, with the rise of 'academic capitalism' (Slaughter & Leslie, 1997), the success in attracting external funding has become crucial both for the institution and academic careers. Due to these interlinked transformation processes, universities have become highly competitive environments in which audits, rankings and performance metrics are flourishing.

In the research literature, there is a growing array of studies investigating how the changes of the institutional context of higher education shape and mould academic work, identities and careers. For the most part, the findings follow a plot of a misery narrative. Studies testify to a severe deterioration of working conditions and career possibilities in academia. Academics work increasingly on short-term and part-time contracts, and lose autonomy to managerial control (e.g. Musselin, 2005; Rhoades, 2010). They encounter intensifying productivity pressures and demands for excellence (e.g. Clarke et al., 2012; Hakala, 2009; Leišytė, 2016) and work under heavy time pressure (e.g. Guzmán-Valenzuela & Di Napoli, 2015; Vostal, 2016; Ylijoki, 2013; Ylijoki & Mäntylä, 2003). The miseries involve also a gendered dimension since the growing pressures pose extra difficulties to female academics (e.g. Acker & Armenti, 2004; Menzies & Newson, 2008; Nikunen, 2012). As a result, academics experience increasing disillusionment, stress, insecurity and anxiety in their work.

However, the misery narrative, although the dominant one, is not the only story embedded in the literature on the effects of university transformations. Several studies point to the polarisation and stratification among the academic staff (e.g. Barry et al., 2006; Fanghanell, 2012; Gornall & Salisbury, 2012; Henkel, 2005; Ylijoki & Ursin, 2013), manifest already among junior academics whose career tracks are strikingly separated (e.g. Herbert & Tienari, 2013; Lund, 2018; Ylijoki & Henriksson, 2017). In accordance with the logic of academic capitalism, there are always those who win and those who lose (Slaughter & Leslie, 1997). Thus, miseries do not touch upon everybody as some groups of academics may be practically untouchable and may even gain from the transformations.

In this article, I focus on the winning academics in the UK national context. The British higher education system is particularly interesting, since it has been at the frontline of neoliberal and managerial transformations. Especially the research assessment system, earlier research assessment exercise (RAE) and now research excellence framework (REF) are sort of global iconic examples of neoliberal managerialism in academia, associated with harsh competition, intensifying productivity pressures, increasing strain, and a fear of becoming labelled as non-research-active. Although this kind of misery narrative is overwhelming both in the literature and in everyday discussions at university coffee tables, there are academics who tell an opposite narrative of happiness, success, satisfaction and joy in the current academia. Their story and its relation to the misery narrative are the core of this article.

Next, I will present my empirical data and analytical lens to explore it. Then, I will describe more in detail the happiness narrative, its moral underpinnings and the ways in which it is legitimised. In the conclusion, I will discuss national differences by mirroring the UK data with interviews with Finnish social scientists. In addition, I will consider the narrative of the happy academics in relation to the misery narrative, and reflect on the growing stratification and polarisation within global academia.

Data and method

The empirical basis of this article is comprised of focussed interviews with 15 eminent academics in two Russell Group universities in the United Kingdom. The interviewees worked in three social scientific fields: sociology, social policy and social work. All had established positions, mainly professorships. Ten interviewees were male, and five were female, representing the gendered bias among the academic staff. The interviews were open in nature, enabling interviewees to freely talk about their experiences and opinions. The themes discussed included work history, the best and worst periods in academia, work motivation, time and space for research work, work-life balance, future hopes and fears, and views on the changes of higher education. All interviews were tape recorded and transcribed.

In this article the interviews are analysed from the elite perspective. The interviewees are considered as members of the scientific elite due to their institutional and intellectual power. They all work at the Russell Group universities in which their fields have a strong position, manifest, for instance, by their excellent success in research assessments. The Russell Group itself has a high status within the higher education system in the United Kingdom. For instance Bowl (2018, p. 674) underlines that already before world rankings 'there was a pecking order among universities, with Oxford, Cambridge and the elite "Russell Group" at the top of that hierarchy'. According to her, this creates 'the elite social ethos'. In a similar way, Evans (2015) emphasises that the universities belonging to the Russell Group produce a special 'elitist identity'.

Apart from institutional prestige, the interviewees have also prominent personal reputation and authority. They hold key gate-keeping positions, for instance, as members of research assessment panels, research funding agencies and recruitment committees and other decision-making bodies in their universities, they act as editors of top journals, and often they have also close linkages outside university to relevant policymaking bodies and networks. Furthermore, the elite perspective springs from data-driven reading of the interview material itself. It became evident that while talking about academic work and their own experiences, these interviewees had a special point of view from which to make sense of academic life and its values and norms. I refer to their way of talking as a happiness narrative.

The happiness narrative is a cultural master narrative (e.g. Elliot, 2005; Polkinghorne, 1988) constructed on the basis of the collectively shared elements of the interviews. It is embedded in a moral order (Harré, 1983) that crystallises what is good and valued, and what is bad and despised in a given community. In this way, the happiness narrative has normative power over individuals as it defines what the right kind of academic work is and what a true academic is. Yet, since each individual always has a particular and unique relation to one's culture, the happiness narrative does not have any one-to-one correspondence with single interviewees. Some interviewees are more deeply attached to the happiness narrative than some others, but in any case, they all identify and acknowledge its basic elements and values. Irrespective of individual differences, the happiness narrative thus forms a shared foundation to make sense of academic work and its transformations among the interviewees.

Based on close reading of the interview material, I will describe the key characteristics of the happiness narrative. I will present plenty of quotes in order to offer a rich and nuanced touch of how the interviewees express themselves. The longer quotes are intended, and the short ones are bracketed in the text. In the interview situations, full anonymity was promised, so all personal and institutional identifiers are omitted. The names mentioned in the text are pseudonyms, but the gender of the speaker is maintained.

The happiness narrative

Love and commitment

The happiness narrative is based on love and passion for work. Academic work is described as so 'satisfying', 'stimulating' and 'absolutely fascinating' that one becomes totally captivated and absorbed by it. For instance Peter says, 'I love what I do' and repeats his declaration of love again and again:

> Oh gosh yeah, I do really love to work. And I would happily do it all the time, really. I really love doing research. I actually really quite like teaching as well. So I would happily work all the time really. (…) The only thing that stops me working more is having other people in the house who I obviously want to interact with, I need to interact with. If those were magically disappeared, you know, if my entire family would die on the car crash, once I got over the grief, which might take me many, many years, I would just work all the time.

Because of profound love, academic work is not really work at all but rather a vocation that is embedded in dedication and commitment. In this way, the happiness narrative builds a distinction from ordinary paid work. By cherishing love, passion, pleasure and enjoyment, it makes one's work superior and unique compared to normal 'five-to-nine work'. Anne, saying that work forms 70% of her commitments, explains her attraction to work in the following way:

> It's a vocation. I mean when I think of what I enjoy doing I don't see it as work. I see work as what I don't like doing. So it's different.

The commitment to academic work results in working long hours, often also in evenings and over weekends. For example, Malcom tells that he normally starts at the university at half past seven and ends at half past nine. Then he frequently continues at home where he has an office too. So work and private become 'seamless entities' for him. Malcolm emphasises that long working hours are by no means 'the fault of the university' but 'a personal choice'. Academics, having a lot of autonomy and freedom, willingly choose to work hard and long because they are enthusiastic and ambitious and just cannot say no to exciting invitations and new work possibilities. However, he points out that not all academics work in this way, saying 'I'm sure I have colleagues who will work nine till five'.

The exact degree of commitment varies, depending especially on the life situation of the narrator. Linda's account presents an extreme. She underlines that she has 'no other life but work'. She does not have any moral obligations outside working life, which enables her to concentrate fully on her work. She considers the situation as a lucky one. She says that she has a lot of control over her timetable and, as a rule, she chooses to work:

> I don't really do anything else in any sustained or commitment way, but that's a choice. (...) I'm very lucky. My mother died at the age of fifty-eight. My step-mother died in the autumn. She was the last relative to whom I had any moral commitment. (...) I've never married. I've never had any children. I never wanted children. I chose not to have children.

Even if the commitment to work is not as complete as in Linda's case, work takes the key role in life. Since work is life and life is work, the notion of work-life balance does not find resonance in the happiness narrative. It is acknowledged as a common discourse everywhere, including in academia, but it is not sensible when thinking about one's own work. There might be some other kind of balancing, like in the case of George. For him, the core issue is keeping 'a balance between doing empirical work and doing more reflective writing', between 'writing for journals and writing books' and balancing 'between solo writing and joint writing'. Instead, the question of work-life balance is pointless in the happiness narrative. This is expressed in a particularly apposite way by Brian:

> I don't find it challenging because I don't balance it. There is no balance there at all. This staff in our university, they are talking about work-life balance. There's no balance. Work wins every time, pretty much every time.

Not all academics follow the ideals of dedication and commitment. The happiness narrative acknowledges that there is a majority of academics who are different and who do not adhere to the same values and working patterns. In this way, it makes a clear-cut distinction between people like me and others. Tony explains the difference between two kinds of academics:

> There are people for whom the academic work is the co-partner in their life and there are those whom the academic work is their job. Now I'm not saying, I don't wish to say that one is more desirable that the other, but I know I would be seen as somebody who is largely my academic work is my life.

Thus, the happiness narrative generates a distinction between sort of 'true' academics (Ylijoki, 2013) who work long hours out of love and dedication, and nine-to-five academics who fail to reach the same standards and values. By doing this, it establishes a demanding normative ideal about what being an academic should mean. This notion follows closely the traditional view of an intellectual life devoted to the quest for truth and wisdom for the sake of love and passion for one's subject (Cannizzo, 2018; Clarke et al., 2012; Ziman, 1998). This notion is detached from place and time, reproducing an image of academic and academic work in a social and societal vacuum. Next, I contextualise the happiness narrative in the current managerial university environment and explore how happiness is constructed under the recent transformations of higher education.

No complaints

In the happiness narrative the managerial changes are more than welcome. Conversely, this means that all kinds of complaining about their disastrous impacts are forbidden. It is emphasised that although people tend to talk so much about increasing stress, strain, pressure and anxiety in academia, this is not an accurate and justified perception. On the contrary, the changes have been beneficial in several ways. For instance, Steven, recalling his recent conference experiences, distances himself from complainers:

> A lot of people of my age think that this is the perversion of intellectual life, the castration of intellectual life. And they complain about it bitterly. I went to a big conference last March, the first speaker was a very eminent, slightly older than me, and he just spent all his time complaining about how he is been treated by his university and how rotten things were. Well yeah you could, you know, but things, the expectations change. I don't complain.

The reflections on changing higher education environment frequently refer to RAE and REF, treated as symbols of all transformations. The happiness narrative underlines that against a common opinion among academics, the benefits of these assessments are abundant. For instance, Roger, presenting himself as different from the majority, highlights that he has personally gained from the assessments:

> The demands of the research assessment exercise, this is not a common thing to hear people say, but for me that has been a positive thing, I was on the RAE panel. (…) You would find more people who would say this has not been for development, that they find it stressful, that they feel it overrates research that has a measurable impact. (…) But for me, I think it has worked well.

Furthermore, the happiness narrative not only makes a distinction from complainers and whiners, it also attaches a moral disapproval on them. Linda, who says that she has very strong moral positions, expresses an extreme view. She stresses that research assessments have been the best thing ever in British higher education. Moreover, she draws a demarcation line between those who do well in the assessments and those who fail. The latter gets no sympathy, but instead a moral accusation as thieves who do not work hard enough to deserve their salaries:

> There are some social scientists in Britain and many people in humanities who see the research assessment exercises since 1985 as a bad thing. I think they have been a wonderful thing. They have been the best that has ever happened in higher education. (…) They have been splendid because they have driven out the people who are in fact thieves because those people didn't do any publications and research (…) Now they don't survive in the universities. They have been either moved to teaching contracts when they have to do a lot more teaching and administration or they have gone. (…) Well, I think that is good.

In this way, the happiness narrative casts severe moral doubts on those academics who complain about the intensifying requirements and deteriorating work conditions. It involves a subtext that these academics are dishonest, incompetent or lazy. This moral criticism is kept hidden since 'you don't go around saying that in public of course because it wouldn't make you popular', as Linda remarks. Yet the moral disapproval is strong. This is made plain, for instance, by Peter who sharply differentiates himself from those who are not productive enough for research assessments:

> I mean, what the hell are academics doing if they can't produce four papers in as many years? I mean that's not much to ask. I don't think people have so much teaching and so many admin that they can't write one paper a year which is all you need to get through the RAE. (…) I think a lot of the changes in universities have been good. I'm not one of these people who think the good old days were in the 1970s.

The maxim of no complaints covers all kinds of whining about academic miseries. The misery discourse, overwhelming in academia, creates irritation and moral indignation. Complainers are described as people who do not fulfil properly their duties, whereas true academics are not only scientifically productive but also carry the heavy responsibility of the overall functioning of the university. For instance, Roger cannot find any justification for complainers:

> I can't stand complaints whether the government is betraying previous principles or whether the university world is going to the dogs, expressions, all these metaphors. I wouldn't take the view that recession, the coalition government and so on and so forth is undermining academic autonomy. I have no patience with those. (…) You look at the people

> who do most research and write most, and on the whole they are the people that are also carrying management burdens. I have quite strong feelings about this. There's no excuse really.

Overall, the happiness narrative differentiates academics into two categories with a moral assessment: a majority of complainers and a chosen few who are happy with the changes. It is striking that the latter category shows hardly any understanding of or sympathy for the complainers. Complaining is seen as irritating, unjust and immoral, which builds a sharp contrast and moral supremacy to the followers of the happiness narrative. Hence, these academics are not only true academics but also academics with high moral standards.

Success and elitism

Academics' happiness in the present day university is also related to success. They have been highly successful in getting grants, creating key networks, producing impressive publication records, reaching recognition in their scientific community, and gaining quick and smooth career advancement. So, they are happy, lucky and satisfied, but 'who wouldn't be', as Anne remarks:

> I've actually been able to carve out, you know, a successful academic career for myself at relatively young age. I mean, you know, I had my personal chair before I was forty. I established myself as a scholar before that. So I am satisfied, I think I'm very lucky. (...) Yes, I'm satisfied, who wouldn't be. I mean I think that in some ways I've reached quite a high level of my career very early on.

In the happiness narrative, academic work conditions allow autonomy, freedom and security, often involving possibilities for blues skies research. These features, representing traditional Humboldtian values and ideals, are highly appreciated and respected, further increasing academics' happiness and satisfaction. There really is nothing to complain. Roger describes his work experiences in the following way:

> I am very satisfied, yeah. I feel very, here in the secure job where I have this level of autonomy and this, I suppose, status really, I feel incredibly lucky. My office overlooks a lake. I have control over my time. I have freedom to do the research that interests me. This is quite wonderful, I'm very lucky.

Although academics have made their own success, the happiness narrative acknowledges that there is also 'a luck element'. Anne, who made fast career advancement to the top, mentions that she has been fortunate to be 'in the right time with the right people'. Especially being in a Russell Group university with high standards, a world-wide reputation and an excellent standing are considered as crucial. Happiness, luck and success accumulate in this particular academic environment. Thus, successful academics and successful institutions match together. John describes how lucky it is to work in the university which has succeeded so well:

> It does feel quite luxury at the moment the kind of life that I've got. (...) I mean our university was certainly among those institutions in social sciences that did very well. So we've had quite privileged life here. (...) I've always been lucky in the sense of being here. We've always been on the right side of the trade-off, I suppose.

In this way, the happiness narrative makes a distinction between Russell Group universities and ordinary and average higher education institutions. It acknowledges that the nature of academic work varies in different institutional settings and establishes a hierarchical order among them. Compared to institutions which do not have much success in rankings and assessments, the Russell Group university offers elitism and privilege. The elite status characterises individual academics too. They often hold influential positions not only within academia but also outside it. Malcolm, having particularly powerful connections to and roles in many sectors, explains his influence in science policymaking:

> I have been so close to the funding councils. I have helped to check their agenda which means that what has come out has been something I'd want to do anyway. So I've been fortunately close to the research councils and being asked to help to shape programmes. The sorts of areas which I think is needed to be done are ones that they identify.

This kind of elitism may evoke doubts of arrogance, selfishness and egocentrism, and the interviewees recognise this. Therefore, this interpretation is strongly denied by pleading to high moral standards in work. The happiness narrative is deeply embedded in a moral order which underlines the dedication to the common good. In this way, elite academics are sharply differentiated from self-seeking careerists. In contrast to morally doubtful and egoistic careerists, they are 'good departmental citizens', who 'love all duties actually' and constantly strive for 'institutional building for younger people'. For instance Anne, having a strong international reputation, assures that she does not want to be a career-oriented 'international research superstar':

> Being kind of international research superstar, I don't think that's what I want to do. I don't think I couldn't do it because I could do it if that's what I decide. (...) I think having, you know, got into more administration and the management side of things, I mean I get quite a lot out of that and I enjoy that and someone's got to do it.

In this way, the happiness narrative underlines the moral supremacy of the devoted, hard-working, successful and happy academics. Their success and elite position are not built at the expense of others or by neglecting their obligations. On the contrary, they take care of the common good, carry their responsibilities willingly and find personal pleasure in all duties they are involved in. So once again, this reinforces the differentiation between the happy ones and the complainers, the true academics and the nine-to-five academics.

Discussion

The happiness narrative is a cultural master narrative constructed from the shared elements in the UK interview material. The individual interviewees attach to it with different degrees. Not all are equally happy among the elite. For instance, an illness can set bodily limits and prevent from working as a true and totally committed academic, at least for a while. Likewise, in a rare occasion, one may fail in fund raising, which turns happiness fragile and shakes the grounding of the elite subjectivity. In addition, a looming retirement poses a special threat. Although the interviewees are confident that they can continue working through their wide networks, for instance as visiting professors abroad, the retirement still is a threat to one's identity as an eminent professor. It gives rise to a basic existential question asked by Acker (2017, p. 637), 'without my work, who would I be?' Yet, also in these cases in which there are threats and challenges, the happiness narrative forms the foundation against which one's divergent experiences are accounted for.

The strength of the happiness narrative is particularly noticeable when compared to similar interviews we carried out with eminent Finnish social scientists (see Ylijoki, 2016). Overall, their accounts are more moderate and internally less coherent. There are very few who follow the plot of the happiness narrative and warmly welcome the rhetoric on excellence, audits, metrics and rankings. Others are more or less critical of these trends. Especially, the Finnish professors show much empathy towards the younger generation of academics who need to build their careers in an increasingly insecure, demanding and competitive environment. Thus, their happiness is much more reserved than in the interviews with UK social scientists.

The differences between the United Kingdom and Finland imply that national contexts matter. The Finnish higher education system is not hierarchical in the same way than the British system, and there is no counterpart to the elite Oxbridge and Russell Group universities. Accordingly, it can be said that there are no elite academics in the same sense than in the United Kingdom. In addition, being a small Nordic welfare state country, equality is one of the ideological cornerstones of the Finnish culture, which acts against the elitist discourse. Hence, there may be differences in feeling rules concerning how to publicly display happiness and success in academia

(Bloch, 2012). Furthermore, Finland has been a latecomer in the managerial transformations of its higher education system. This may partly explain that the Finnish professors still lack coherent and shared ways to respond to changing work conditions and are only in a process of reshaping common narrative resources to make sense of them.

Notwithstanding national differences, there are signs of homogenisation of the academic elite in different countries, resembling the emergence of international elites and 'command posts' in general (Zald & Lounsbury, 2010). Based on the analysis of highly productive academics in 11 European countries, Kwiek (2016) reports that the European research elite is a very homogeneous group. The results corroborate the 10/50 rule, meaning that 10% of academics produce 50% of all publications. Kwiek (2016, p. 395) argues that these top performers form 'a universal academic species'. They have similar working patterns and they share similar academic attitudes, which substantially differ intra-nationally from their lower-performing colleagues. These top performers are much more cosmopolitan, much more research-oriented and work much longer hours than the rest of European academics included in his study.

The existence of the academic elite itself is not a new phenomenon since the science system is by nature hierarchical. As Mulkay (1976, p. 453) underlines, academic science has a well-defined elite who is able to exert power over the professional activities of non-elite members. In science studies, this is often referred by the Matthew effect (Merton, 1968): the rich get richer and the poor get poorer. Thus, the key academic credits, especially top publications, grant funding and university posts, tend to accumulate and thereby further strengthen the position of those who are on the winning side. In the current increasingly competitive university environment, this becomes all the more apparent. What is more, Mulkay (1976) points out that the scientific elite actively engage in regulating the relationship between government and academic research. In this study too, the elite interviewees are entangled in several ways with managerial power, for instance in their roles in research assessment panels, science policy networks, research funding agencies and university decision-making bodies. Doing this, they are able to protect and promote their views and values concerning what it takes to be a top academic. As a result, the elite members are actively involved in co-producing the changes in academia, meaning that academic power and managerial power are intermingled (see Gläser, 2007).

The happiness narrative of the academic elite, discerned in this study, presents a remarkably different picture of the nature of the current academic work than the prevailing misery narrative. These two narratives are embedded in opposite moral orders concerning who are the morally virtuous and respectable academics. Interestingly, the views on moral virtues and vices have similar features, highlighting the contribution to the common good. As Fernando (2018) stresses, there seems to be a rather general agreement on what constitutes 'good character', that is good academic work and workers. She states that good character, drawing on socially defined and historically inscribed rules of ethical conduct, involves responsibilities to students, organisational citizenship and serving the wider community. However, it is apparent that the opposite narratives entail radically different views as to who belongs to the category of good character.

The happiness narrative makes a sharp distinction between true academics and complainers. True academics are hard-working, committed and high performing members of the elite who carry all their duties happily and uncomplaining. Although they work extreme hours, they are not presented as workaholics but engaged workers who enjoy what they are doing (Torp et al., 2018; see also Gornall & Salisbury, 2012). Working out of joy and dedication, the happy academics carry responsibility of the success of both their disciplinary field and institution, thereby taking care of the common good. The complainers, for their part, do not meet these high standards and requirements. Accordingly, they are treated as morally suspicious, not motivated enough, lazy or incompetent in their work. This distinction builds moral superiority to the followers of the happiness narrative.

However, this view is challenged from the point of view of non-elite academics. For instance, Brew et al. (2017, p. 217) strongly argue that the common view of the low research performance group of academics as 'deficient, lacking the necessary skills or drive to engage in research' is mistaken and wrong. They introduce the concept 'academic artisans', which refers to ordinary academics who craft their roles creatively to provide 'a service to the institution by going beyond necessary tasks and contributing to a bigger whole' (Brew et al., 2017, p. 123). So, from this point of departure, it is academic artisans who are good corporate citizens, committed to the common good, often with a caring attitude. Likewise, Fernando (2018) says that a good character is in tension with career progression in the current competitive university context, which stresses individual achievement in measurable outputs. Thus, according to her study with senior lectures in research-intensive universities in the United Kingdom, communal and individual interests are incompatible. This implies that elites, having advanced to the top of the career ladder, are perceived as morally doubtful careerists pursuing only their individual interests (see Clarke & Knights, 2015), and the moral superiority as good departmental citizens is accorded to the less elite academics.

It can be summarised that there is a sort of moral struggle taking place in academia concerning what party is contributing most to the common good and deserves the credit for high morality. Irrespective of the opposite views, it is noteworthy that moral standing and good character still are a significant source of legitimacy in academic work, as Fernando (2018) mentions. The interviewees of this study frequently make reference to moral aspects of their work, thereby justifying their privileged position and denying in advance potential accusations of careerist and egoistic pursuits. It might be suggested that this kind of impression management is all the more important since, as social scientists, the interviewees are fully aware of the importance of structures in human agency, including career building.

Finally, it can be concluded that along with the increasing stratification and polarisation of the academic staff, the life-worlds of different parties become more and more separated. In the happiness narrative, the elite subjectivity is built on a sharp distinction from the rest of academics. It is striking that this narrative shows hardly any compassion or empathy to those who draw upon the misery narrative. The happiness narrative poses a very demanding normative ideal on what it means to be a successful academic, yet it shows little understanding of those who fail or are not willing to comply with it. As a result, it seems that mutual understanding and dialogue between these opposite narratives becomes all the more difficult.

Acknowledgements

The majority of the interviews have been carried out by PhD Virve Kallioniemi-Chambers and doctoral student Johanna Hokka, few by Oili-Helena Ylijoki.

References

Acker, S. (2017). Being an academic is the key to who I am – a memoir. *Higher Education Research & Development*, *36*(3), 637–639.

Acker, S., & Armenti, C. (2004). Sleepless in academia. *Gender and Education*, *16*(1), 3–24.

Barry, J., Berg, E., & Chandler, J. (2006). Academic shape sifting: Gender, management and identities in Sweden and England. *Organization*, *13*(2), 275–298.

Bloch, C. (2012). *Passion and paranoia: Emotions and the culture of emotion in academia*. Farnham: Ashgate.

Bowl, M. (2018). Differentiation, distinction and equality – or diversity? The language of the marketised university: An England, New Zealand comparison. *Studies in Higher Education*, *43*(4), 671–688.

Brew, A., Boud, D., Lucas, L., & Crawford, K. (2018). Academic artisans in the research university. *Higher Education*, *76*(1), 115–127.

Cannizzo, F. (2018). 'You've got to love what you do': Academic labour in a culture of authenticity. *The Sociological Review*, *66*(1), 91–106.

Clarke, C., & Knights, D. (2015). Careering through academia: Securing identities or engaging ethical subjectivities? *Human Relations*, *68*(12), 1865–1888.

Clarke, C., Knights, D., & Jarvis, C. (2012). A labour of love? Academics in business schools. *Scandinavian Journal of Management*, *28*(1), 5–15.

Elliot, J. (2005). *Using narrative in social research*. London: Sage.

Evans, L. (2015). Competitiveness, elitism and neoliberal performativity: The formation of a Russell Group academic identity. In L. Evans & J. Nixon (Eds.), *Academic identities in higher education* (pp. 149–166). London: Bloomsbury.

Fanghanel, J. (2012). *Being an academic*. London: Routledge.

Fernando, W. D. A. (2018). Exploring character in the new capitalism: A study of mid-level academics in a British research-intensive university. *Studies in Higher Education*, *43*(6), 1045–1057.

Gläser, J. (2007). The social orders of research evaluation systems. In R. Whitley & J. Gläser (Eds.), *The changing governance of the sciences* (pp. 245–266). Dordrecht: Springer.

Gornall, L., & Salisbury, J. (2012). Compulsive working, 'hyperprofessionality' and the unseen pleasures of academic work. *Higher Education Quarterly*, *66*(2), 135–154.

Guzmán-Valenzuela, C., & Di Napoli, R. (2015). Competing narratives of time in the managerial university. In P. Gibbs, O.-H. Ylijoki, C. Guzmán-Valenzuela, & R. Barnett (Eds.), *Universities in the flux of time* (pp. 154–167). London: Routledge.

Hakala, J. (2009). The future of the academic calling? Junior researchers in the entrepreneurial university. *Higher Education*, *57*(2), 173–190.

Harré, R. (1983). *Personal being*. Oxford: Basil Blackwell.

Henkel, M. (2005). Academic identity and autonomy in a changing policy environment. *Higher Education*, *49*(1–2), 155–176.

Herbert, A., & Tienari, J. (2013). Transplanting tenure and (re)constructing academic freedoms. *Studies in Higher Education*, *38*(2), 157–173.

Kwiek, M. (2016). The European research elite: A cross-national study of highly productive academics in 11 countries. *Higher Education*, *71*(3), 379–397.

Leišytė, L. (2016). New public management and research productivity – a precarious state of affairs of academic work in the Netherlands. *Studies in Higher Education*, *41*(5), 828–846.

Lund, R. (2018). The social organisation of boasting in the neoliberal university. *Gender and Education*. Advance online publication. doi:10.1080/09540253.2018.1482412

Menzies, H., & Newson, J. (2008). Time, stress and intellectual engagement in academic work: Exploring gender difference. *Gender, Work and Organization*, *15*(5), 504–522.

Merton, R. K. (1968). *Social theory and social structure*. New York, NY: The Free Press.

Mulkay, M. (1976). The mediating role of the scientific elite. *Social Studies of Science*, *6*(3/4), 445–470.

Musselin, C. (2005). European academic labor markets in transition. *Higher Education*, *49*(1–2), 135–154.

Nikunen, M. (2012). Changing university work, freedom, flexibility and family. *Studies in Higher Education*, *37*(6), 713–729.

Polkinghorne, D. E. (1988). *Narrative knowing and the human sciences*. Albany, NY: State University of New York Press.

Rhoades, G. (2010). Envisioning invisible workforces. In G. Gordon & C. Whitchurch (Eds.), *Academic and professional identities in higher education* (pp. 36–53). New York, NY: Routledge.

Slaughter, S., & Leslie, L. (1997). *Academic capitalism*. Baltimore, MA: The Johns Hopkins University Press.

Torp, S., Lysfjord, L., & Midje, H. H. (2018). Workaholism and work-family conflict among university academics. *Higher Education*. Advance online publication. doi:10.1007/s10734-018-0247-0

Vostal, F. (2016). *Accelerating academia*. Basingstoke: Palgrave Macmillan.
Ylijoki, O.-H. (2013). Boundary work between work and life in the high-speed university. *Studies in Higher Education*, *38*(2), 242–255.
Ylijoki, O.-H. (2016). Projectification and conflicting temporalities in academic knowledge production. *Theorie Vedy/Theory of Science*, *38*(1), 7–26.
Ylijoki, O.-H., & Henriksson, L. (2017). Tribal, proletarian and entrepreneurial career stories – junior academics as a case in point. *Studies in Higher Education*, *42*(7), 1292–1308.
Ylijoki, O.-H., & Mäntylä, H. (2003). Conflicting time perspectives in academic work. *Time & Society*, *12*(1), 55–78.
Ylijoki, O.-H., & Ursin, J. (2013). The construction of academic identity in the changes of Finnish higher education. *Studies in Higher Education*, *38*(8), 1135–1149.
Zald, M. N., & Lounsbury, M. (2010). The wizards of Oz: Towards an institutional approach to elites, expertise and command posts. *Organization Studies*, *31*(7), 963–996.
Ziman, J. (1998). Basically, it's purely academic. *Interdisciplinary Science Reviews*, *23*(2), 161–168.

Part III

Funding and metrics

Chapter 8

Early career academics and evaluative metrics

Ambivalence, resistance and strategies

Gaby Haddow and Björn Hammarfelt

Introduction

The reputation-based economy in which scholars compete for positions, grants and visibility is not unique to the present day, and neither are discussions and complaints about a 'publish or perish' culture in academia. In fact, the tradition of researchers being compared and ranked based on their writings, as well as the principle of focussing on publications as a key merit can be traced back to the origins of the modern university in eighteenth-century Germany (Josephson, 2014). Since then the primary method of valuing research outputs has been peer-review in various forms. However, it seems that the proliferation of measures and indicators of research impact in recent years marks, if not a completely different evaluative landscape, at least a remarkable intensification of measuring and counting in that landscape.

This intensification of measurement is visible both in the manifold of indicators, services and products that provide metrics and data on research outputs, and on the many levels – from country comparisons to individual level bibliometrics – that these indicators and evaluation systems are used. From being a rather specialised and obscure activity, which was largely dependent on a few data sources (mainly the citation databases provided by Institute for Scientific Information (ISI), now *Clarivate Analytics*), we now have a situation where many actors compete in providing a vast array of more traditional citation-based indicators as well as new, alternative, ways of measuring (altmetrics). Paired with growing demands for accountability and evaluation across society (Dahler-Larsen, 2011; Power, 1997) this has led to increased reliance on metrics across all levels of academia. Reliance on metrics can be seen at a macro level of highly visible university rankings and country comparisons that influence research policy and strategies, at a meso level where institutions allocate resources based on performance measures, and through individual (micro) uses of metrics when hiring or applying for funds. Increasingly the 'quantification' of research is also instigated by researchers themselves when monitoring their own performance through Google Scholar or by creating profiles in services such as *Research-Gate* and *Academia.edu* (Hammarfelt et al., 2016).

The increasing use of bibliometric measures and indicators, described as a metric tide (Wouters et al., 2015), has prompted further interest in the possible effects that these measures might have on research and researchers. Starting with Linda Butlers's (2003) landmark study of the Australian research evaluation system, which suggested an increase in the number of publications but not in 'impact', we have seen a range of studies trying to distinguish distinct effects. While it has been difficult to pinpoint direct effects of specific systems (for an in-depth discussion on the difficulties of studying effects see the special issue of *Journal of Informetrics* [Waltman, 2017]), it is evident that metrics and indicators have an influence on practices and decisions on a range of levels (de Rijcke et al., 2016). One reason as to why it is challenging to isolate specific effects is that indicators and evaluation systems operate in a complex evaluative landscape (Brandtner, 2017) in which assemblages of measures and values interact. Moreover, depending on an institution's, or an individual's, position in the evaluative landscape the reaction to performance measurement is likely to take different forms. For example, an esteemed and already highly ranked university may respond differently to ranking lists compared to less well-known institutions. Similarly, the reaction of a tenured professor to the demands of evaluation systems and metrification will differ to that of a young researcher without secure employment.

Hence, the rather complex and multifaceted landscape of evaluation in academia suggest that a fruitful approach to investigate the consequences of metric use is to focus on specific groups and contexts rather than on effects of the research system as a whole. One such group, which we deem particularly interesting to study, is 'early career researchers' (ECRs) as these have been identified as especially perceptive to outside pressures (Hammarfelt & de Rijcke, 2015; Herschberg et al., 2018). The questions we seek to answer is how ECRs use, and respond to, evaluation systems and indicators, and how such interactions inform strategies and ambitions for the future. The influence of evaluation systems and bibliometric indicators on the work practices and strategies of young researchers has been discussed in previous research (Müller & de Rijcke, 2017). While we are inspired by these accounts, our work adds a further dimension by focussing on a set of fields, the social sciences and humanities (SSH), which has attracted less attention, and where both the concept of 'early career academics' (ECAs) and the evaluative landscape are shaped quite differently compared to STEM fields.

The study draws on in-depth interviews with Australian academics in the SSH. We are particularly interested in how competing 'orders of worth' (Boltanski & Thévenot, 2006) come to the fore in these accounts, and how researchers negotiate rivalling demands and expectations. In contextualising our findings we also relate to a broader literature on ECRs and the consequences that 'narrow regimes of worth' might have on the epistemological and social organisation of research (Fochler et al., 2016).

The chapter is organised as follows: first, a background section provides an introduction to research on ECRs, metrics use and the wider evaluative landscape. In this section we also describe the material we have used, and the context, SSH in Australia, from which the data were gathered. The findings are then presented thematically in four sections – ambivalences, resistances, strategies and identities – which represent different, but not mutually exclusive, ways of approaching indicators and evaluation systems found in our material. Ambivalence about indicator use occurs across disciplines and academic career stages (Wouters, 2014), but resistance and identity are themes that are connected more directly with young academics (Archer, 2008; Clegg, 2008; Malsch & Tessier, 2015; Osbaldiston et al., 2016). The strategies theme was explored to illustrate how this younger cohort is actively engaging with the evaluation landscape. Finally, we present some concluding thoughts on how different values are negotiated within a complex ecology of measures and indicators, and we also discuss our findings in relation to a broader evaluative landscape.

Background

Early career academics

ECRs – generally referring to researchers in a transition phase from newly minted PhDs to senior positions and stable employment – form a group that has recently been of great interest in relation to research policy and higher education. There is no agreed upon definition for what constitutes an 'early career researcher', but the label is generally applied to researchers who have finished their doctoral dissertation (PhD students are not included). To delimit when researchers leave this early phase is more difficult, and to a large degree this is dependent on possibilities of more stable employment and funding. Thus, the length of this period may be longer or shorter depending on the research field in question and national context. For example, the potential for securing a permanent contract (tenure) is significantly higher in England where 86% of staff have permanent contracts than in Germany where only 30% of staff are permanent (Wöhrer, 2014). Sometimes the 'early career' period can be as long as nine years (Hakala, 2009, p. 179), while others draw a line at five years after a PhD is completed (Petersen, 2011, p. 35). As our study concerns a range of fields we opted for a fairly generous definition by setting the limit to seven years after receiving a PhD. In relation to the terminology we use, it is important to acknowledge that 'early career researchers' is a concept that is often used to describe the natural and medical sciences. In these fields the notion is closely connected to a 'postdoctoral phase', and even if such positions are becoming more common in the

SSH they are still not a mandatory step in an academic career. In fact, many young academics in SSH are heavily involved in teaching after receiving their PhDs, and their situation is rather different from a postdoc that spends most of their time on research. Thus, we suggest that 'early career academics' (ECAs) might be a more accurate label when the concept is used in SSH.

Topics such as the precarity of ECAs (Enright & Facer, 2017), gender discrimination (White, 2004) and mental health problems (Signoret et al., 2018) are among the issues that have been explored by researchers interested in ECAs. Furthermore, as argued by Fochler and colleagues (2016, p. 177), young researchers are an interesting group to study as they are strongly affected by competition and changes in how research is evaluated. This focus on young researchers also opens the possibility for studying how these scholars are socialised into a specific academic culture.

For Archer (2008) these young academics are caught in an 'audit culture' in which they are positioned as 'neoliberal' subjects, and as one of her respondent's comments 'You can't argue against a lot of the audit culture' (Archer, 2008, p. 282). Still, young academics are able to formulate critique and resistance while reflecting on their own role and identities. The imagined 'future self' becomes a key for understanding how young academics orient themselves in a complex and competitive environment (Osbaldiston et al., 2016). Metrics in the form of publications, citations and grants become important in guiding scholars towards a future idealised self. The 'quantified academic self', which is perhaps most evidently manifested on platforms such as ResearchGate, is then increasingly important for the formation of academic identity (Hammarfelt et al., 2016). Metrics also becomes a way of mitigating risk and uncertainty, and as argued by Cannizzo (2018), the decision to place the responsibility of handling risk on the individual rather than the institution is a deliberate strategy. Young academics, without permanent contracts, are the ones who most evidently feel the pressure of managing the uncertainty of career prospects and employment. Consequently, many accounts given by ECRs are not so much about hopes of a bright future, but concerns about failure and exclusion.

Mind the gap: SSH and rivalling orders of worth

'The evaluation gap' is a concept introduced by Paul Wouters (2017) and it describes a situation of mismatch between evaluation tools (e.g. bibliometric indicators) and notions of what constitutes quality by those who are evaluated. For most SSH fields the 'gap' between what metrics such as citations or journal impact factors measure and what actually is valued within the field is wide (Haddow & Hammarfelt, 2019; Hammarfelt & Haddow, 2018). One reason for this mismatch is due to inadequate database coverage resulting from more diverse publication practices in many SSH disciplines (Hicks, 2004), but epistemological factors are important to consider as well.

On a more general level the inadequacy of bibliometrics to capture and reflect research quality in the humanities can be discussed in term of rivalling 'orders of worth' (Hammarfelt & Haddow, 2018). Building on Boltanski and Thévenot's distinction between different 'orders of worth' it becomes evident that the 'evaluation gap' is, in part, attributable to a clash between rivalling value systems. Following their conceptual framework, bibliometric indicators and various journal rankings foremost relate to 'industry' and the 'market' where statistics, global circulation and competition are central manifestations. The order of worth that characterises the 'world of industry' is described through words such as 'performance', 'efficiency' and 'productivity'. Thus, the mere concept of 'performance measures' signals the type of worth that is at stake when such indicators are introduced. The main objective is to promote the productive 'man of action' and foil the inactive and wasteful (Boltanski & Thévenot, 2006, p. 204f). The evaluative gaze is here directed towards the future, and what has worked traditionally is of little importance. If the key concept of the world of industry is performance, then the most distinctive notion in the realm of the 'market' is competition. In this logic, nations, universities and scholars compete in a 'marketplace of ideas', which has global reach. While it might be debated whether researchers, especially in SSH, really compete in a universal market the possibility of such competition (and comparison) is assumed when universities, journals and even scholars are globally ranked and compared.

Although the kind of worth expressed in the worlds of 'industry' and 'the market' clearly has an influence in SSH disciplines these fields draw on additional 'orders of worth' originating in spheres of the 'inspired' (singularity and creativity) and 'the domestic' (local and authority). 'The inspired world' is in many ways a shielded one, where outsiders have little say and where few measures and general rules exist. What is valued here, and this is also the reason why bibliometric measures are seldom applicable in research fields associated with 'the inspired world', is uniqueness and originality. The relative independence in relation to other orders of worth makes this kind of value system fragile and somewhat unstable, and the inspired world constantly needs to 'confront the paradox of a worth that eludes measure' (Boltanski & Thévenot, 2006, p. 159).

The domestic world reflects the importance of the local, and traditions, for assigning worth. Authority and seniority are important as 'hierarchical superiors supply the worth of inferiors and define their identity' (Boltanski & Thévenot, 2006, p. 171). This system of assigning worth is well recognised in the academic system more generally, and it is especially notable in the manner in which the traditional university has been organised. What makes the domestic sphere more relevant to SSH disciplines compared to their colleagues in STEM is the more local orientation of research and teaching which elevates the importance of a confined elite.

Tensions between 'orders of worth' vary considerably between fields in SSH, and scholars in a largely internationally oriented field like economics might experience these tensions less than those in more nationally oriented fields such as literature or history. Here it is important to acknowledge that the individual researchers interviewed in this study are positioned in an 'evaluative landscape' in which bibliometric indicators are joined by many other evaluation practices. In the same way as Brandtner (2017) suggests that evaluative landscapes, rather than single evaluative practice, should be in focus when studying organisational responses, we propose that a broader plurality of evaluative practices must be considered when studying responses to and effects of bibliometric measures. The full plurality of evaluation practices of SSH research in Australia cannot be captured in this study alone, and our ambition is not to map a complete landscape. Rather the purpose of incorporating the concept of evaluative landscapes is to show how bibliometric measures and indicators come to interact and compete with other types of evaluative practices. In this study we zoom in on one particular component of a wider evaluative landscape, and by necessity this means that other, possibly important aspects, remain uncharted.

Methodology

Our data were drawn from interviews with Australian SSH scholars, conducted in early 2017. These followed a widely distributed online survey in Australia and Sweden (Haddow & Hammarfelt, 2019; Hammarfelt & Haddow, 2018), in which Australian scholars were asked to indicate their willingness to participate further in the study. Of the scholars who were interviewed (51 in total), ten met our criteria for ECA status. The time since being awarded their PhD ranged from 1.5 to 7 years and most scholars (six) were in lecturer positions. An equal number of male and female participants comprised the ECA group, and their research areas spanned the SSH spectrum: literary studies, anthropology, sociology, education, linguistics, communication, law and workplace safety. Their employing universities are representative of the different types of institutions in the Australian higher education sector.

The interviews explored two main topics: the influence of research evaluation (at any level – institutional, national or international) on publishing and/or creative practice activities; and opinions about evaluative metrics and their relevance to the scholars' research fields. An unstructured approach was taken to allow participants to discuss their thoughts on each topic, with occasional prompts from the researcher (Haddow). Each interview was recorded and subsequently transcribed, providing rich descriptive data for analysis.

NVivo, the qualitative analysis software tool, was used to code the data. The data were initially coded into broad categories, such as 'publishing practices', 'evaluative metrics' and 'research culture'. Sub-categories that captured specific aspects of the topic, for example 'strategies', 'ranked journal lists' and 'identity and exposure', were then coded. Using the query function of NVivo, we exported sets of quotes by category and sub-category into document files. These data were subjected to repeated reading and identification of common threads to arrive at the themes discussed in this chapter. Direct quotes are used to illustrate the themes. The participant identification number and research field are noted against the longer quotes to provide context.

It is acknowledged that the act of qualitative data collection and analysis is not an objective process. Our interpretation is bound by the interview discussion, in which both interviewer and interviewee are influenced by their own constructed knowledge and understandings of the evaluation landscape. Similarly, we bring our existing knowledge and opinions to the interpretation of data, which has the potential to 'highlight' particular topics (Denzin & Lincoln, 2008). The themes we determined are situated in our perspectives of the evaluation landscape and would almost certainly differ from other interpretations. In addition, the themes share blurred and overlapping boundaries, illustrating, we believe, the complex and multifaceted nature of the evaluation landscape in which the ECAs are working.

Findings

In the following section, we discuss the responses of ECAs to evaluative metrics in their academic life. These responses relate very directly to the new researchers' identities as scholars and employees, and they reflect an environment in which competing 'orders of worth' (Boltanski & Thévenot, 2006; Hammarfelt & Haddow, 2018) are experienced. For some this is expressed as ambivalence and possibly resistance, while others choose to ignore the expectations to be measured as per the status quo. However, quantification in academic work also results in playing 'the games of academic politics' (Malsch & Tessier, 2015, p. 85) and developing strategies to demonstrate alternative measures of worth. In the final part of the section we present the ECAs' reflections on identity in relation to the use of evaluative metrics.

Ambivalences

Ambivalent attitudes to the use of evaluative metrics as a performance and assessment measure is said to stem from 'the interaction between individual and structural factors' (Wouters, 2014, p. 57). While the use of metrics has the potential to challenge an individual scholar's sense of worth at any stage in their career, the often-precarious circumstances of ECAs, with a focus on their future in a research field and academic employment, can intensify the importance of structural factors.

For ECAs to secure ongoing positions in academia they are likely to have to demonstrate research achievements according to criteria that include metrics of some kind. In Australia, ranked journal lists are frequently used, along with citations and Impact Factors. Promotion and grant applications also require scholars to attend to evaluative metrics as evidence of 'quality' research (Hammarfelt & Haddow, 2018). Illustrating an appreciation of these imperatives, but with a lack of conviction about their value, one young academic said, 'I'm not sure that I really am chasing the numbers, although I'm aware that that probably is a good career move to do that' (P22: Education), and another commented, 'I don't feel like I can just ignore the various different measures that we're given on those things' (P5: Communication). Metrics for these young academics are reluctantly acknowledged as a facet of their work.

Researchers also interact with structural factors relating to their discipline, such as scholarly communication traditions and accepted research practices. Although research conventions differ across fields, many young academics in SSH have entered academia valuing books and book chapters, as well as creative works and practitioner-oriented research. For one ECA this is expressed as a 'tension between what … universities want compared to what people in their own particular disciplines need' (P23: Education). 'What universities want' is often at odds with the norms of SSH research, and although the national research evaluation model includes books and other non-traditional outputs for assessment, it is journal articles that are the preferred publication for many institutions (Hammarfelt & Haddow, 2018).

The ambivalence experienced by most of the Australian ECAs in SSH is not dissimilar to Malsch and Tessier's (2015, p. 87) 'identity fragmentation' and 'loyalty dilemma', with the former being closely aligned with Boltanski and Thévenot's (2006) competing 'orders of worth'. In some cases, ECAs expressed some helplessness in the face of the evaluative landscape: 'I feel like, while I can look for quality journals, there are also other factors that I have less influence over' (P5: Communication). In others the competing 'orders of worth' extend into the realm of an 'evaluation gap' (Wouters, 2017). These ECAs question the appropriateness of some metrics, or indeed metrics in any form, and regard them as inadequate and potentially inequitable criteria for assessment in a research field. An ECA in the field of education made the point:

> Those things [metrics], I think, have gained increasing weight in the system … but as I say I'm very specific to the field of education because what I don't like seeing, which sometimes happens, is when the norms or the values of one discipline start to invade another.
>
> (P23: Communication)

Hence, evaluation criteria and metric use are very much dependent on disciplinary cultures, and the adoption of norms and values from other contexts might be experienced as an 'invasion'. Withstanding the pressure of conforming to specific indicators or measures thus becomes an act of independence, and devising alternative criteria for assessment is part of being a sovereign and resourceful research field.

An important component of the Australian evaluation landscape is the use of ranked journal lists, and Australian scholars are acutely aware of them. This is, in part, a result of the introduction and then discarding of a list of ranked journals for the national research evaluation model, Excellence for Research in Australia (ERA). Its continued use, as well as the regularly updated Australian Business Deans Council (ABDC) ranked journal list, as a quality assessment tool is evident in our survey results (Hammarfelt & Haddow, 2018; Haddow & Hammarfelt, 2019) and emerged as an issue of equity in the use of indicators. A comment by the 'earliest' of the ECAs interviewed illustrates this point:

> people do compare academics, and there's all those h-scores, or different methods of rating academics, so is it actually a fair way to do it when you can't publish in journals that are highly rated because they just don't exist in your areas?
>
> (P37: Workplace safety)

A mismatch between institutional expectations and an ECA's disciplinary values was linked to the ranked journal list in 'frankly I only publish in it because it's got an A rating. I don't publish in it in order to influence either my peers or practitioners in my field. So we end up with I think some perverse incentives' (P42: Law). On the issue of metrics and academic work, another scholar remarked, 'I despair at an academy that is becoming more and more exclusive and not just metricised'. This ECA had earlier expressed their opinion of metrics and broader social influence:

> It seems particularly hierarchical and power laden and problematic that the printed word, as reflected in metrics and exclusive to not very broadly read academic journals, as an exclusive measure, I think that that is very much a part of the policing of knowledge globally, and socially in our own society and I have a real problem with it.
>
> (P36: Anthropology)

In this quote we see how the use of metrics is related to a broader rhetoric of 'excellence' where attention is directed to top ranked journals or institutions. The ranked list of journals is perhaps the most salient example in our material, but criteria such as 'being indexed in Web of Science' also denote an exclusive set of journals that direct themselves foremost to an international and scholarly audience.

Whether related to institutional performance measures, disciplinary factors or broader notions of excellence, the use of evaluative metrics in SSH fields has the potential to generate ambivalent attitudes. Individual ECAs respond to this experience in different ways, with resistance, either active or passive, being one.

Resistances

Archer (2008) refers to the term 'resistance' in her discussion about how some scholars construct their academic identity in the neo-liberal academy. In a paper published in the same year, Clegg (2008 p. 340) noted that 'covert resistance could co-exist alongside a strong sense of practising with integrity'. We use 'resistance' to represent the ECAs' frustrations with an evaluation landscape and an instinct to challenge, criticise or work within that system in the recognition that metrics play into career considerations regardless of their worth.

The direct connection between ranked journal lists and preferred publishing channels in SSH meant that some ECAs expressed their resistance to evaluative metrics as a facet of their publication practices: 'Although my focus should be on A and A star in the ABDC I'll also quite happily write for other journals that I think have impact in my area of research' (P42: Law). The reference to reaching a particular audience was echoed by several ECAs. It indicates a tension between the channels that produce desirable outcomes in one evaluative landscape, such as a particular institution, and channels that may have longer-term disciplinary impact, and is clearly articulated in the comment:

> I'm a little bit cynical of them, but I guess that is the system of which we work in.... I guess you've got to play by the rules of that game, but for me, I'd rather publish in a journal where my peers and the people that I read, and the scholars, and the thinkers that I respect, they publish in that. To me, I'd rather 50 people that I rate read my work than 5,000 people.
>
> (P22: Education)

However, the sheer number of publishing channels and evaluative metrics available was also a source of frustration for one ECA, who commented, 'five or six different platforms plus Academia.edu. I've just given up on those. I can't continue monitoring those and doing publications for that' (P31: Linguistics). The level of inherent bias (gender and nationality) in evaluative metrics was the basis for another young academic's concerns: 'there's a lot of disparity built into publishing systems and all the metrics then have those disparities built into them too. So that's one of the biggest reasons why I'm very sceptical about it' (P36: Anthropology).

While resistance, frustration and scepticism were expressed by some, pragmatic attitudes towards evaluative metrics were also evident in the

ECAs' comments. Metrics are used because that is what is required – at the same time as being regarded as a poor indicator of research quality. The terms 'cynical' and 'contrived' were used by ECAs to describe their opinion of metrics, alongside a recognition that 'those are the rules of the game' (P31: Linguistics). We suggest this response to 'playing the game' to advance an academic career is a form of covert resistance for some ECAs, and is expressed clearly in:

> My opinion about the quantitative measurable stuff is pretty low at a personal level, although I do take impact factors into consideration – and this is really something that impacts on whether you get a promotion or not, or something that you have to place in an ARC grant application.
>
> (P32: Sociology)

The structural factors in the evaluation landscape, such as promotions and grants, are a means to reduce career uncertainty. However, these structures are driven by metrics that new academics have little power to influence and, in many cases, do not value. Individuals manifest their ambivalence and resistance to the evaluation landscape in different ways, often balancing their integrity as a scholar with 'playing the game'. The ECAs' responses demonstrate there are tensions relating to competing orders of worth, but these tensions also have the potential to generate creative strategies that embrace metrics in a range of forms.

Strategies

In an evaluative landscape that values the 'world of industry', ECAs in SSH have developed a number of strategies to establish themselves and demonstrate their 'worth'. For an ECA only two years post-PhD completion, the strategy involved developing a 'résumé to get the ongoing job' (P22: Education), which was not necessarily in the institution where they were currently employed. The role of evaluative metrics during this period is illustrated in the comments:

> Early on the first few years out of my PhD I spent a lot of time on the ERA page researching journal names and figuring out which ones I should go for. I used that, too, to find a couple of A star journals.
>
> (P36: Anthropology)

> In the first couple of years out of PhD I was pretty well 100% driven by these policy drivers and these institutional expectations and lists. I'm now probably 80% driven by them. Still primarily driven by them, but a bit more flexible.
>
> (P23: Education)

That flexibility appears to come with a foothold in the academy so that ECAs with more years of experience feel they can risk a strategy that accommodates the 'inspired' and 'domestic' spheres of their academic identity. The previous quote and the comment 'my strategy has evolved via what I want to do personally, and also what I feel like I have to do instrumentally, from a university perspective' (P32: Sociology) were made by ECAs with more than five years' experience since their doctoral studies.

Impact Factors and 'all sorts of other measures' were regarded, by some, as another layer of knowledge that must be acquired to perform effectively in academia. That knowledge informs publishing decisions that align with the evaluation landscape's criteria and many of the ECAs associated 'significance in the world', 'Impact Factors' and ERA journals with research rewards, often expressed as 'points'. We suggest that competing orders of worth, combined with the manifold of evaluative metrics available results in creative strategies that incorporate measures in similar, but different forms. Scholarly communication networks, such as *Academia.edu* and *ResearchGate*, have provided an alternative to citation-based metrics while still delivering the 'numbers' that are valued by management. Due to their potential for improving research visibility these alternative approaches are viewed as feeding into, as well as complementing, traditional evaluative metrics. Several ECAs talked about uploading publications to scholarly communication networks in order to 'get more citations', 'see views' and 'hits', and that these metrics might be used for promotion applications and other performance assessment activities. The alternative metrics are not immune from criticism, however, and the potential for 'gaming the system' and questionable correlation with quality was raised. Despite it all, the attraction of metrics – or the worth of metrics in the evaluation landscape – is palpable in the remark:

> So I look at those metrics and I always get pleased when I get a good mark on one of those sites, you know. When they pick up another citation it makes me feel like, you know, tick, tick, tick, you know, keep going.
>
> (P36: Anthropology)

Clearly, the strategic use of metrics feeds into the general insecurity of an academic career (getting a job, embarking on a career), but it also thrives on a more general anxiety regarding the value of one's own work. Thus, scoring well in terms of metrics might for a young researcher suggest that they are on the right path, and that others value the work. Yet, as the previous quote suggests, metrics can deliver a sense of reward; checking the scores might for many be an act associated more with joy and pleasure than anxiety.

Existing evaluative metrics are central to most of the strategies discussed earlier, but recent changes in the Australian evaluation landscape may enable the inspired and domestic spheres to emerge as alternative orders of worth. In the next section we explore these alternative strategies and the ECAs' thoughts on how worth might be demonstrated.

Engagements

After a trial in 2017, the ERA 2018 is taking submissions on engagement and impact to assess research. This component of the ERA will run parallel to the research quality assessment model that has been in operation since 2012 (Australian Research Council, 2018). With a focus on research that contributes beyond the academy, this component of the ERA will run parallel to the quality assessment model that has been in operation since 2012 (Australian Research Council, 2018). While the outcomes are not yet known, the discussion around engagement and impact has generated interest in the possibilities of proving value outside the predominantly publication-based model.

The opportunity that impact might offer was discussed by a number of the ECAs, although metrics remained a feature in some cases. Reflecting our earlier discussion about ambivalences and research visibility, one ECA commented:

> What's increasingly coming is you look at broader evidence of whether your message is being read by people so you're looking at Google Scholar or you're writing articles for The Conversation or public media. Again, it's not perfect, but you preference things that are visible. Things that are web-based that you can record the number of visits, the number of reads, etcetera, ... because it's measurable. Again, it's not correct and it's not fair, but it's measurable and therefore you can at least look at it.
> (P23: Education)

Indeed, the impact associated with reaching a wider audience was identified as a feature of this shift in the evaluation landscape and this had a liberating effect, illustrated in an ECA's remark that they 'no longer hold as strongly to the fear that I have to focus on the really top prestige publications' (P36: Anthropology).

Although impact beyond academia is slowly being recognised in national research evaluation systems, institutions appear to be retaining a metrics focus, as an ECR involved in informing government policy noted:

> significant impact that occurs from discussions either with people who are making formal submissions to influence and help their [government] thinking. ...It is hard to overstate how important that influence is and it's equally hard to actually convert it into some sort of metric that you can say this is the value of my research. ... Lots and lots of us do it all very quietly and get no recognition for it but it's not something we

> should stop doing just because there's no recognition. So research can have impact outside of journals, outside of questions about impact factor of journals or number of citations and I don't think we have mechanisms to collect that.
>
> (P42: Law)

The difficulty of 'converting' impact into a metric of some form is echoed in the comment: 'I think impact – I don't think you can ever measure it to be honest. But I think impact matters a lot more than citation numbers' (P36: Anthropology), and for an ECA who works with activists, impact 'comes in far more diffuse ways that aren't necessarily closely tied to the publication itself'. The impacts described, such as creating or being a catalyst for 'shifts with activist groups through my conversations and through my connections with them on a personal level' (P5: Communication), won't result in metrics like citations or tweets. Whether these are of value in demonstrating impact was queried by another ECA, whose school was encouraging 'other' publications to improve impact, in addition to peer-reviewed articles. Their observation, 'I'm still not perfectly convinced as to what the impact is. Broadly it's media impact' (P42: Law), describes the challenge for scholars in this alternative approach to evaluation. It is a point reiterated in

> Academia needs to remember that good quality public engagement isn't how many times your paper gets tweeted. It's on the ground stuff that you do within community, within local stakeholders, and various other things, especially in social science.
>
> (P32: Sociology)

Whilst attempts to measure alternative impact are generally welcomed it is evident that our respondents question the capacity of their evaluative landscape to fully grasp the broader influence that their research has on society. In many ways these alternative metrics – for example usage statistics derived from the web – fail to capture what they intend to measure, and yet these numbers, which are neither 'fair' nor 'correct', are better than not having any numbers at all. For some SSH disciplines, such as philosophy, these metrics demonstrate the paradox referred to by Boltanski and Thévenot (2006, p. 159). That is, the 'worth' – or 'impact' in the language of the evaluation landscape – of research in these disciplines 'eludes measure' so that any metrics produced bear little relationship to the scholarly value of that work.

Identities

While academic identity is closely related to the points raised in the previous discussion, some of the ECAs made more direct connections between academic identity, scholarship and evaluative metrics. If they use metrics 'to provide pathways' to their 'idealised sense of self' (Osbaldiston et al., 2016, p. 15), they also recognise the potential damage to their academic identity and the sustainability of their discipline, as a consequence of adhering to the 'market's' orders of worth. These concerns are articulated in the following comments:

> I think ... writing about those things that are quite interesting to you helps to continue to authenticate you as an academic person, especially in my discipline, where you can get caught up in the numbers game, and start publishing things for rather instrumental reasons that appease university goals and whatever else.
>
> (P32: Sociology)

> I've seen very renowned scholars produce fairly shallow work because they produce such a volume of it, because that helps their citation rates and that helps their indices, and I find that very disappointing that that happens in my discipline.
>
> (P36: Anthropology)

The ECAs' concerns also extended to contemplating the 'worth' of evaluative metrics and the focus on prestigious journal publications in relation to scholarship. The following reflection on the influence of an evaluative landscape on epistemic processes and the future of knowledge production illustrates the extent to which metrics are perceived as a threat to scholarly work.

> I know a lot of universities say, 'No, no. It is about quality.' But the reality is, their version of quality is that you publish in the top 10% of journals or something like that in terms of impact factor ... We need to have a discussion about slow, deliberate thinking that goes into scholarship. I really do worry about the way we are going and the way we are trending, actually.
>
> (P32: Sociology)

This respondent connects the use of metrics with the broader trend of 'acceleration' of work and practices in contemporary academia (Vostal, 2016). Hence, changing temporalities, which also are due to funding arrangements and work conditions more generally (Ylijoki & Mäntylä, 2003), are here intertwined with discussions on measures and performance. As so often is the case, evaluative metrics thus comes to be interpreted as a 'symptom' of more general developments – 'acceleration', 'elitism' or 'academic capitalism' – haunting academic life.

Concluding remarks

Traditionally measurement, and especially numbers, has been seen as one of the main ways to reduce uncertainty (Porter, 1996). In the context of assessing scholarly output however, it seems that metrics thrive on existing uncertainties in how research should be evaluated. Bibliometric indicators can thus, in the same way as university rankings, be described as 'engines of anxiety' (Espeland & Sauder, 2016). For many young academics in our study these measures do not provide a bridge over the 'evaluation gap' but rather they reinforce and widen divisions between different orders of worth. The result is a fractured evaluative landscape where values rarely align, and while this opens windows of opportunity for some (engaging, resisting), others might resort to 'playing the game' or just giving up. Manifesting as ambivalence, resistance and strategies, the responses to metrics and other indicators of 'quality' by the ECAs suggest that for many the evaluation gap will be bridged by strategies that incorporate alternative approaches to demonstrate scholarly 'value'. Yet, for some scholars and fields – especially those where the 'domestic' and the 'inspired' orders of worth play a central role, the 'gap' might become so wide that it becomes futile even to attempt to bridge it. This sense of futility is not far-fetched or just a possibility; it is in fact very real for teachers working within similar measures-based environments (Ball, 2003). In contextualising such conclusions, however, it is of great importance to acknowledge that SSH consists of large heterogeneous fields of research, which should not be reduced to just being the significant other in relation to STEM fields (Hammarfelt & Haddow, 2018). Hence, our findings should be read in the light of the diversity of fields under study, and we acknowledge that there are vast differences in evaluative cultures between, for example, the fields of economics and literary studies.

Studying (and worrying) about a younger generation easily results in a largely unproductive 'nostalgia' for the 'golden days' (Ylijoki, 2005). Such descriptions of a not so distant past without indicators and evaluation often accompany the extensive criticism of neoliberalism, audits and new public management in contemporary academia. We draw on key insights from such criticism, but at the same time we are careful not to depict the use of metrics in black and white. As indicated by our respondents, metrics are experienced as obtrusive and damaging, yet at the same time they can bring pleasure and reward. In fact, recognising that bibliometric indicators and rankings do play an important role in the daily life of these researchers means that we must study them as integrated in a larger evaluative repertoire, as part of an evaluative landscape.

Metrics, we argue, can be viewed as signposts in this academic landscape, used to assess achievement and to navigate a pathway to the 'idealised sense of self'. The many forms of metrics available allow for creative approaches to demonstrate 'success' and develop an academic identity. There is a risk, however, that metrics will undermine that identity at a time when it is most precarious. Several quotes from young academics in SSH reflect the challenges of navigating this landscape of measures, rankings and indicators while maintaining a strong sense of self and 'loyalty' to their discipline and to scholarship more broadly. A degree of powerlessness is evident at times, but so too is intellectual resistance (Malsch & Tessier, 2015). It is unlikely that we will see the demise of the 'industry' and 'marketplace' spheres of academic work in the near future, so this resistance as well as the strategies to work within the evaluative landscape might be viewed as positive forces. Certainly, the value and 'worth' ascribed to scholarship by ECAs, compared to their opinions of metrics as a measure of quality, suggests that the 'inspired' and 'domestic' spheres will not submit easily.

Acknowledgements

We would like to express our gratitude to the early career researchers who gave their time to participate in our study and consented to the use of their quotes in this chapter. This study received support from Riksbankens Jubileumsfond: the Swedish Foundation for the Social Sciences and Humanities) (grant number SGO14–1153:1).

References

Archer, L. (2008). The new neoliberal subjects? Young/er academics' constructions of professional identity. *Journal of Education Policy*, *23*(3), 265–285.

Australian Research Council. (2018). *Engagement and impact assessment*. Retrieved from http://www.arc.gov.au/engagement-and-impact-assessment

Ball, S. J. (2003). The teacher's soul and the terror of performativity. *Journal of Education Policy*, *18*(2), 215–228.

Boltanski, L., & Thévenot, L. (2006). *On justification: Economies of worth*. Princeton, NJ and Oxford: Princeton University Press.

Brandtner, C. (2017). Putting the world in orders: Plurality in organizational evaluation. *Sociological Theory*, *35*(3), 200–227.

Butler, L. (2003). Explaining Australia's increased share of ISI publications—the effects of a funding formula based on publication counts. *Research Policy*, *32*(1), 143–155.

Cannizzo, F. (2018). Tactical evaluations: Everyday neoliberalism in academia. *Journal of Sociology*, *54*(1), 77–91.

Clegg, S. (2008). Academic identities under threat? *British Educational Research Journal*, *34*(3), 329–345.

Dahler-Larsen, P. (2011). *The evaluation society*. Stanford, CA: Stanford University Press.

Denzin, N. K., & Lincoln, Y. S. (2008). *Strategies of qualitative inquiry*. Thousand Oaks, CA: Sage Publications.

Enright, B., & Facer, K. (2017). Developing reflexive identities through collaborative, interdisciplinary and precarious work: The experience of early career researchers. *Globalisation, Societies and Education*, *15*(5), 621–634.

Espeland, W. N., & Sauder, M. (2016). *Engines of anxiety: Academic rankings, reputation, and accountability*. New York, NY: Russell Sage Foundation.

Fochler, M., Felt, U., & Müller, R. (2016). Unsustainable growth, hyper-competition, and worth in Life Science research: Narrowing evaluative repertoires in doctoral and postdoctoral scientists' work and lives. *Minerva*, *54*(2), 175–200.

Haddow, G., & Hammarfelt, B. (2019). Quality, impact and quantification: Indicators and metrics use by social scientists. *Journal of the Association for Information Science and Technology*, *71*(1), 16–26.

Hakala, J. (2009). The future of the academic calling? Junior researchers in the entrepreneurial university. *Higher Education*, *57*(2), 173–190. doi:10.1007/s10734-008-9140-6

Hammarfelt, B., & de Rijcke, S. (2015). Accountability in context: Effects of research evaluation systems on publication practices, disciplinary norms, and individual working routines in the faculty of Arts at Uppsala University. *Research Evaluation*, *24*(1), 63–77.

Hammarfelt, B., de Rijcke, S., & Rushforth, A. (2016). Quantified academic selves: The gamification of research through social networking services. *Information Research*, *21*(2), paper SM1. Retrieved from http://InformationR.net/ir/21-2/SM1.html

Hammarfelt, B., & Haddow, G. (2018). Conflicting measures and values: How humanities scholars in Australia and Sweden use and react to bibliometric indicators. *Journal of the Association for Information Science and Technology*, *69*(7), 924–935.

Herschberg, C., Benschop, Y., & van den Brink, M. (2018). Selecting early-career researchers: The influence of discourses of internationalisation and excellence on formal and applied selection criteria in academia. *Higher Education*. Advance online publication. doi:10.1007/s10734-018-0237-2

Hicks, D. (2004). The four literatures of social science. In H. F. Moed, W. Glänzel, & U. Schmoch (Eds.), *Handbook of quantitative science and technology research* (pp. 473–496). Dordrecht: Kluwer Academic Publishers.

Josephson, P. (2014). The publication mill: The beginnings of publication history as an academic merit in German universities, 1750–1810. In P. Josephson, T. Karlsohn, & J. Östling (Eds.), *The Humboldtian tradition: Origins and legacies* (pp. 23–43). Leiden: Brill Academic Publishers.

Malsch, B., & Tessier, S. (2015). Journal ranking effects on junior academics: Identity fragmentation and politicization. *Critical Perspectives on Accounting*, *26*, 84–98.

Müller, R., & de Rijcke, S. (2017). Thinking with indicators: Exploring the epistemic impacts of academic performance indicators in the life sciences. *Research Evaluation*, *26*(3), 157–168.

Osbaldiston, N., Cannizzo, F., & Mauri, C. (2016). "I love my work but I hate my job"—Early career academic perspective on academic times in Australia. *Time & Society*. Advance online publication. doi:10.1177/0961463X16682516

Petersen, E. B. (2011). Staying or going? Australian early career researchers' narratives of academic work, exit options and coping strategies. *Australian Universities' Review*, *53*(2), 34–42.

Porter, T. M. (1996). *Trust in numbers: The pursuit of objectivity in science and public life*. Princeton, NJ: Princeton University Press.

Power, M. (1997). *The audit society: Rituals of verification*. Oxford: Oxford University Press.

de Rijcke, S., Wouters, P. F., Rushforth, A. D., Franssen, T. P., & Hammarfelt, B. (2016). Evaluation practices and effects of indicator use—a literature review. *Research Evaluation*, *25*(2), 161–169.

Signoret, C., Ng, E., Silva, S. D., Tack, A., Voss, U., Lidö, H. H., ... Balachandran, C. (2018). Well-being of early-career researchers: Insights from a Swedish survey. *Higher Education Policy*. Advance online publication. doi:10.1057/s41307-018-0080-1

Vostal, F. (2016). *Accelerating academia: The changing structure of academic time*. Basingstoke: Palgrave Macmillan.

Waltman, L. (2017). Special section on performance-based research funding systems. *Journal of Informetrics, 11*(3), 904.

White, K. (2004). The leaking pipeline: Women postgraduate and early career researchers in Australia. *Tertiary Education and Management, 10*(3), 227–241.

Wouters, P. (2014). The citation: From culture to infrastructure. In B. Cronin, & C. R. Sugimoto (Eds.), *Beyond bibliometrics: Harnessing multidimensional indicators of scholarly impact* (pp. 47–66). Cambridge, MA: MIT Press.

Wouters, P. (2017). Bridging the evaluation gap. *Engaging Science, Technology, and Society, 3*(1), 108–118.

Wouters, P., Thelwall, M., Kousha, K., Waltman, L., de Rijcke, S., Rushforth, A., & Franssen, T. (2015). *The metric tide. Literature review. Supplementary report I to the independent review of the role of metrics in research assessment and management*. Bristol: HEFCE. Retrieved from http://blogs.lse.ac.uk/impactofsocialsciences/files/2015/07/2015_metrictideS1.pdf

Wöhrer, V. (2014). To stay or to go? Narratives of early-stage sociologists about persisting in academia. *Higher Education Policy, 27*(4), 469–487.

Ylijoki, O.-H. (2005). Academic nostalgia: A narrative approach to academic work. *Human Relations, 58*(5), 555–576.

Ylijoki, O.-H., & Mäntylä, H. (2003). Conflicting time perspectives in academic work. *Time & Society, 12*(1), 55–78.

Chapter 9

The rise of project funding and its effects on the social structure of academia

Thomas Franssen and Sarah de Rijcke

Introduction

The distribution of funding for scientific research has changed over the past decades due to an increasing governmental involvement in the governance of research and innovation (Gläser & Laudel, 2016). This has resulted in the introduction of performance-based and project funding mechanisms (Auranen & Nieminen, 2010) and had a differentiating effect on the distribution of research funding across universities, departments and individual researchers (Masso & Ukrainski, 2009). The competitive distribution of research funding leads to concentration due to the Matthew effect (Merton, 1968), which is strengthened on the organisational level by the increase in grant size aimed at creating critical mass at a select number of organisations (Bloch & Sørensen, 2015). Consequently, the social structure of some research groups has changed due to the influx of a large number of PhD students and other temporary staff members. For all researchers it has increased time spent on grant proposal writing and an administrative burden to provide increasingly detailed information on output activities for these grant applications as well as formal evaluations (de Rijcke et al., 2015).

Previous research on the effect of the rise of project funding points to a range of detrimental effects on the science system as a whole, including increasing short-term employment, hyper-competition and the narrowing of valuation regimes (Fochler et al., 2016) as well as increasing anxiety and career uncertainty (Sigl, 2016) – especially among early career researchers. However, an understanding of the mechanisms through which project funding changes the social structure of research groups is missing.

In this chapter we analyse the mechanisms through which negative consequences of project funding come about, building on the existing literature and an in-depth case study of a, in terms of project funding, particularly successful research group in the social sciences. We focus on the structural effects of the rise of temporary positions due to incoming project funding, and on the experiences of early career researchers in such temporary positions.

In the last section we discuss a response of senior staff members that try to counter the individuating force (Knorr-Cetina, 1999) of project funding by promoting communitarian values in hiring committees. While such a response is useful and necessary to establish the research group as a community, it also introduces another set of demands to the already long list of what early career researchers are expected to do. This suggests that communitarian ideals are not straightforwardly positive (Stöckelová, 2014), as communitarian demands can be circumvented by obtaining a project grant. This increases the inequality of expectations between those with project grants and those without. We conclude that because of the structural nature of the mechanisms we describe, individual research groups will be unlikely to be able to solve these problems and a more radical shift in the distribution of research funding is necessary.

The effects of project funding: a model

In this chapter we present an in-depth case study of a Dutch research group in a social science discipline. By combining our empirical analysis with prior research on the effects of funding, we aim to develop a model of the effects of the rise of project funding on the social structure of research groups. In Figure 9.1 we present our model and in the following sections we will take the reader through each element of the model as well as explain the relations

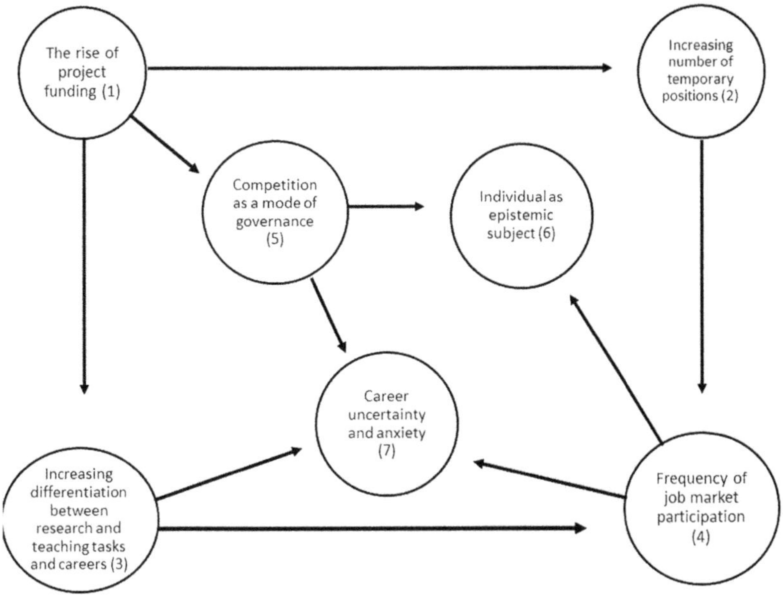

Figure 9.1 Model of the effects of the rise of project funding.

(the arrows) between each element. Our aim, and contribution to the literature, is to analytically and empirically clarify these relations and their underlying mechanisms.

To summarise the model, we argue that the rise of project funding (1) has increased the number of temporary positions (2) as well as the length of the temporary career phase. The increase in temporary positions means that the frequency with which early career scholars participate in the job market (4) increases drastically. This is heightened by the increasing differentiation between research and teaching tasks (3), and research-intensive and teaching-intensive career scripts and trajectories, which push early career scholars to try to increase their research time continuously.

The rise of project funding (1) also introduces competitions for funding as a mode of governance (5). With this we point not just to the rise of competitive behaviour but specifically to the outsourcing of epistemic authority (i.e. the authority over what kind of research is being done and who becomes part of the research group) to funding bodies that effectively determine whether or not an early career researcher gets a position (through granting someone a project grant).

Both job market participation (4) and project funding competition (5) establish and reaffirm the individual as the primary epistemic subject (6) in the science system. We show that early career researchers think about the science system in individualised terms that highlight their CV, grants and publications and pushes them towards entrepreneurial behaviour.

The differentiation between teaching and research (3), the frequency of job market participation (4) and the competition for project funding (5) as a means to secure a position all increase career uncertainty and anxiety (7) as early career researchers do not know what is enough to secure a permanent academic position.

Project funding and the social structure of a research group

The rise of project funding (1): the Dutch situation

In OECD countries, science funding has changed considerably over the last decades. Most importantly, there has been a rise in project funding which shifted control over large amounts of research funds towards funding agencies (Auranen & Nieminen, 2010) that distribute these funds across groups or individuals. The distribution of funds usually takes place through a competitive selection procedure for which scholars have to apply by writing a project proposal (however see Franssen et al., 2018 on prize funding). Project proposals are reviewed by either employees of the funding organisation or, as is much more usual, through a peer-review committee that also draws on external peer-reviews of project proposals (e.g. Gläser & Laudel, 2016, pp. 122–125; Luukkonen, 2012 for an overview of the literature).

In the Dutch higher education system, project funding is part of a three-tier funding system (see Koier et al., 2016 for a detailed description). The first flow, from the Ministry of Education, Culture and Science, is traditionally the largest. The first funding flow is composed of a student-dependent and a student-independent part and is allocated by the Ministry to the universities. The university divides these funds across faculties. In both the allocation mechanism used by the Ministry and those used by universities, natural and life science disciplines are systemically prioritised over social science and humanities disciplines due to historical developed differences. The second component, the student-dependent factor, is based on student numbers and includes not only funding for teaching but also some additional research funding. This means that in social scientific disciplines in the Netherlands, more than among natural and life science disciplines, research time and staff are linked to student numbers.

The second flow is research funding distributed through the Netherlands Organization for Scientific Research (NWO) and the European Committee (currently Horizon 2020). As noted earlier, this funding flow has become more important over the past decades and is also the main focus in our case. It is important to note that funding through the second flow needs to be 'matched' by universities. The matching funds are relocated from the first flow and therefore diminish the funds available for research from the first flow even further (Koier et al., 2016).

Next to individual- and group-based project funding that is distributed through funding agencies, additional competitive funding mechanisms have been introduced at the university and faculty level (Versleijen et al., 2007). On these levels the allocation of research funds from the first flow is increasingly based on past performance or, again, open competition. Examples of this phenomenon are university-wide research priority areas, additional funding for 'excellent' institutes or graduate schools, or competitions within research institutes for project funding.

The third flow funds are acquired through contract research for private partners and (non-)governmental organisations that operate in the public domain. For the department under study this was a major source of funding in the 1990s and early 2000s, but its importance has declined over the last ten years.

The rise of temporary positions (2)

The case

The research group we studied is part of a prominent social science department of a major Dutch university. We selected this research group because of its success in acquiring project funding. Between 2009 and 2015 members of the group obtained seven individual grants from NWO or the ERC, participated in a number of Horizon 2020 projects and obtained additional funding for PhD students through competitive individual PhD-funding programmes and funding assigned to the institute or graduate school as part of different 'excellence' initiatives.

We conducted interviews with 17 group members and one junior research manager. We interviewed the group's professor at the start and the end of the project. Also, we were given the opportunity to observe research seminars and group meetings on a number of occasions. At one of the meetings we presented our research as a 'member check'. At the time of conducting the research project (November 2014–May 2015), great upheaval characterised Dutch academia as the building housing the central board of one of the universities was occupied by students and faculty (Blaustein, 2015). This gave great urgency to the issues we were analysing for the group members and other academics working in the Netherlands. Group members tended to reflect on the topic of research governance outside the context of interviews, for instance in faculty-wide email discussions. In some cases, these emails were publicly available (sent out to a large number of staff or even university-wide) and we were able to collect them. We also collected other relevant documentation regarding the group.

The composition of the group

At the time of analysis, the research group consisted of one professor, five associate professors, eight assistant professors, four postdocs and eight PhD students. In addition, two lecturers without research time had permanent contracts in the department and were part of the group. The professor and associate professors had tenured contracts. Of the eight assistant professors, only three had a tenured contract and the others had contracts of approximately three years – without tenure or other form of extension. The postdocs had temporary contracts (often 1–3 years) while the PhD students had three-year contracts.

The rise of project funding has resulted in a new composition of this research group around the group leader, who was PI of many of the external projects and supervisor of most PhD students. This new structure resembles the natural science labs (e.g. Knorr-Cetina, 1999) but is a relative novelty in the social sciences. The size of the research group is a direct result of competitive funding as usually all or most temporary positions are funded externally. While PIs often have permanent or tenure-track positions, the much larger group of postdocs and PhD students does not (Müller, 2012, 2014; Sigl, 2016). In this case all temporary staff (five of the assistant professors, four postdocs, eight PhD students) were funded through external project funding, which created a large group of highly skilled, highly motivated early career researchers. Researchers on the associate level did have permanent contracts and had often been successful in acquiring project funding themselves.

The group leader was aware of the increase in temporary positions due to project funding and the difficulties temporary staff members experience. He explained:

GROUP LEADER: Someone who has a permanent contract can, first of all, probably hire a postdoc him or herself, a temporary person, and then we have the policy that a replacement must be found, but the teaching should not be done by a temporary lecturer so then an assistant professor for 4 or 5 years comes in, so you have two temporary members to be able to give a permanent staff member the possibility to, for a while, teach less, and that increases the dynamic because we succeed in bringing in good, talented people for these temporary positions.

INTERVIEWER: A large temporary basis.

GROUP LEADER: And I mean, we really cannot go in any direction, because there wasn't even a job to begin with. And that is in this whole discussion the rock hard message, because I understand the frustration and I see it, and at the same time, that we are having this conversation is because a temporary position has been created because of a grant, otherwise this conversation would not take place.

'There wasn't even a job to begin with', as the group leader explains, characterises the contradiction inherent in the positions created through project funding. It is only first flow funding that provides continuous funds, provided that student numbers remain relatively stable, for permanent positions. All other funding creates temporary positions that will terminate after the funded project ends. However, as he notes, this dynamic is intensified because the people that come in on temporary positions themselves also acquire additional project funding. This cumulative effect of temporary positions acquiring new external funding is an effect that the literature has not addressed in any detail yet. The rise of project funding implies that, because of the Matthew effect, funding becomes increasingly concentrated with certain individuals or groups. As such, temporary positions become equally concentrated and new temporary staff members acquire project funding of their own, thereby increasing concentration even further.

Increasing differentiation (3): teaching-intensive and research-intensive career trajectories

Contracts of staff members in social science disciplines in the Netherlands will typically consist of a 60%/40% time allocation between teaching and management on the one hand and research on the other. This means that a staff member will, based on a full-time contract, have 1,000 hours of teaching and 666 hours of research time.

Acquired project funding can be used by staff members to 'buy' themselves out of teaching, a common strategy in the social sciences. The buy-out is restricted in this particular research group because staff members are not allowed to buy-out fully. However, taking into account managerial tasks and PhD supervision, senior staff members do not carry a large teaching load. The professor in the group was involved in one course in the academic year 2014–2015 (based on the online study guide of the university), and associate professors with grant funding also had a minimal teaching load. Consequently, there is a large teaching load that does not rest on the senior staff members.

The rise of project funding, and, related, the teaching buy-out in the social sciences, leads to increasing differentiation and specialisation among university staff and to either teaching-intensive or research-intensive careers (Leisyte & Dee, 2012; Musselin, 2011). In this research group, and the institute at large, this was perceived as an unwelcome development that the institute aimed to counter. As such, there were only two lecturers with little to no research time in the department, and management had developed a strategy to deal with the potential separation between teaching and research staff. The organisational solution to this differentiation was the development of a new temporary position, the temporary assistant professor (TAP). This temporary position introduces a new hierarchical layer between the postdoc and assistant professor position and increases the length of the 'early career' phase in academia as characterised by temporary contracts. Where the assistant professor position traditionally was the start of the tenure track in the social sciences, this is no longer the case. These TAPs have contracts that themselves consist of 60% teaching and 40% research. TAPs cover the teaching load of senior staff members who used project funding for a buy-out. The development of the TAP showed an organisational commitment to the academic ideal of the intimate relation between research and teaching in the social sciences. However, as we will show, this did not dissolve the tendency towards specialisation, as project grants increasingly determine both research time and career trajectories of early career researchers. The TAP is therefore a temporary solution to extend the early career phase. However, scholars who are able to obtain a tenure-track assistant professorship are primarily those who obtain more research time and project funding.

Crucially, early career researchers are increasingly socialised with a particular research-intensive career script as the ideal career (Müller, 2012). The rise of project funding changes how researchers think about who has a right to research time. We find that early career researchers have a fear of missing the boat of the research-intensive career if they don't get particular grants that allow them to devote more time to research and publishing. The story of one TAP who was transitioning to a teaching-intensive position shows how continuing a research-intensive career is becoming increasingly limited to those researchers that can do research (and publish) in a particular, high paced, way.

ELENA: I prefer to make sure something's really good. I think of high quality, theory-heavy slowly built papers. Slow has nothing to do with it, but it takes time to do that, I do not feel rushed to just try to crank out publications. But here, I felt that right away, and I was like "shit I am never going to catch up". It is sort of this vicious cycle too, because if you do not have enough papers you cannot get a grant, and then if you do not have a grant you cannot get data to get 27 papers out.

Elena explains later on that she does feel appreciated at the institute for her teaching skills and in general for her role in the group. In the social sciences the importance of teaching, compared to the life sciences, might prevent a narrowing of valuation regimes (Fochler et al., 2016, see the last section on communitarian values). However, what is important here is how she contrasts her abilities (doing theory-heavy slowly built papers) to the much faster paced (27 papers) research practices of those that are allowed to continue doing research as assistant professors in the Netherlands, and the importance of the cycle of publications-grant-data-publications they need to sustain for a research-intensive career.

Increasing frequency of job market participation (4)

The rise of temporary positions and the increasing length of the temporary career stage force early career researchers onto the labour market much more often. The early career scholars in this research group all applied to the same internal positions for postdocs, temporary assistant professorships and tenure-track assistant professorships. This was often not to get an entirely new position, but rather to make their current position more research intensive. In the following we quote a TAP and a postdoc who talk about their job history within the research group which gives a particular good insight in how 'patchworked' academic positions are becoming:

DAVID: I had a lectureship for 4 days a week, 100% teaching. (...) After a while, I applied for research time. This was a policy that a number of lecturers could get 20% research time. I applied for that, and I got it. So after half a year, 9 months that I just taught, I got a contract in which I taught 3 days and did research on 1 day. After I had let them know a number of times I wanted to become an assistant professor (AP), and also applied for an AP 2 or 3 times without getting it, I finally got a contract in which I worked 5 days a week with 40% research time and 60% teaching. Then an official AP position came up and I applied for that, and for that, so since August I'm officially an [temporary] AP (...)

If someone would leave now who has a tenure-track contract as an AP, and if a job application procedure would arise, then I will apply for that and hope I get it.

DANIELLE: The postdoc is coming to an end. Last year there was a vacancy, a formal vacancy for an open rank. I applied for that to become AP, but I didn't get it, but I did get a lectureship [meaning a teaching-only position]. And then, last November there was a postdoc vacancy because of the research priority area, I applied for that as well. That consisted of 0.8 FTE research time, and they have split that between me and [name of temporary AP]. So we both got 0.4 FTE to do research within that project. (...) I will have 0.4 FTE teaching and 0.4 FTE research.
INTERVIEWER: For how long?
DANIELLE: 2 years.
INTERVIEWER: Okay, and when did that postdoc start?
DANIELLE: I am still working on the old postdoc.
INTERVIEWER: You were hired as a lecturer but you have not yet taken that up?
DANIELLE: No I didn't. But that will be my official title. Lecturer, but with research time.

Project funding has introduced, through short-term contracts, a much greater sense of competition for early career researchers. As these quotes show, early career researchers are constantly in competition. These experiences of competition also mark the moments where early career researchers feel evaluated. Danielle explains that the length of contracts prevents the yearly appraisal from being a significant moment:

DANIELLE: It [the yearly appraisal] has never really been relevant for me because my contracts were so short. Right after the yearly appraisal a new contract would start. For me the job application is the evaluation moment, not the yearly appraisal. I have another one coming up about my current post but after three months that will seize to exist, so I don't really care what the appraisal is about.
INTERVIEWER: but you do feel you are being evaluated?
DANIELLE: Yes, in the job applications.

Competition as a mode of governance (5)

Competition is a more recurrent phenomenon not only due to participation on the job market but also because competition for project funding is, increasingly, used as a mode of governance (De Boer et al., 2007; Felt, 2009). That is, the competition for project funding is increasingly a means to govern who becomes part of the research group, or more broadly speaking who is allowed to stay in academia by creating a job for oneself (Müller, 2014), or whose career progresses after the early career phase (Bloch et al., 2014).

In our case too successful grant applications could be used by early career researchers to negotiate a position in the research group, possibly even a tenure-track one (in case of large grants). One postdoc explains how grant applications increase her worth, in terms of her CV, and give her leverage towards the university to obtain a position:

INTERVIEWER: How do you see funding applications, as a way to get a job somewhere? Or is it a way to create a job for yourself?

MAGS: (...) If you get a Veni, and that's also what people tell me, then you're much more ... You're WORTH more in academia, because "wow, you got that". There is a lot of pressure of course involved in it. So, yeah, it's not only your money or you know, I guess people ... I mean ... Not in my position, but who actually have a job, or at least a contract for a bit longer, and don't get the Veni are also very much under pressure, because this is something that counts a lot. And this was something that someone from [project] in the first few months told me, that if you get that, you can have a good career here. It's very special.

INTERVIEWER: If you would get it, the Veni, would you then become assistant professor?

MAGS: That would be a condition yeah. (...) Then you're worth much more here, you offer something, and I understand that the university also ... Yeah, basically, they are proud of having Veni-researchers. The [university] advertised it last summer: "this is how many of them we got" so this is a good thing for them.

The increasing importance of project funding as income to the university also means that the research group and group leader become increasingly important institutionally. Group leaders are nodes through which competitive project funding comes into the university (Edler et al., 2014; Raudla et al., 2015; Whitley, 2014). This means that high-performing group leaders can direct the course of research, through successful funding applications, to an increasingly large extent. Epistemic authority thus shifts in two ways: to funding bodies and to group or project leaders.

Individuation: the individual as the primary epistemic subject (6)

In being on the job and grant market, in competition with peers, the individual is constantly established and reproduced as the primary epistemic subject (Knorr-Cetina, 1999, p. 205). This individuating force, and the way early career scholars respond to it, calls to mind the process of individualisation that characterises late modernity (Beck, 1992; Beck & Beck-Gernsheim, 2002). Beck's individualisation theory points to individualisation as a process in which people learn to see themselves as 'the centre of action'

(Beck, 1992, p. 135) in which society becomes a set of 'environmental variables' (136) that need to be dealt with to build the life one desires. Rather than relate what happens in the life course, for instance failure in terms of social mobility, to systemic contradictions, it is reconceptualised as a set of individual risks and opportunities (Beck & Beck-Gernsheim, 2002). The individualisation of precarity, where this is felt as a personal failure rather than a sign of system failure, is a particular harmful outcome of this process (Gill, 2010; Loveday, 2017; Sigl, 2016).

Moreover, the reflexive biographies that early career scholars are building follow an increasingly narrow career script (Müller, 2012) as they report a narrowing of valuation regimes, towards a single form of academic worth, focussed on high-impact publication output (Fochler et al., 2016; Müller, 2014). This was true also for our early career researchers when they talked about continuing a research-intensive career. The insecurity of fixed-term positions pushes the early career researchers in the group towards an entrepreneurial and reflexive strategy. They are reflexive about their careers, what is lacking on their CV, what needs to happen and how they can improve their position. As they are in a constant competition, for jobs or grants, they feel a constant need to appear attractive as candidates for a new (tenure-track) position or a project grant. Denise reflects on how she does this:

DENISE: I think it is really important as an assistant professor to find your niche, about that there might be comparison going on between each other.

INTERVIEWER: And then others gauge whether you are in their way, in a manner of speaking?

DENISE: Yes exactly, because everyone wants to find his or her niche. If we all go towards [subarea], that is [group leader] his main topic, you cannot raise your profile with that theme. My profile is really being in between [two sub areas]. I think everyone is looking for his or her own niche (…) You are also really thinking about your CV. And it is really important. And besides that I want to function well [in the department]. I like organising things, and I think it is important to get good student evaluations, because I want to be a good teacher and a good academic. It is also really about output, indeed about publications. (…)

INTERVIEWER: I aim to understand what it is like to be in a 3-year contract, when you have to publish a lot, but it doesn't seem to affect you, do you think it influences your research?

DENISE: Maybe it does. Maybe you want to publish even more, you want to do as many different things as you can I think. I really enjoy working with others, so I like saying to people "Maybe we can write a paper about this and this." Whether we will really get to write it, that is the next question of course, but you try to keep balls in the air in the sense of "we could do this and this". At the moment for the yearly [global disciplinary organisation]-deadline, a big conference deadline, I try to finish stuff, now there are five papers and they can be submitted.

Denise clearly shows reflexivity about her CV and what needs to be on it to make it. She reflects on what it takes to be an enterprise or a brand that needs to be visible and needs to show potential. It is this continuous showing of potential and worth that is important in a science system in which research time is increasingly distributed on a competitive basis rather than part of the job. This also makes for a strong focus on the individual. Research time is understood as something that an individual can receive, rather than acquired through collective effort. Indeed, while some grants are collective in nature, the individual grants offer greater prestige and larger funds which puts one in a position to secure a tenure-track position. The seeming certainty of employment a grant implies is the main reason for its desirability. The importance of publication is derived from the grant competitions in which publication counts are said to be crucial in judging ones CV.

Anxiety and career uncertainty (7)

The short-term contracts and constant competition on the basis of individual merits create immense pressure on early career researchers (Fochler & Sigl, 2018; Müller, 2014; Sigl, 2016). Early career researchers tend to do as much as possible without a clear idea of what is enough. This is well documented in the literature and came up often in our interviews about the pressure early career researchers put on themselves. As one example among many Ron illustrates this reflecting on why the work is never finished:

RON: I work hard yes, that is a bit of a problem sometimes.

INTERVIEWER: Do you have on the weekend, a morning, afternoon or day of?

RON: Yes I do. I notice that I do have to take a bit of rest this week. That is the disadvantage of the postdoc-life: that there is an endless stream of work. And much of it us just for yourself. I have 20 students, that is manageable, and other than that I don't HAVE TO do anything. Everything I do, I do for myself. That makes it very alluring to just continue. But I don't work 7 days a week, and I sleep in, but I have to be careful I don't exaggerate it.

INTERVIEWER: that you don't work too hard and too much… is that a problem with postdocs?

RON: For me it is. Look if you put me in one of those work surveys, then I will score high on stress and… but I have a temporary contract, if I want to continue in the academic world then this is the moment to step on it for a bit. Not endless. Last summer I was on a holiday for three weeks, and this summer I will go for a month so it isn't like. I do take a holiday. For sure. But like this during the week (…) it is often that nearly every day, also in the weekend, you have something to do, that isn't always nice.

Countering individuation by promoting communitarian ideals in hiring committees

In this research group, senior staff members aim to counter the individuating effect of the rise of project funding by promoting communitarian ideals and merit-based (rather than publication count-based) hiring procedures. The group leader explains that publication counts are not all that matters when a position opens up:

GROUP LEADER: I will dare to say out loud that our selection committees are not blind and stupid. It is not the case that if there are 4 internal candidates and you see that one has 7 publications and the other has 1, 'oh weird that person has 7 publications within [name] VICI-project, or [name] ERC-project', that nobody thinks 'oh well, it is convenient to have data on 25 countries being embedded within such a large team'. So that person with 1 publication can be compared to the person with 7. People are not blind to those things. What is more, often you have a different assistant professor-selection criterion: you do not want to have 7 APs who all do the same thing. So maybe that person who has 1 publication, who represents a different sub-area, maybe has a competitive advantage in a different area, can teach broader for instance, which is 60% of an AP-position. So it might look like it, but for 8 years I have been in almost all selection committees and they can see through that. If someone comes from a big project, and is co-author on 5 things within the project, then you can still compare that to someone who almost did a solo project.

What matters according to senior members of the research group is the extent to which group members contribute group work and act collegially. In almost all interviews the issue of collegiality came up. Interviewees argued that collegiality was very important for them, and that they appreciated this in others as well. This senior staff member feared collegiality was not valued in job application procedures, and he contrasts collegiality with publications, but his experience in the institute proved otherwise:

CHRISTOPH: I feel there has been discussion the last years about that it cannot be only publications, and of course there always already was some criticism from outside that we would be soulless publication monsters. My feeling is, and I have been through many job application procedures here, my feeling is that it has become increasingly important what you do for the group, the softer things, that that plays a role. I was always afraid that that would not be the case, but my feeling is that it does matter, that is my experience.

INTERVIEWER: Is that being made explicit, that that is important?

CHRISTOPH: Well, the other way around. It is never stated that it is only about publications. There is no official guideline that says 'If you have this and this and this and this, then you will be successful' or something like that.

A second senior member explains that a research group needs a diverse group in terms of topics but also in what people are willing to do, for the group to function:

SARAH: I think definitely. I think output of course is number 1. I think there is an awareness that you can't just run a department on loners who can publish 50 articles per year, that's impossible, it will implode. You need a couple of people who keep it together.

The staff members in temporary positions also understand that helping out in the group is part of their job and doing so has helped them or will help them in job application procedures. David explains:

DAVID: If I look at my own trajectory, then I see that, after my PhD, I solved a lot of tasks that had to be solved, but that a lot of people could not or did not want to do. There was a course for which within 1 month a new lecturer had to be found. I am someone who says 'yes' quickly with these kinds of things. (...) How flexible you are in terms of teaching, helping your colleagues, being present (...) In the end that is something that plays an important role. You have to look at the group as a whole, and that is what I mean with the idea that I have an important role, in a way, within the group. Because I teach certain courses, have a certain expertise, and maybe I do other things very badly, that could be, but this type of position within the group you cannot account for that by measuring output or measuring student evaluations.

The senior members quoted earlier, including the group leader, all declare that collegiality is important next to publication output. The two senior members both call into imagination an image of a 'publication monster' and a 'loner who can publish 50 articles per year', the type of academic they might feel fits with today's academic reward structures. This becomes clear because collegiality is seen as something that does not show up in quantitative measures, it is never visible but crucial to 'run a department'. Without staff members that do 'group work', organise seminars, are very active in teaching and coordination, the group could not function. But this also adds to the already lengthy list of what makes a good scholar. A TAP from a different group concluded:

> We spend a lot of time wondering what the criteria are but I'm not sure there are any criteria at all. Like they see a person and think, oh I like this person, I like his work, so let's hire him. We can say this hire was based on X, Y, Z. but then next time it is D, E, F. There is no transparency who we want to hire, and based on what criteria we want to do that.
>
> (fieldnotes, 12–3–2015)

The communitarian ideals make hiring procedures less transparent as they add a new valuation regime that can be used, but does not have to be used, in selecting candidates (see also Lamont, 2009). As Stöckelová (2014) shows, a plurality of ideals is not necessarily better for early career researchers. In this case, in hiring and promotion decisions made based on successful grant applications communitarian ideals do not necessarily apply. Communitarian ideals seem to be important for scholars who do not obtain a grant which increases the inequality of expectations between those with project grants and those without.

Conclusion: the limits of valuation heterarchy without structural change

In this chapter we analysed the effects of the rise of project funding on the social structure of academia. We show that more temporary positions are created and the temporary phase in the career is extended. Short-term contracts make it so that early career researchers are more often on the job and grant market, which, in turn, increases experiences of competition, establishes competition as a mode of governance, reaffirms the individual as the primary epistemic subject and increases anxiety and career uncertainty. All of which impacts the social fabric of research groups and departments.

In high-performing research groups such as the one we studied the effects of project funding are visible to a larger extent. In such groups the amount of project funding is very large leading to a bigger group of early career researchers in temporary positions. To establish a community the group leader and senior staff members promote communitarian ideals in hiring committees, making clear that it is not just publications that determine whether someone receives a job offer.

While a heterarchy of valuation regimes (e.g. Rushforth et al., 2018; Stark, 2011) might be a way to counter the negative effects of project funding our analysis shows important limitations. Following the analysis of Stöckelová (2014) we find that valuation regimes are not inherently bad or good. Promoting communitarian values also adds to the lists of expectations early career researchers have to deal with. Moreover, these hiring committees can be circumvented by researchers that obtain individual grants who can negotiate a position. It also decreases the transparency of criteria, which, while narrow, are at least clear when focussed solely on publication counts. This analysis teaches us that in a heterarchy of valuation regimes a crucial question becomes what values count, when and for whom.

Moreover, in high-performing research groups such as this one, the effects of project funding are not incidental but structural. Success in obtaining competitive project grants will always lead to more temporary positions, both PhD positions and post-PhD positions. The short term of these contracts will always push these early career scholars to the job and grant market. As the amount of temporary staff members greatly surpasses the needs of any research group, based on their first flow financing, for new permanent staff these temporary staff members will have to seek employment elsewhere.

It is an important question to what extent the concentration of funding (and therefore of early career researchers) in a small number of research groups negatively effects the discipline as a whole on an epistemic level. The skills of any scholar are by definition limited. It might therefore, in terms of epistemic diversity, be useful to spread research funding across a larger number of groups.

Acknowledgements

This chapter was supported by the KNOWSCIENCE project (https://www.fek.lu.se/en/research/research-groups/knowscience), funded by the Riksbankens Jubileumsfond Sweden, grant FSK15–0881:1 and the R-Quest project (https://www.r-quest.no/) funded by the Research Council of Norway, grant 256223. We thank Francisca Grommé and the editors for their helpful comments.

References

Auranen, O., & Nieminen, M. (2010). University research funding and publication performance—an international comparison. *Research Policy*, *39*(6), 822–834.

Blaustein, G. (2015). Letter from Amsterdam. Retrieved from https://nplusonemag.com/online-only/online-only/letter-from-amsterdam/

Beck, U. (1992). *Risk society: Towards a new modernity.* London: Sage.

Beck, U., & Beck-Gernsheim, E. (2002). *Individualization.* London: Sage.

Bloch, C., Graversen, E. K., & Pedersen, H. S. (2014). Competitive research grants and their impact on career performance. *Minerva*, *52*(1), 77–96.

Bloch, C., & Sørensen, M. P. (2015). The size of research funding: Trends and implications. *Science and Public Policy*, *42*(1), 30–43.

De Boer, H. F., Enders, J., & Leisyte, L. (2007). Public sector reform in Dutch higher education: The organizational transformation of the university. *Public Administration*, *85*(1), 27–46.

de Rijcke, S., Wouters, P. F., Rushforth, A. D., Franssen, T. P., & Hammarfelt, B. (2015). Evaluation practices and effects of indicator use—a literature review. *Research Evaluation*, *25*(2), 161–169.

Edler, J., Frischer, D., Glanz, M., & Stampfer, M. (2014). Funding individuals–Changing organisations: The impact of the ERC on universities. In R. Whitley & J. Gläser (Eds.), *Organizational transformation and scientific change: The impact of institutional restructuring on universities and intellectual innovation* (pp. 77–109). Bingley, UK: Emerald Group Publishing Limited.

Felt, U. (Ed.). (2009). *Knowing and living in academic research: Convergences and heterogeneity in research cultures in the European context.* Prague: Institute of Sociology of the Academy of Sciences of the Czech Republic.

Fochler, M., Felt, U., & Müller, R. (2016). Unsustainable growth, hyper-competition, and worth in life science research: Narrowing evaluative repertoires in doctoral and postdoctoral scientists' work and lives. *Minerva*, *54*(2), 175–200.

Fochler, M., & Sigl, L. (2018). Anticipatory uncertainty: How academic and industry researchers in the life sciences experience and manage the uncertainties of the research process differently. *Science as Culture*, *27*(3), 349–374.

Franssen, T., Scholten, W., Hessels, L. K., & de Rijcke, S. (2018). The drawbacks of project funding for epistemic innovation: Comparing institutional affordances and constraints of different types of research funding. *Minerva*, *56*(1), 11–33.

Gill, R. (2010). Breaking the silence: The hidden injuries of the neoliberal university. In R. Flood & R. Gill (Eds.), *Secrecy and silence in the research process: Feminist reflections* (pp. 228–244). London: Routledge.

Gläser, J., & Laudel, G. (2016). Governing science. *European Journal of Sociology*, *57*(1), 117–168.

Koier, E., Van der Meulen, B., Horlings, E., & Belder, R. (2016). *Chinese borden – Financiële stromen en prioriteringsbeleid in het Nederlandse universitaire onderzoek*. Den Haag: Rathenau Instituut.

Knorr-Cetina, K. (1999). *Epistemic cultures: How scientists make sense*. Chicago, IL: University of Chicago Press.

Lamont, M. (2009) *How professors think: Inside the Curious World of Academic judgment*. Cambridge, MA: Harvard University Press.

Leisyte, L., & Dee, J. R. (2012). Understanding academic work in a changing institutional environment. In L. W. Perna, R. D. Perry, S. L. Thomas, & M. A. Titus (Eds.), *Higher education: Handbook of theory and research* (pp. 123–206). Netherlands: Springer.

Loveday, V. (2017). Luck, chance, and happenstance? Perceptions of success and failure amongst fixed-term academic staff in UK higher education. *The British Journal of Sociology*. Advance online publication. doi:10.1111/1468–4446.12307

Luukkonen, T. (2012). Conservatism and risk-taking in peer review: Emerging ERC practices. *Research Evaluation*, *21*(1), 48–60.

Masso, J., & Ukrainski, K. (2009). Competition for public project funding in a small research system: the case of Estonia. *Science and Public Policy*, *36*(9), 683–695.

Merton, R. K. (1968). The Matthew effect in science. *Science*, *159*(3810), 56–63.

Müller, R. (2012). Collaborating in life science research groups: The question of authorship. *Higher Education Policy*, *25*(3), 289–311.

Müller, R. (2014). Postdoctoral life scientists and supervision work in the contemporary university: A case study of changes in the cultural norms of science. *Minerva*, *52*(3), 329–349.

Musselin, C. (2011). The academic workplace: What we already know, what we still do not know, and what we would like to know. In D. Rhoten & C. Calhoun (Eds.), *Knowledge matters: The public mission of the research university* (pp. 423–457). New York, NY: Columbia University Press.

Raudla, R., Karo, E., Valdmaa, K., & Kattel, R. (2015). Implications of project-based funding of research on budgeting and financial management in public universities. *Higher Education*, *70*(6), 957–971.

Rushforth, A., Franssen, T., & de Rijcke, S. (2018). Portfolios of worth: Capitalizing on basic and clinical problems in biomedical research groups. *Science, Technology, & Human Values*. Advance online publication. doi:10.1177/0162243918786431

Sigl, L. (2016). On the tacit governance of research by uncertainty: How early stage researchers contribute to the governance of life science research. *Science, Technology, & Human Values*, *41*(3), 347–374.

Stark, D. (2011). *The sense of dissonance: Accounts of worth in economic life*. Princeton, NJ: Princeton University Press.

Stöckelová, T. (2014). Power at the interfaces: The contested orderings of academic presents and futures in a social science department. *Higher Education Policy*, *27*(4), 435–451.

Versleijen, A., van der Meulen, B., van der Steen, J., Kloprogge, P., Braam, R., Mamphuis, R., & van den Besselaar, P. A. A. (2007). *Dertig jaar publieke onderzoeksfinanciering – trends, beleid en implicaties*. Den Haag: Rathenau Instituut.

Whitley, R. (2014). How do institutional changes affect scientific innovations? The effects of shifts in authority relationships, protected space, and flexibility. In R. Whitley & J. Glaser (Eds.), *Organisational transformation and scientific change: The impact of institutional restructuring on universities and intellectual innovation* (pp. 367–406). Bingley, UK: Emerald Group Publishing.

Chapter 10

Racing for what? Anticipation and acceleration in the work and career practices of academic life science postdocs*

Ruth Müller

Introduction

In contemporary research cultures, as in industrialized societies in general, it often goes unquestioned that *fast is always better* (Adam, 2003). After all, who could object to more knowledge in a shorter period of time? Narratives about science's indispensable role in society are often narratives about *urgent* necessity: we need to understand more in order to cure, prevent, construct, excel, and survive. Particularly today, as ever more pressing global challenges such as climate change, rapid loss of ecological diversity and an economic downturn seem to demand instantaneous responses, swift scientific progress is often portrayed as the only possible answer. Prime examples of this rhetoric include, e.g., contemporary European Union science policy documents such as Horizon 2020 (European Commission, 2011). Yet, at the same time, some voices in academia are questioning whether more speed in research will actually help us to get where we want to be going. Academia, they argue, is already dominated by a culture of speed that would produce growing heaps of publications, but which would also marginalize time for slow creative thought and reflection. The proponents of 'slow science' worry that science operating under the conditions of constant acceleration might move fast, but rather headlessly and hence not necessarily towards the right goals. 'Bear with us, while we think,' the authors of The Slow Science Manifesto (2010) urge their audience, emphasizing the necessity of slow and thorough thought about goals, means and processes for the beneficial advance of science. The Slow University initiative that is the background for this special section (O'Neill, 2014a; b) takes up this plea for slow and wants to

* Chapter 10 was originally published as: Müller, R. (2014). Racing for what? Anticipation and acceleration in the work and career practices of academic life science postdocs. Forum Qualitative Sozialforschung / Forum: Qualitative Social Research, 15(3), Art. 15, http://dx.doi.org/10.17169/fqs-15.3.2245. For this reprint, the article has undergone additional language editing and thus differs slightly from its original version.

think through what a focus on slow could entail for the organization of contemporary universities.

My interest in slow science is academic and personal. It builds on my research about how career structures and working conditions in academia affect the knowledge production practices of scientists in the life sciences, and more recently the climate sciences. I first started experimenting with the term 'slow science' in 2010, in conversations with Jenny Reardon, Jake Metcalf and Martha Kenney at the Science & Justice Research Centre, UC Santa Cruz. While the term seems to have emerged rather simultaneously in different national and intellectual contexts around that time (McCabe, 2012), in our context we remember it being coined, rather playfully and casually in conversation, by feminist science studies scholar Donna Haraway, as a possible antidote to the frenzy of speed in contemporary academia. While the term slow science can embrace many things, which is both a strength and a weakness, in the context of my work it serves as a shorthand for imaginaries about a counter culture to the current fast-paced, metric-oriented research worlds I encountered in my research. Cultures that appear to worship and reward competition, mobility, individualism and speed above all else; that exhibit, as Barbara Adam put it, 'speed fetishism' (2003, p. 101).

To date, there is a rich corpus of work discussing the multitude of changes academic institutions have been undergoing in the wake of what is mostly summarized as 'new public management' (NPM) transformations during, depending on national context, the last two to three decades (e.g. Deem, 1998; Felt, 2009; Ferlie, Musselin & Andresani, 2008; Jacob & Hellström, 2000; Slaughter & Leslie, 1997). Central to virtually all changes instigated by the market-oriented management techniques of NPM is the introduction of a pervasive focus on efficiency and competition into almost all areas of academic work. Throughout the literature, increasing time pressures, the fragmentation of time into projects and work-packages, and a general sense of there being too little time for thorough thought is pointed to as among the consequences of this refocusing. Yet, only a few studies have explored the empirical details of these perceived shifts in the temporalities of academic work. Scholars who have, such as Ylijoki and Mäntylä (2003), suggest that investigating what they call an emerging new (academic) 'time consciousness' (Hassard, 1991) may be central to understanding the social and epistemic consequences of NPM transformations for academia more broadly.

A key feature of the changes, which all of the rather few studies of temporality in contemporary academic work ascertain, is an increase in experienced tempo of academic work, and a continuous demand to further speed up that already accelerated pace (Garforth & Cervinková, 2009; Vostal, 2015; Ylijoki & Mäntylä, 2003). In the context of contemporary academic NPM inspired audit cultures (Power, 1997; Strathern, 2000), the *accelerated pace* of academic work refers to an *increase of countable academic output per predefined unit of time*, e.g. per year, such as data produced, articles written, volumes edited, grant proposals submitted, lectures given, students passed, etc. While *quality* of output is certainly still an important issue, in contemporary universities the question of *quantity*, of '*How much countable output per unit of time?*' is becoming an increasingly important assessment criterion, particularly in processes such as hiring or promotion of scholars.

Vostal (2015) proposes that junior scholars, who often work on temporary contracts and aim at establishing themselves in academia, are particularly exposed to the demand to produce more units per time. 'It seems that early career academics are particularly vulnerable to the restructuring of higher education in comparison with more established and tenured/permanently employed senior scholars and professoriate' (p. 12f.). This includes a heightened vulnerability to the changing temporal frameworks of academic cultures. Similar to the differences between career stages, the focus on speed appears to be pronounced more or less strongly in different fields. While the imperative to 'Speed up!' seems to interpellate a wide range of scholars across the disciplines and faculties, fast-growing fields that are receiving high policy attention and investments, often due to hopes of economic return, and that are exhibiting high degrees of internationalization and competition, appear to be particularly prone to processes of acceleration. One such field is the life sciences. Garforth and Cervinková (2009) point out that scholars in this field are faced with a growing standardization of possible career trajectories in the context of increasing international competition. This would result in a 'rigid, narrow and increasingly formalised career path [...] in the biosciences' (p. 172) along which particularly junior scholars must run as fast as possible to outpace a growing number of known and unknown, local and international competitors. The article at hand focuses on a distinct category of junior scholars[1] in the life sciences who are, as the empirical work shows, particularly strongly affected by experiences of competition and hence acceleration: postdoctoral researchers.

Building on qualitative interviews with 38 life science postdocs in Austria, this article investigates how postdocs experience the temporal dimensions of their work and their careers. Questions of pace, of how fast one can and needs to work; the experience of being in a competitive race and questions of possible futures within and beyond this race will be central to these narratives. I will discuss a number of social and epistemic consequences of working in a race-like situation, e.g. regarding the social structure of life science labs, the design and organization of research projects and the life of postdocs beyond the lab. In conclusion I will reflect on how racing for a career in the life sciences relates to other goals traditionally associated with scientific inquiry, such as developing a greater basic understanding of the animated and unanimated world and creating societally relevant knowledge and practical problem solutions.

Theoretical perspectives: Anticipation, acceleration and the entrepreneurial self

To lay the groundwork for making sense of the distinct temporal experiences of life science postdocs elaborated in the empirical analysis, I will now discuss a number of important concepts from the sociology of time and social theory that explore and theorize distinctive, overarching features of time and temporality in contemporary (Western) society. These are mainly Adams et al.'s (2009) work on anticipation as form of contemporary governance, Hartmut Rosa's (2003, 2005) reflections on acceleration as a pervasive societal mode of operation and experience and Ulrich Bröckling's (2007) concept of the 'entrepreneurial self' as form of self-governance under the conditions of neoliberal governmentality and omnipresent competition.

In a 2009 paper on *anticipation* as a mode of governance, Adams et al. argue that 'one defining quality of our current moment is its characteristic state of anticipation, of thinking and living toward the future' (p. 246). They further elaborate:

> The present is governed, at almost every scale, as if the future is what matters most. [...] As an affective state, anticipation is not just a reaction, but a way of actively orienting oneself temporally. [...] Regimes of anticipation are distributed and extensive formations that interpellate, situate, attract and mobilize subjects individually and collectively.
> (p. 248)

In an age of growing uncertainty on many levels, anticipation as the attempt to make the future controllable through certain actions in the present becomes an ever more dominant mode of being in the world. The present increasingly becomes a resource to reach or avoid desired or dreaded futures. Imagined futures can induce highly affective states that govern individual and collective behaviours in the present. The making of certain futures often legitimizes a pervasive *resourcification* of the present.

Yet, what is not part of these anticipatory calculations is that the present has a future life of its own that is often unexpected and goes beyond that which is anticipated, feared or desired. Lived presents are always more than resources to be translated into anticipated futures. They are complex social phenomena that pass on every detail of their existence in one way or another. Adams et al. (2009) argue that in the anticipatory mode, the present is often ignored—it is glossed over by the eye fixed on the future. However, it is exactly this inattentiveness and devaluation of lived presents that tend to sabotage even the most beautifully pictured futures. In his book 'Seeing like a State: How Certain Schemes to Improve the Human Condition Have Failed,' James C. Scott (1998) gives striking historical examples of how future-oriented projects have failed in the past—ranging from the radical restructuring of farming practices in the Soviet Union or attempts to conjure a modern Brazil overnight by means of modernist city planning. What all of these projects had in common is a certain disregard for the present: The present was figured not as important in and of itself, but as valuable because of its potential to *become* the future. Discomfort and sacrifice in the present were hence normatively acceptable and reframed as potentially beneficial. If the present is only a moment of transition towards a golden future, no serious attention needs to be paid to the trials and tribulations of the now. Uneasiness with a new system is recast as a period of adaptation, critique is washed away with the final argument of where we need to go. Scott shows how, with their eyes fixed on the future, the planners of the past cropped and mutilated the present, attempting to fit the complexities of human life into their schematic visions of the time to come.

Adams et al. (2009) as well as Scott (1998) point to the modalities and effects of a pervasive orientation towards the future, and of anticipatory practices that think the present mainly in relation to and as a resource for certain futures. In the contemporary context, the overwhelming authority of the future over the present needs to be considered in relation to what Hartmut Rosa (2003, 2005) describes as a comprehensive *acceleration* of society. Anticipation as a mode of governing the self and others becomes dominant in a society that is, in general, considered to speed up. Rosa (2003) argues that there is evidence for three interrelated forms of acceleration taking place: technological acceleration (e.g. in transportation, communication, production); acceleration of social change (changes in social constellations and structures); and acceleration of the pace of life (increase in events/activities per time; an ethics of and desire for 'do[ing] *more* things in *less* time' [p. 9]). With growing rates of change, anticipating the future becomes ever more important. Indeed, Rosa argues, the present itself might even be shrinking in the context of an accelerating society, becoming less of a wide playing field and more of a narrow ridge between fleeing past and fast-approaching future, offering only little ground to stand on. Here Rosa draws on conceptualizations of past, future and present developed by philosopher Hermann Lübbe (1998) and historian Reinhart Koselleck (1985). He writes

> Lübbe claims that Western societies experience what he calls the 'contraction of the present' (*Gegenwartsschrumpfung*) [...] For Lübbe, the past is defined as that which [...] *is no longer valid* while the future denotes that which [...] *is not yet valid.* The present, then, is the time-span for which (to use an idea developed by Reinhart Koselleck) the horizons of experience and expectation coincide. Only within these time-spans of relative stability can we draw on past experiences to orient our actions and infer conclusions from the past with regard to the future. Only

> within these time-spans is there some certainty of orientation, evaluation, and expectation.
>
> (Rosa, 2003, p. 7)

Under the conditions of comprehensive acceleration, the time spans in which expectation and experience coincide are becoming shorter and shorter. Rosa hence argues that social acceleration is both defined and made palpable 'by an increase in the decay-rates of the reliability of experiences and expectations and by the contraction of the timespans definable as the "present"' (p. 7). On individual as well as collective levels, the experience of a shrinking and fast-decaying present can in turn induce a stronger orientation towards the future, an anticipatory orientation that aims to create future possibilities and tentative certainties, and to ensure an ongoing trajectory that is somewhat recognizable as a good (future) life. The resources this anticipatory mode of (self-) governance can put to use lie in the present: the shrinking present, whose currencies of today might be worthless tomorrow, and in the present selves that, like their time, might easily become obsolete and outdated, if they don't keep up with the times.

This narrative about acceleration as sketched by Rosa, Lübbe and others is implicitly—and sometimes explicitly—built on the assumption that the selves of the accelerating society exist in a condition of almost ubiquitous competition. Here, theories of social acceleration can be productively linked with scholarship on processes of subjectification in contemporary societies in the field of governmentality studies (Bröckling, Krassmann & Lemke, 2000; Bührmann, 2005). With regard to the nexus of acceleration and competition, Bröckling's (2005, 2007) work on the 'entrepreneurial self' as an important mode of contemporary subjectification is particularly interesting. Bröckling builds on the works of Michel Foucault, who argued that neoliberal governmentality would increasingly produce subjects who understand and conduct themselves as if they were *entrepreneurs of themselves*, 'who [are their] own capital, [their] own producer, [their] own source of property' (2004, p. 314). This entrepreneurial self emerges as a form of *self-governance* and *governance of the self* in late modern societies, in which states take over less and less responsibility for their citizens and employing institutions for their employees, but instead they appeal to them to take their lives into their own hands and make something of themselves on the free and open market of local and global opportunities. Inherent to this appeal is a strong temporal dimension, suggesting continuous self-improvement and adaptation to market needs and trends. The entrepreneurial self is, at most, only good enough for the already fading moment of the now, as the conditions, opportunities, exposures and perils it needs to exploit and master are already changing again. In that sense, the entrepreneurial self is less of a state of being than of becoming. As Bröckling (2005, p. 12) writes, the entrepreneurial self

> [...] marks a direction for the way in which individuals are to change and be changed. It exists only in the gerund as something being produced and optimized. One is not an enterprising self, but is rather becoming one. Speaking of this self is never a description, but rather an interpellation.

The entrepreneurial self is hence always on the run, becoming what it is supposed to already be. Under the conditions of acceleration and market-economic competition, *being* an entrepreneurial self 'implies being compelled to permanently achieve more [...] [b]ecause one can assert his position only for the moment and only in relation to his competitors [...]. Today's recipe for success is tomorrow's path to ruin' (p. 15). Here we find a clear resonance with Lübbe's and Rosa's diagnosis that the present as a point of reference and reliability is shrinking, and with Adams et al.'s conclusion that anticipation is becoming a pervasive mode of temporal orientation of contemporary subjects. The future in all its uncertainty is lurking and looming, and wants to be tamed by strategic, efficient and most of all prompt anticipatory action in the present. The shrinking space of the present that provides momentary orientation and congruency of expectations and experiences needs to be put to good use to prepare as best as possible for a future that cannot be known, but must be anticipated, and is sure to come.

In the empirical part of this article, I will show how life science postdocs in Austria can, as they are trying to build a career in academia, be understood as entrepreneurial selves that operate significantly in a mode of future-orientation that can be sketched as, first, *anticipatory acceleration* and second, *latent individualization*. I will draw out social and empirical consequences of these modes of self-governance, and in conclusion discuss these in connection to other, more societal than individual, hopes and expectations projected onto scientific research.

Material and methods

For its analysis, the article draws on 38 interviews with postdoctoral life scientists, conducted between 2007 and 2013, as its main material. 21 of these interviews[2] have been conducted in the course of the ELSA-research project[3] 'Living Changes in the Life Sciences. Tracing the 'ethical' and 'social' in scientific practice and work culture'[4] in 2008 and 2009. This project investigated how changes in the framework conditions of life science research—such as changes in funding structures, the increasing projectification of scientific work and the integration of multiple audit mechanisms—are reflected and negotiated within the work cultures and research practices of life scientists in Austria. The core methodological approach of this project consists of biography-oriented, semi-structured interviews with life scientists. The sample included life scientists from different sub-fields (biomedical, plant biotech, microbial, bioinformatics) and different career stages (PhD students, postdocs and research group leaders). The project team always interviewed several researchers within one lab, starting with the group leader. Labs of interest were identified through interviews with the seven members of the project's life science advisory network. These interviews were conducted at the beginning of the project in order to map the Austrian life science landscape.

Each interview was about 2–3 hours in length and consisted of three main parts: a first part aimed to evoke a biographical narrative about the researchers' ways into science up to their current position and about their possible future paths, a second part focused on their current research practices, discussing both their social and their epistemic dimensions, and a final part invited the interviewees to discuss certain buzz words in science policy, such as excellence, mobility, societal relevance, etc., and their concrete meaning within their everyday work and lives as life science scholars. As the interviews encouraged reflection regarding the interplay between policy, institutional structures and personal experience/practice, and constituted, among other things, a conversation between academic peers, the project team named them 'reflexive peer-to-peer interviews.' A more detailed discussion of this methodological approach can be found in Felt, Fochler and Strassnig (2010) and in Müller and Kenney (2014).

Beyond the 21 interviews with postdocs conducted in the initial study, this article draws on two additional group interviews with four life science postdocs conducted during research stays in the United States in 2010 and 2011. These group interviews followed an adapted version of the one-to-one interview guideline for the reflexive peer-to-peer interview. This article is further informed by interviews with 17 life science postdocs in an Austrian postdoc excellence program conducted in a study in 2013[5] that followed a context-sensitive variation of the initial interview guideline.

The key focus of my analysis as part of the initial project and in the follow-up research was how values, norms and structures of making a career in academia affect researchers' working practices. Postdocs are a particularly interesting group of researchers for exploring these questions. The increasing prominence of this rather new type of scholar is in itself a symptom of changing patterns of organizing academic work, lives and careers. Today, significantly more people are acquiring a PhD, particularly in fields of policy interest and investment such as the life sciences, and aim for an academic career, but compared to these numbers, there are far fewer senior positions available (Benderly, 2005). Hence, an increasing number of people are working as postdoctoral researchers for an increasing number of years, a status that is often loosely defined as being an academically employed researcher holding a PhD, but not a senior or faculty position. Postdocs are typically employed on short-term contracts (1–3 years). A high degree of international mobility is usually characteristic for this period of academic work, caused by both pull factors (the attractiveness of certain international research institutions) and push factors (not enough positions available in the home country, going abroad as a norm and value of career development, see Ackers, 2008). Competition and career pressures, particularly in terms of expected research productivity and publication output, are high during these years, and chances of transitioning into more stable, senior academic employment are at best uncertain, if not plain slim.

Hence, precariously located at this narrowest 'bottleneck' (Russo, 2003) of contemporary scientific careers, postdocs' accounts offer dense narratives about how contemporary career rationales influence their ways of working and living in life science research. I analyzed this nexus with a grounded theory-based approach, with multiple consecutive rounds of coding and analysis (Charmaz, 2006; Strauss & Corbin, 1998).[6] This article draws together those aspects of the analysis, in which questions of temporality and particularly acceleration of work pace figure prominently. I further incorporate relevant analyses and arguments from the published work of two colleagues (Ulrike Felt, Maximilian Fochler), with whom I collaborated in the initial research project 'Living Changes in the Life Sciences'.

Empirical findings

In this empirical section, I will develop two main arguments about life science postdocs' temporal orientations. The first is that under the conditions of current largely metric-based and internationalized academic competition, postdoctoral life scientists adopt a set of future-oriented behaviours that I will subsume under the notion of *anticipatory acceleration*. Second, I will argue that in relation to *anticipatory acceleration* postdocs' social relations in and to life science research groups and institutions are shaped by a state of *latent individualization*.[7] Throughout the section, I will be understanding postdoctoral subjectivities as distinctive context-dependent instantiations of the contemporary form of subjectivation that Bröckling (2005, 2007) describes as the entrepreneurial self. To give the reader a sense of the contexts in which both anticipatory acceleration and latent individualization emerge, I will start the section with a description of how postdocs perceive the trajectories and rationalities of contemporary academic life science careers, and of the specific role of the postdoc period within this career path.

Academic careers as linear and exclusive trajectories

To understand postdocs' temporal orientations, it is crucial to first outline their understanding of what an academic career is or can be. First, as Garforth and Cervinková (2009) elaborate to be the case for early career researchers in the life sciences in a number of European countries, postdocs in the life sciences in Austria have a highly standardized vision of what an academic career path looks like. After a PhD that should ideally be completed in 3–4 years (usually the timeframe of available funding) in either one's home country or abroad, an aspiring life science researcher will hold 1–2 consecutive international postdoc positions of 1–3 years each, preferably at prestigious institutions in Western European or North American countries, and then make the leap to becoming an independent junior group leader, and from there at some point to becoming a senior group leader. While this envisioned career track in itself might not be very surprising, it is important to note that, first, this is the *only* way postdocs think an academic career can be done. For example, taking breaks along this path, working in non-academic research or trying out a different, non-research career at some point, are all perceived as practically impossible deviations that would significantly diminish academic career chances.

Second, it is important to note how this career path is normatively imagined as international. The postdocs interviewed in both studies this article draws on, no matter if they were born in Austria or came to Austria for academic employment, considered a career without significant periods of international mobility to be virtually impossible. Personal restrictions or reluctances to be internationally mobile were seen as severely hindering career prospects. This high degree of expected and experienced mobility is important to keep in mind for understanding how postdocs related to their current local working and living context.

There is a third important and distinctive feature of how the academic career path is perceived, that is yet less described in the literature: the academic career path is not only perceived as highly linear, but also as rendering those who wander it increasingly unfit for other careers. As junior scholars progress from PhD to postdoc, they increasingly assume that their particular training makes them fairly unattractive for non-academic employment. Comparing interviews with PhD students with postdoc interviews, the latter appear much more unsure of what they would have to offer to employers outside academia.[8] Additionally, academic enculturation in the life sciences provides a mindset in which academic work is normatively superior to other types of employment and hence leaving academia is considered a failure of either desire or capability.[9] Even expressing interest in non-academic employment among peers or particularly towards superiors is considered to be potentially damaging to one's reputation as a serious scholar. Hence, other professional options beyond academia mostly remain unexplored and even unimagined. This means that in practice, postdocs' impressions of their future options are characterized by a relatively clear-cut, yet highly uncertain academic path standing out against a vague background of mostly undetermined other professional possibilities. Depending on personality type and particular subfield, this leads some postdocs to consider their job prospects beyond academia dull and unattractive, while others fear that there is not really anything for them out there, and that if they had to leave academia they might end up in long-term unemployment. Hardly any postdoc interviewed in the studies this article draws on considered their job prospects beyond academia good or exciting.

The postdoc period: Competing for a group leader position by increasing the impact per time ratio

Along this linear, internationally mobile and exclusive academic career path, the postdoc period is considered to be of unique importance: it is envisioned to be the moment of highest selection in terms of people being selected out of the academic career, and hence assumed to be the time of the highest competition along the track. This perspective is not only brought forward by postdocs themselves, but also echoed in the interviews with PhD students and research group leaders in the initial study, as well as in discussion pieces in key scientific media such as Benderly (2005) or Russo (2003). In this mindset, the postdoc period becomes primarily a time-space that needs to be successfully traversed.

This makes the postdoc significantly different from the PhD period (Fochler, Felt & Müller, 2016). Doing a PhD is seen as an aim in itself that might give rise to an academic career, but still possibly also to other professional trajectories. Life science PhD students in our study also hardly feared that they might fail to complete the PhD; it might take a bit longer than expected or ideal, but their supervisors would ensure that they would ultimately have enough academic capital in terms of data and results to pass. Doing a postdoc on the other hand is hardly seen as an aim in itself and its completion—the transition to the research group leader stage—is considered to be highly uncertain. The possibility of this transition is perceived to depend on *acquired academic capital per time*, not on academic capital *per se*. A PhD can be extended and still passed with the same amount of capital, but as time moves on in an extended postdoc period, the increment in capital needs to be rather steep to make up for the additional time. Moreover, in times of *increasing* competition, standards of what counts as possibly enough capital for the transition might rise as time passes, and catching up might also mean catching up to already again elevated expectations. Finally, there are perceived cut-off points in terms of age for transitioning from the postdoc to the group leader stage: 35 is often considered the age at which one should have made the transition. Someone who is a postdoc at or after the age 40 is suspicious in and of him/herself, because that 'is somehow a sign that this person is not very successful, is not motivated' (PDoc_1m 203).[10] Hence, postdocs critically depend on and are attuned to the *pace* of their productivity: on how many units of output they can produce within what is perceived to be an acceptable time span of postdoc existence.

What are these units of output? The answer is as simple as it might obvious: publications, or more precisely, impact factors of publications. Put bluntly, publishing at a (cumulative) high impact is the key goal of postdoctoral activity. This aim can be reached, often preferably, through one or a few publications of high impact each, or if this is not possible, through a higher number of publications at lower impact. While a publication in the big three of life sciences journals—*Nature*, *Science* or *Cell*—will go a long way to increasing career prospects and high impact is generally aimed at, overall, it is the cumulative impact factor of a researcher's publications *per unit of time* that increasingly becomes the measure of his or her productivity and hence quality. As one postdoc put it (capturing in his speech pattern much of the breathlessness that often goes along with keeping this ratio up):

> You need to keep publishing papers, you need to publish, you need to make sure you publish papers over a year. If you don't have papers over a year then you are toast. [...] I need at least one, two papers a year [...] or one really good one every few years.
>
> (PDF_2m 1058)

In postdocs' narratives, publication often is no longer something that possibly happens at the end of a research process that might take a number of years, but it rather becomes a *continuous* activity. Gaps in publication patterns come to indicate not periods of intense research, but rather inertia, lack of motivation or capability. Research processes hence need to be planned and staggered in ways that allow for a rather continuous flux of publications. Here the epistemic and social impacts of the demand to work at a high pace of output production start to become tangible. In the following two subsections, I will first discuss key epistemic consequences of this, and then crucial effects on the social organization of research labs.[11]

Epistemic consequences: Working in a state of anticipatory acceleration

In this subsection, I will develop the notion of *anticipatory acceleration* to refer to the temporal orientation in which postdocs are making decisions about the epistemic content of their research. With regard to the overbearing question of publication output per time, questions of epistemic risk, i.e. the predictability or openness of the outcomes of research processes, becomes paramount in these decision processes. I will use this discussion of risk and predictability to elaborate what is meant by anticipatory acceleration.

Under the conditions described above, research processes tend to become mainly vehicles for the fast-paced production of publications. This is how one rather senior postdoc explained how she goes about developing her research projects:

> You already need to plan in the very beginning what papers you will be able to publish, which experiments do I need for that. It sounds way more calculating than you think when you naively start your research career. But you just have to focus on what's good for the papers.
>
> (PDoc_6f, 1319)[12]

The question of how to ensure regular publication output and avoid gaps in the publication record governs research processes right from the start, influencing already the choice of a research question. Asked what the 'ideal' postdoc project would look like, this PhD student at the transition to becoming a postdoc answers:

> One that gives me a good paper in a year! [laughter] Well, you can never entirely cancel out all risks. But what I mean with 'risks' is how predictable it is what will come out of the research in a certain frame of time.
>
> (PhD_2m 971)

Predictability of results and hence publication within a certain, foreseeable time span becomes a marker of an attractive postdoc project. Risk, in terms of less predictability and a greater openness of possible results becomes problematic in a research culture in which keeping up the relentless pace of publication is paramount. Epistemic risk needs to be avoided or at least tamed.[13] Many postdocs employ the first strategy of choosing a rather safe project with somewhat predictable outcomes. Some postdocs, who speculate on a paper of particularly high impact (*Science*, *Nature*, *Cell*), attempt the latter: they work simultaneously on one safe and one high-risk project.[14] In the case of two postdocs in our interview sample who had received a particularly generous fellowship from a leading Austrian research institution, working in such a twofold manner was even mandated. Attached to the high-risk project is the individual—and in the case of these two fellowships also the institutional—hope of achieving the kind of groundbreaking results that allow for a publication in the big three, while the safe project shall guarantee a rather continuous flux of lower-impact publications and hence provide a career fallback. Yet, as can be easily imagined, such a strategy requires exhaustively expanding working hours, often to and beyond postdocs' physical limits. This strategy is essentially a form of extensive multi-tasking, one of the phenomena Rosa (2003) describes as central to the acceleration of the pace of life.

The parallelization of two differently natured research endeavours as well as the initial example of focusing on one safe, quickly realizable project during the postdoc are two examples of epistemic decisions shaped by what I shall term *anticipatory acceleration*. Postdocs accelerate their working practices, i.e. increase the amount of events per time, to their very limits not primarily because of concrete and time-limited time pressures (e.g. a person somewhere else in the world working on exactly the same topic; a specific deadline), but habitually and because of a profound anticipatory orientation that suggests that however much they are currently doing might not be enough and can still be optimized. Only research questions that can have a fit with this orientation or can be made to fit are considered possible choices. Inherently lengthy, speculative or highly unpredictable research projects can hardly be the sole focus of a postdoc researcher's attention under these conditions.

The aim of postdocs' anticipatory acceleration is to make the future more controllable and to improve one's position in the intense and threatening postdoctoral competition. Yet, as Bröckling (2007) points out regarding such attempts of the entrepreneurial self to create some certainty, in the end no amount of effort can really overcome the fear of failure. Instead, the high investments and sacrifice weigh heavy on the postdocs. The long hours of work are shrinking their perspective on their future options ever more, resulting in a 'vicious cycle' (PDoc_16f, 1052) of emotional dependency on and investment in academic success. Working in state of anticipatory acceleration shapes postdocs' research processes deeply, rendering epistemic decisions largely subject to the imperatives of this career-focused, anxious mode of anticipation that demands continuous acceleration.

Social consequences: Working in a state of latent individualization

What does this imply for the social setting of the life science laboratory? Here, we need to remember that life science career trajectories are not only characterized by acceleration and anticipation, but also by international mobility. In most cases, the current laboratory hence figures mainly as a momentary stopping point along an internationalized, fast-paced career trajectory. Under the conditions of anticipatory acceleration, everyday time is always scarce and desired to be devoted to those activities that can increase the output per time ratio. Rosa (2003) argues that processes of acceleration are often linked to conditions of individualization,[15] as the individual can accelerate more easily than the collective. In the case of life science postdocs this is reflected in a condition that I have described in an earlier article as a state of *latent individualization* (Müller, 2014). The terminology of latent individualization tries to capture how postdocs' decision-making practices within their current institutions and groups are also almost always crucially shaped by considerations of and for a future self that is no longer part of its current collective contexts. *Latent* describes the state of something not being there yet, but still, as a probable future, acting upon the present. In this case, it is postdocs' future selves, who will have to prevail in the international academic labour market on their own, that become crucial reference points for postdocs' actions and decisions in the present. This specific anticipatory orientation towards their individual futures guides how postdocs relate to the collective contexts of their presents. Institutions, groups and colleagues become, despite the existence of and desire for emotional bonds such as friendships and loyalty, also and often foremost resources for their future scholarly survival. A research lab is only a good space to be in as long as it allows for ample and high-quality results to be produced in a short period of time. A collaboration is only then desirable if it warrants publications of high impact or number in the next year or two.[16] Supervising a student is only then advisable if chances are that the practice of advising will also produce co-authorships on the student's papers. The needs of the latent future self are decisively governing the present.

Across the two studies, only a very small number of postdocs had any more long-term prospects at their current institutions. The prevalently nomadic postdocs' prime focus hence rested on how to translate as much of their work performed during their temporary engagements in a certain lab as possible into the quantitative, metric-based language of publication numbers and impact factors that dominates contemporary international academic labour markets. The question moulding social relationships to and in research groups and institutions then becomes how these relations can be used to increase the ever-decisive ratio of impact per time. At the end of a contract, the postdoc researcher must have reached escape velocity: that is, enough impact per time to either transition to a group leader position or at least to another postdoctoral position that promises to be good enough to possibly allow for the desired transition to happen at the end of the next contract period.

A note on postdocs and their relation to local societal contexts

Needless to say, anticipatory acceleration and latent individualization also have effects on postdocs' lives beyond the lab. One aspect of this, which is less discussed than the more common issues of family life and child care, is how postdocs relate to the societal contexts they live in during periods abroad. Most postdocs will live in a country other than their home country at some point, for a number of years, possibly in a place where they don't speak the common language. Fochler (2010) argues that instead of creating a transnational, cosmopolitan research community that lives in and engages with different national contexts, international mobility as performed in current speed-fetishizing research cultures rather produces 'cosmo-idiots': people, who travel but hardly get to know where they are; who move around the globe, but exist in a bubble of work and more work, without ever really engaging with local communities or the national political systems. In the Austrian case studies, young scholars frequently mentioned that they had no time to learn the local language, read the newspaper or engage in any political debates, even if these debates concerned science. This suggests that an increasing number of scholars per country are not actively participating in civil society, which, given the traditional role of academia as a source of critical thought and political activism, gives reason for concern.

Conclusions: What are we racing for?

In this concluding section, I will briefly recap the concepts developed in this article to describe the temporal orientation of life science postdocs in their academic career-making practices and the ways they are affecting the epistemic and social dimensions of their work. Then I will infer speculative conclusions about the broader contexts and impacts of these phenomena.

Anticipatory acceleration is a type of acceleration that aims at increasing units of output per units of time that is not developed in response to a certain event or specific time horizon, but rather constitutes a generalized response to a state of pervasive competition in the academic life sciences that primarily selects along the question of 'how much per time?' Anticipatory acceleration of this kind tends to privilege research questions and approaches that are predictable in terms of their outcomes, or requires highly elaborate and exhaustive individual risk management strategies to engage projects bearing more epistemic uncertainty, and hence potential for novelty.

Latent individualization is a type of relation between the individual and its collective (working) contexts that emerges in life sciences laboratories under the condition of high international mobility, metric-based competition and respectively anticipatory acceleration. It indicates that researchers relate to their current collective contexts decisively through the perspective of the career needs of their future individual self that is no longer part of these contexts, but which must prevail on the international academic labour market by itself. Latent individualization tends to render social relations to individuals, groups and institutions instrumental and tentative.

What can be inferred from the prevalence of these two interdependent temporal orientations in postdocs' accounts about their academic working practices? I offer speculative conclusions on two levels: the future of knowledge production and the importance of the slow science movement. The first one concerns the question of which types of research cultures might be emerging with these temporal orientations, if one speculates that they are becoming increasingly pervasive. Adams et al. (2009) as well as Scott (1998) remind us that lived presents always also generate unexpected futures that go beyond those futures which they have attempted to anticipate. Felt (2013)[17] captures this in her concept of 'collateral futures' that she develops, inter alia, out of her studies of contemporary research cultures. These collateral futures have not been anticipated, but still they are materializing instead of or alongside the desired effects. In the case of the contemporary life sciences, and the ways in which they are currently temporally governed, what becomes apparent are the consequences of a pervasive focus on metrics-based competition enacted in science policy and institutional management for the research practices and the academic socialization of the coming generation of researchers. If researchers need to pass an increasing number of checkpoints at which the quality of their work and their scholarly biographies is inspected in terms of their productivity per time, researchers will develop social and epistemic habits that allow them to accommodate these demands. Extrapolating from the material at hand, this might mean a reduction of the complexity of problems addressed and a focus on meeting the outlined criteria of performance rather than on originality; it might also include an exhaustive focus on individual achievement and tendency towards the instrumentalisation of others. The first could be a threat to academic inventiveness (Osborne, 2003; Vostal, 2015), the second to the social cohesion, collegiality and knowledge exchange in academic institutions.

Here, we find a certain tension between expressed policy goals such as fostering original thought, collaboration and creative innovation, and the practice of attempting to achieve these goals through an ever-increasing amount of metric-based competition. If, for example, science funders, on which academics are so increasingly dependent in their working life, regularly reject fellowships and grant proposals because the curriculum vitae of the applicant does not show enough quality in terms of numbers and impacts of publications and citations counts, *regardless* of the content of the proposal, what does this say about the relationship between metrics and ideas in current science policy and administration? This is not to disavow quality control in academia, nor to suggest that performance metrics are generally useless. On the contrary, I find it of uttermost importance that academic institutions and funding bodies develop ways of actually assessing the quality that rests behind the few or many lines of a CV. The current pervasive focus on metrics-based competition however seems not to be the way to go, as this study and an emerging body of literature suggest.

What can be the place of the Slow Science movement or most recently the Slow University initiative within these debates about the quality of academic work and the future of academic institutions? While other contributions in this special section and elsewhere criticize the term as conservative (Mendick, 2014), distracting from more analysis of cause and effect (Martell, 2014) or plain toothless (Vostal, 2015) and suggest switching to a different, more complex vocabulary, I propose that if we do not only focus on the experiences and knowledge cultures of the social sciences and humanities, but also take into account natural science and engineering cultures, the term is useful because it speaks to the experiences of a broad variety of scholars across the fields. It is in that sense not necessarily satisfactory as an analytical category of social science research, but useful as a vector of intra- and inter-university mobilization. This is confirmed by the overwhelming interest in the two Slow University workshops at Durham University in 2013 and 2014 that gave rise to this special section. I think *slow* can serve as a sensible shorthand for relating critically within and to ongoing transformations in the university, because for scholars across the disciplines many of the problematic trends in current academia become tangible on the *experiential level* as questions of pace: as experiences of and demands for acceleration; as tensions between fragmentation of time, time pressures and creative and thorough academic practice; and as the demand to be an anticipating, flexible entrepreneurial self that is always a step ahead of its time in order to succeed in the pyramid scheme[18] of academic careers. Slow, in the way in which it is used in the Slow Science movement and the Slow University initiative, and before that in the Slow Food or Slow Cities movements, understands slowing down as form of instigating a critical reflection on the values that are encompassed by the often unmarked fast. Starting a discussion about slowing down in academia in this sense is hence not necessarily to address the root of the problem, but can be a useful means to invoke and unpack the experiences of many scholars in different disciplinary contexts, and relate and rally across the divisions to develop models of resistance and change. It could lead to asking the question of *Cui bono currimus?*[19] – To whose benefit is it that we are racing? Is it primarily to our own, in terms of our careers? To that of *science*? The *economy*? The *public good*? Answers to these questions and their alternatives can of course only form tentatively and will possibly bristle with cynicism at first. Yet, this just shows that it is time to pose the question.

Acknowledgments

This article is based on research conducted in the research project 'Living Changes in the Life Sciences,' funded by GEN-AU/BMWF (Project leader: Ulrike Felt; main collaborators: Maximilian Fochler, Ruth Müller; September 2007 to December 2010); and on research conducted in the course of the study 'VIPS Impact Assessment Study' (May to June 2013), funded by the Vienna International Postdoc Program, Vienna Biocenter. Many thanks to Maximilian Fochler, Cornelia Schadler, Kay Felder, Thomas Völker and Maggie O'Neill for their comments and feedback on earlier versions of this article. An initial outline of the article was first presented at the workshop 'The Slow University?' Durham University, November 6, 2013. Thank you, Maggie, for taking the initiative and bringing us all together. For the reprint, I thank Mike Holohan for additional language editing.

Notes

1 A rather vague, and in itself politically problematic container term, see Pain (2014).

2 This number includes 16 postdocs working as group member scientists, 2 postdocs with special fellowships that allowed them to have a small research group for themselves, and 3 researchers, who had not formally finished their PhD research at the moment of the interview, but were already focused on the postdoctoral academic labour market. The postdocs' ages ranged from their late twenties to their mid-forties, with the majority aged between 30 and 35. With one exception, all aimed at succeeding in an academic career, with the goal of becoming an established senior scientist (group leader, professor, research director).

3 ELSA = 'Ethical, Legal and Social Aspects of Science.'

4 Conducted from September 2007 to December 2010 at the Department of Science and Technology Studies, University of Vienna, Austria. The project was funded by the Austrian Genome Program GEN-AU; project leader: Prof. Ulrike Felt; main collaborators: Maximilian Fochler and Ruth Müller.

5 VIPS (Vienna International Postdoc Program) Impact Assessment Study, funded by VIPS from May to June 2013.

6 In the initial rounds of open coding the nexus of career considerations and postdocs' working and living practices emerged as a key theme that became the topic of my research work between 2008 and 2012. Within this broad topic, the relationship between individuality (e.g. individual career aspirations and trajectories) and collectivity (e.g. collective working contexts) became a focal point and sensitizing concept (Blumer, 1954; Bowen, 2006) for the following rounds of analysis.

7 I first developed this analytical concept in a study on how postdocs engage in supervision work of PhD students (Müller, 2014).

8 This is not least a product of academic ways of measuring a person's worth. Hardly ever is a scholar's worth measured in abilities and skills, but rather only in units of output, a form of evaluation and self-evaluation that does not easily translate into private sector forms of assessing a possible employee's potentials.

9 It is interesting to note that postdocs appear to often lose sight of peers who have left academia: what those people might be doing now often remains a mystery to academic postdocs. This situation has, for example, led postdoc representatives at the renowned European Molecular Biology Organization (EMBO), to actively invite former postdocs, who are now pursuing non-academic careers, to come back and give talks about their work so current postdocs could develop ideas of what else they could do.

10 This abbreviation depicts: career stage, interview number, gender and line in interview transcript.

11 Please bear in mind that the distinction between the epistemic and the social is somewhat artificial. Aspects of research work that are usually discussed as social (e.g. whether to work on a project individually or collaboratively) of course have effects on the epistemic level. In turn, issues usually addressed as epistemic (e.g. such as selecting a research question) can have impacts on the social structure of a lab (e.g. depending on how this question relates to what others in the lab work on). Yet, for clarifying that an increase in working pace does not only have social, but also epistemic impacts, I chose to separate these categories for now.

12 This passage was also quoted in: Müller and Kenney (2014, p. 545).

13 In this particular interview, the soon-to-be postdoc tells a narrative of ever-declining possibilities to take risks along an academic career. Risk in his narrative is something only PhD students, who are allowed to operate in time-space that has less pressure to publish and more temporal freedom, can take. Senior scholars again can experience and engage with risk through their PhD students, while their postdocs need to be assigned rather safe questions and projects.
14 See Sigl (2012) for a detailed elaboration of different risk management strategies among early-career life science researchers.
15 Rosa (2003) makes a more linear argument, suggesting that it is social acceleration that has created the phenomenon of individualization in modern societies (as described e.g. by Beck & Beck-Gernsheim, 2002). I do not wish to take a stand in this ongoing debate, but while I agree that there is a link between both phenomena, I am inclined to consider the connection to rather be a two-way than a one-way street.
16 See also Müller (2012) on the nexus of career and collaboration in life science labs.
17 In developing this concept Felt draws on and adapts John Law's (2011) concept of 'collateral realities,' introducing a focus on questions of temporalities and particularly future-making practices.
18 Pyramid scheme (in German: ['Pyramidenspiel']): A fraudulent investment scheme in which new investors are attracted to the operation by being promised unrealistically high returns for their investments after a certain amount of time. The scheme depends on a constantly growing number of new investors on the base of a pyramid structure, whose invested capital is transferred to those on top of the pyramid. New members are encouraged to attract new investors themselves, so they can move towards the top of the pyramid.
19 Feminist science studies scholar Susan Leigh Star (e.g. 1995), a relentless explorer and critic of the seemingly given and self-evident, reminds us throughout her life's work never to forget to pose the question: *Cui bono?* To whose benefit?

References

Ackers, L. (2008). Internationalisation, mobility and metrics: A new form of indirect discrimination? *Minerva*, *46*(4), 411–435.

Adam, B. (2003). When time is money: Contested rationalities of time in the theory and practice of work. *Theoria*, *50*(102), 94–125.

Adams, V., Murphy, M., & Clarke, A. (2009). Anticipation: Technoscience, life, affect, temporality. *Subjectivity*, *28*(1), 246–265.

Beck, U., & Beck-Gernsheim, E. (2002). *Individualization: Institutionalized individualism and its social and political consequences.* London: Sage

Benderly, B. L. (2005). Not your father's postdoc. Editorial feature. *Science*, *308*(5722), 717–718.

Blumer, H. (1954). What is wrong with social theory? *American Sociological Review*, *18*(1), 3–10.

Bowen, G. A. (2006). Grounded theory and sensitizing concepts. *International Journal of Qualitative Methods*, *5*(3), 1–9.

Bröckling, U. (2005). Gendering the enterprising self. Subjectification programs and gender differences in guides to success. *Distinktion: Scandinavian Journal of Social Theory*, *6*(2), 7–25.

Bröckling, U. (2007). *Das unternehmerische Selbst: Soziologie einer Subjektivierungsform*. Frankfurt: Suhrkamp.

Bröckling, U., Krassmann, S., & Lemke, T. (Eds.) (2000). *Gouvernementalität der Gegenwart*. Frankfurt: Suhrkamp.

Bührmann, A. D. (2005). The emerging of the entrepreneurial self and it's contemporary hegemonic status: Some fundamental observations for an analysis of the (trans-) formational process of modern forms of subjectivation. *Forum Qualitative Sozialforschung / Forum: Qualitative Social Research*, *6*(1), Art. 16. Retrieved from http://nbn-resolving.de/urn:nbn:de:0114-fqs0501165

Charmaz, K. (2006). *Constructing grounded theory: A practical guide for qualitative analysis*. London: Sage.

Deem, R. (1998). "New managerialism" and higher education: The management of performances and cultures in universities in the United Kingdom. *International Studies in Sociology of Education*, *8*(1), 47–70.

European Commission. (2011). *Horizon 2020*. Retrieved from http://ec.europa.eu/research/horizon2020/

Felt, U. (Ed.) (2009). *Knowing and living in academic research. Convergence and heterogeneity in research cultures in the European Context*. Prague: Institute of Sociology of the Academy of Sciences of the Czech Republic.

Felt, U. (2013). Kollaterale Zukünfte: Zu den (An)Ordnungen von Morgen. Paper presented at the conference *Zukunftsexpertise. Zur Generierung, Legitimierung, Verwendung und Anerkennung von Zukunftswissen, Bielefeld, Germany, January 25, 2013*.

Felt, U., Fochler, M., & Strassnig, M. (2010). Experimente partizipativer ELSA-Forschung. Eine methodenpolitische Reflexion. In E. Grießler, & H. Rohracher (Eds.), *Genomforschung – Politik – Gesellschaft. Perspektiven auf ethische, rechtliche und soziale Aspekte der Genomforschung* (pp. 33–67). Wiesbaden: VS Verlag.

Ferlie, E., Musselin, C., & Andresani, G. (2008). The steering of higher education systems: A public management perspective. *Higher Education*, *56*(3), 325–348.

Fochler, M. (2010). Responsibility on the move: Societal responsiveness in shifting epistemic living spaces in the life sciences. Paper presented at the *Conference Risky entanglements? Contemporary research cultures imagined and practised, Vienna, Austria, June 11, 2010*.

Fochler, M., Felt, U. & Müller, R. (2016) Unsustainable Growth, Hyper-Competition, and Worth in Life Science Research: Narrowing Evaluative Repertoires in Doctoral and Postdoctoral Scientists' Work and Lives. *Minerva, 54*(2), 175–200.

Foucault, M. (2004). *Geschichte der Gouvernementalität II: Die Geburt der Biopolitik. Vorlesung am College de France 1978–1979*. Frankfurt: Suhrkamp.

Garforth, L., & Cervinková, A. (2009). Times and trajectories in academic knowledge production. In U. Felt (Ed.), *Knowing and living in academic research: Convergence and heterogeneity in research cultures in the European Context* (pp. 169–224). Prague: Institute of Sociology of the Academy of Sciences of the Czech Republic.

Hassard, J. (1991). Aspects of time in organization. *Human Relations*, *44*(2), 105–125.

Jacob, M., & Hellström, T. (Eds.) (2000). *The future of knowledge production in the academy*. Buckingham: Open University Press.

Koselleck, R. (1985). *Futures past: On the semantics of historical time*. Cambridge, MA: MIT Press.

Law, J. (2011). Collateral realities. In F. D. Rubio, & P. Baert (Eds.), *The politics of knowledge* (pp. 156–178). London: Routledge.

Lübbe, H. (1998). Gegenwartsschrumpfung. In K. Backhaus, & H. Bonus (Eds.), *Die Beschleunigungsfalle oder der Triumph der Schildkröte* (pp. 129–164). Stuttgart: Schäffer/Pöschel.

McCabe, D. (2012). The slow science movement. *University Affairs Magazine, December 5 2012.* Retrieved from http://www.universityaffairs.ca/the-slow-science-movement.aspx

Martell, L. (2014). The slow university: Inequality, power and alternatives. *Forum Qualitative Sozialforschung / Forum: Qualitative Social Research, 15*(3), Art. 10. Retrieved from http://nbn-resolving.de/urn:nbn:de:0114-fqs1403102

Mendick, H. (2014). Social class, gender and the pace of academic life: What kind of solution is slow? *Forum Qualitative Sozialforschung / Forum: Qualitative Social Research, 15*(3), Art. 7. Retrieved from http://nbn-resolving.de/urn:nbn:de:0114-fqs140374

Müller, R. (2012). Collaborating in life science research groups: The question of authorship. *Higher Education Policy, 25*(3), 289–311.

Müller, R. (2014) Postdoctoral life scientists and supervision work in the contemporary university: A case study of changes in the cultural norms of science. *Minerva, 52*(3), 329–349.

Müller, R., & Kenney, M. (2014). Agential conversations: On interviewing life scientists and the politics of mundane research practices. *Science as Culture, 23*(4), 537–559.

O'Neill, M. (2014a). The SLOW University—Work, time and well being. *Discover Society, June 3 2014.* Retrieved from http://www.discoversociety.org/2014/06/03/the-slow-university-work-time-and-well-being/

O'Neill, M. (2014b). The slow university: Work, time and well-being. *Forum Qualitative Sozialforschung / Forum: Qualitative Social Research, 15*(3), Art. 14. Retrieved from http://nbn-resolving.de/urn:nbn:de:0114-fqs1403146

Osborne, T. (2003). Against "creativity": A philistine rant. *Economy and Society, 32*(4), 507–525.

Pain, E. (2014). An emerging global picture of early-career scientists. *Science Careers, January 27.* Retrieved from http://sciencecareers.sciencemag.org/career_magazine/previous_issues/articles/2014_01_27/caredit.a1400023

Power, M. (1997). From risk society to audit society. *Soziale Systeme, 3*(1), 3–21.

Rosa, H. (2003). Social acceleration: Ethical and political consequences of a desynchronized highspeed society. *Constellations, 10*(1), 3–33.

Rosa, H. (2005). *Beschleunigung. Die Veränderung der Zeitstrukturen in der Moderne.* Frankfurt/M.: Suhrkamp.

Russo, E. (2003). Victims of success. *Nature, 422*(6929), 354–355.

Scott, J. C. (1998). *Seeing like a state: How certain schemes to improve the human condition have failed.* New Haven, CT: Yale University Press.

Sigl, L. (2012). Embodied anxiety: On experiences of living and coping with (conditions of) precarity in research cultures of the academic life sciences. *Doctoral Thesis, Department of Science and Technology Studies, University of Vienna, Austria.*

Slaughter, S., & Leslie, Larry L. (1997). *Academic capitalism.* Baltimore, MD: Johns Hopkins University Press.

Star, S. L. (Ed.) (1995). *Ecologies of knowledge: Work and politics in science and technology*. Albany, NY: State of New York University Press.
Strathern, M. (Ed.) (2000). *Audit cultures. Anthropological studies in accountability, ethics and the academy*. London: Routledge.
Strauss, A. L., & Corbin, J. M. (1998). *Basics of qualitative research. Techniques and procedures for developing grounded theory* (2nd ed.). London: Sage.
Vostal, F. (2015). Academic life in the fast lane: The experience of time and speed in British academia. *Time and Society*, *24*(1), 71–95.
Ylijoki, O.-H., & Mäntylä, H. (2003). Conflicting time perspectives in academic work. *Time & Society*, *12*(1), 55–78.

Part IV

Agency and control

Chapter 11

Formulating the academic precariat

Christian Mauri

Introduction

According to the British economist, Guy Standing (2011, p. 7), the spread of insecure employment and the erosion of occupational identities under neoliberalism have led to the emergence of the precarious proletariat, or *precariat*, as a 'class in the making'. While this contention has been criticised in respect to more traditional approaches to class analysis (Alberti et al., 2018; Munck, 2013; Wright, 2015), it has received mounting attention in discussions on the employment and work situations of the highly skilled and educated (Frase, 2013; Ivancheva, 2015; Miller, 2010). As Jørgensen (2016, p. 963) observes, the emerging interest in the precariat as a 'class in the making' is tied to the 'realization by some groups (middle-class, highly educated, non-migrants) that they also belong to groups in both real and potentially precarious positions'. This is tied to the fact that, as Standing (2015, p. 7) puts it, 'this is the first class in history for which the norm is having a higher level of educational qualifications than the labour the person can expect to obtain and be obliged to do'. As in the United States and the United Kingdom (Cryanoski et al., 2011; Foti, 2017), this is borne out in Australia, where universities and employers are grappling with an unpredictable environment that ostensibly requires graduates to be more capable communicators and flexible and agile workers than ever before (Harman, 2010; Norton, 2012; PwC and AHEIA, 2016). In this respect, discussions of the precariat can be viewed as the expression of a kind of class shock regarding declining securities and opportunities across various sectors and professions, and as a critique of the structural conditions behind this decline.

Just as the portmanteau 'precariat' brings together precarious and proletariat, so too can casualisation and proletarianisation be viewed in tandem via the processes of 'precarisation', which, as Alberti et al. (2018, p. 449; also see Kalleberg, 2009) puts it, is used to describe 'increasing insecurity in both subjective and objective respects, which can be identified across modern capitalist economies including in ostensibly privileged strata'. Hence, discussions of the academic precariat can be viewed as an attempt to conceptualise and critique the proletarianisation and casualisation of academic workforces in universities around the world. Connections have already been made between these neoliberal trends (Olssen & Peters, 2015; Ward, 2012) and the growing organisational divisions between, for instance, academics and administrators, as well as between academics in ongoing positions and the burgeoning reserve army of sessional – typically teaching – academics (Andrews et al., 2016; Berry, 2003; Brown & Yasukawa, 2010; Goldsworthy, 1990; Kimber, 2010; May et al., 2013; Rothengatter & Hil, 2013; Ryan & Bhattacharyya, 2016). To contribute to these conversations and to aid its newcomers, this chapter draws on Standing's formulation of the precariat to give an idea of how the situations, experiences and growth of sessional academics can be usefully discussed in terms of precarisation, as well as how these developments are tied to the contemporary structures and context of global academia.

The chapter begins with an overview of the casualisation and the proletarianisation of academics, with an emphasis on the segmentation of academics into the salariat and the precariat, which occupy what Kimber (2010) calls the tenured core and the tenuous periphery of universities. Along with securely employed professional and administrative staff, the core is made up by the real faculty who are in or on a clear track towards ongoing positions. While the redundancy rounds that many universities go through, ostensibly to cut down on unnecessary expenditure, means that positions that were previously counted as secure are always subject to the threat of dissolution, the core is nonetheless, comparatively speaking, the domain of the secure salariat. The periphery is inhabited by sessional academics, who are casualised in so far that they are employed as part of a 'reserve army' of labour on casual or limited-term contracts for years at a time, and proletarianised in so far that their experience and expertise can be rendered irrelevant by the administrators and the proxy-employers of the core that they depend on for employment. Note that the intention here is not to explain at length how these conditions have come about, but to outline the effect that they are having on the situations of, and relations between, academics. We then turn to Standing's formulation of the precariat as a broad though distinctive sub-class, comprised of factions that, despite their differences, tend to be subject to structural conditions and modal characteristics that set them apart from his formulations of the salariat and proletariat. In outlining these conditions and characteristics, an emphasis is placed on treating Standing's formulation as an ideal type (as in a conceptual model for drawing attention to certain connected features of social reality) that is suitable to neo-Weberian class-analysis (i.e. for the analysis of the situations and opportunities of groups in contemporary organisational contexts). The chapter then applies this formulation to casual and limited-term teaching (i.e. sessional) academics, to show how, while not a perfect conceptual fit, the notion can help to conceptualise and look beyond this new majority of teaching academics.

Academia and precarisation

Proletarianisation speaks to the shift to closely managed work oriented to the production of goods and the delivery of services. This shift, which can also be called deprofessionalisation, corresponds with what Berry (2003, p. 58) describes as a 'loss of autonomy, loss of control of work process, and finally, loss of the craft ('professional') perquisites that have traditionally gone along with the work…'. These processes overlap through the unbundling of full-time roles and the piecemeal redistribution of work based on ostensibly measurable demand. One manifestation of this in academe is what McCarthy et al. (2017, p. 2) describe as 'the break-up of the research–teaching nexus so as to segment and capture academic skills, the first stage of which was the casualisation of the academic labour force'. As Coaldrake and Stedman (1998, p. 114) observe, this has allowed universities to distribute the various functions of academic work in the form of limited-term contracts to workers who do not necessarily need specialist academic skills and experience to carry out and retain their job. The result is that university teaching is increasingly delivered by sessional academics who may have no background in the subject and no real say in the construction and logistics of the course, with such academics thereby becoming deprofessionalised, on-demand service-providers.

Proletarianisation is closely tied to casualisation, which is the trend of escalating casual and limited-term appointments, relative to declining continuing appointments, resulting in less financial and employment security across the effected workforce (Andrews et al., 2016; Brown et al., 2010; Junor, 2004). For Kogan et al. (1994, p. 53). This reflects the tendency for managers to view ongoing employment (and thus ongoing staff) as potentially unnecessary expenses and avoidable responsibilities. Connecting this trend to managerialism and proletarianisation, Dearlove (1997, p. 61) notes how this 'keenly reveals the weakening position of many academics in relation to their employers'. Taken together, the loss of security and certainty associated with casualisation, and the reduction in professional autonomy and recognition that comes with proletarianisation, reflect an overall process of precarisation.

According to Kimber (2010) a key effect of these processes is a growing divide between the shrinking tenured core and the burgeoning tenuous periphery within academic workforces. This is supported by numerous studies showing that sessional academics are often not seen (and sometimes do not self-identify) as real faculty members; are excluded from collegial forums and events; and are rendered invisible in ways ranging from office space (where, unlike those in the core, even sessionals that are given a space are not permitted to have their name on the door) to recognition for contributions to course-development and recognition in university workforce statistics (Brown et al., 2010; May et al., 2013; Rothengatter & Hil, 2013; Ryan et al., 2013). Moreover, furthering the theme of proletarianisation, Berry (2003, p. 59) points out that, due to their reduced autonomy and their dependence on the academics of the core for employment, the sessional academics of the periphery often come to see their core-based colleagues as 'bosses'.

It is in these respects that class-based analogies are employed in the analysis of contemporary academe, with the new majority faculty (Berry, 2003) that has emerged within contemporary universities being cast as the 'proletariat of the academic profession' (Percy et al., 2008, p. 2). This is understandable, for such staff are typically recruited by academics-as-proxy-employers and work under exploitative conditions set by managers in the economic interest of the university (Brown et al., 2006). That said, many in the academic proletariat work on a casual or limited-term basis, and so lack many of the securities that the proletariat held throughout the better half of the twentieth century – hence, 'precariat' may be more appropriate (Standing, 2011, p. 10). The following section introduces Standing's formulation of the precariat, which is treated as an ideal type 'in which groups are defined by their modal characteristics', which includes material situations along with the experiences that typically accompany them (Standing, 2014, p. 2). In a neo-Weberian fashion – that is, as a model for comparing the situations of groups in contemporary organisational contexts – this is then applied to sessional academics.

Standing and the precariat

Standing presents a loose hierarchy of classes based on differences in wealth and status, as well as employment and work situations and opportunities. At the top are the super wealthy elite: the tiny and well-connected plutocracy that influences economies, governments and other institutions, such as the media. With them are the wealthy elites who aspire to enter this plutocracy: the high-ranking administrators and bosses of successful business. The proficians are the new idealised workers: the agile contractors of the knowledge economy, the jet-setting entrepreneurs and innovators of niche markets. The salariat are the educated professionals who generally tend to have careers, as opposed to just jobs, and enjoy benefits, professional autonomy and clear opportunities for advancement. The proletariat sell their labour to get by, and enjoy a certain measure of security, though they typically have jobs as workers, rather than as career professionals. In part due to their lack of exclusive, specialised skills, the proletariat tend to be lower on organisational hierarchies than the salariat, more disposable, and attract less pay, benefits and status. The precariat is excluded from the salariat and broadly distinguished from the proletariat in respect to securities and status, which reflects their marginalised employment and work situations, and, by extension, their limited opportunities when it comes to advancement.

Standing identifies three factions of the precariat using temporal adjectives. The atavists are the old, native and under-educated working class, so-called because they would have once been among the proletariat and recall to the conditions of those earlier days. The nostalgics are typically migrant and ethnic minorities (such as the Romani peoples). This faction does not look back to the working conditions that the atavists remember – rather, they 'have a strong sense of relative deprivation by virtue of having no present, no home', and so they keep their head down and focus on short-term economic survival (Standing, 2015, p. 8). It is among the progressives that we locate the academic precariat. These are the educated, typically younger people, who are 'plunged into a precariat existence after being promised the opposite, a bright career of personal development and satisfaction' (Standing, 2014, p. 30). This speaks to the graduates who did everything that was expected of them, and in so doing incurred large debts, only to end up in casual jobs, unpaid-internships, or contemplating returning to university for costly courses that will supposedly make them more competitive. While members of this educated precariat are mostly in their twenties and thirties, older professionals are 'drifting out of a salariat existence' to join them (Standing, 2014, p. 30). They are called progressives because their education, networks and social media skills make them the precariat's most probable mouthpiece for civil and political engagement (see Foti, 2017).

While Standing (2011, pp. 13–14) acknowledges that the precariat is far from homogeneous, he insists that these groups 'share a sense that their labour is instrumental (to live), opportunistic (taking what comes) and precarious (insecure)'. Moreover, Standing (2014, pp. 16–17) observes that while 'the proletarian norm was habituation to stable labour, the precariat is being habituated to unstable labour'. This insecurity is coupled with a marginality whereby members of the precariat pursue work along the periphery as a transient organisational denizenry. Hence, for Standing (2011, p. 14), to be 'precariatised' is to be 'subject to pressures and experiences that lead to a precariat existence, of living in the present, without a secure identity or sense of development achieved through work and lifestyle'. While all the characteristics of the precariat laid out by Standing are not addressed here, the following sections address four dimensions that are particularly relevant to the precarisation occurring in academia: *employment and advancement*, *securities*, *unpaid work-for-labour*, and *relative deprivation* and *occupational identity*.

Employment and advancement

According to Standing (2014, p. 16), because the precariat is being 'habituated to unstable labour', they must routinely seek out work and take the work that comes (Standing, 2011, p. 14). To understand how this plays out for the sessional academics of the periphery and the effect that this has on their relations to the salariat of the core and the university administration, it is worth looking at the structural differences in how such academics gain and advance their employment. While those on the periphery generally want entry into the core (Ryan et al., 2013), such transitions are limited by the fact that, rather than being recruited through what might have formerly been entry-level positions within a broader academic career, sessional academics are increasingly treated by universities as a secondary labour market (May et al., 2013, p. 265). Hence, a distinction that can viewed in terms of *formal* and *informal* (or secondary) 'markets'.[1]

The formal market involves opportunities for continuing-employment and for limited-term appointments that might lead to continuing appointments. This is the proper channel for transitioning from the periphery into the core as a faculty member, advancing through the organisational hierarchy and developing a career. It is a large and highly competitive market, for universities can advertise positions both nationally and internationally. Positions are seemingly filled according to the merits of the applicants, along with how well their skills and stated views align with the values and mission of the institution. This is assessed through lengthy application processes, which can involve explicit criteria, the provision of documentation and references, interviews, lunches and numerous reviews. Academic capital, such as formal credentials and specialised expertise, publications and citations, funding history, professional affiliations and personal references from established academic referees all factor into successful applications. Beyond the explicit criteria for the position, the social capital of who one knows, the cultural capital of familiarity with the prospective institutional and collegial culture, qualities that might be deemed relevant to matters of social justice, and the plain luck can also factor into the review process.

The informal market is the primary source of contingent academic jobs, such as with limited-term contracts for teaching. In contrast to the formal market, it tends to operate under ad hoc and pressurised circumstances, with contracts being offered around unpaid non-teaching periods when student numbers – and thus the demand for labour – are still uncertain. The casual-nepotism of 'who you know' is central, as contracts are typically offered or asked for in-person or over emails based on existing relationships and networks, rather than through more transparent processes (Ryan et al., 2013). In this respect, the more secure academics that coordinate units operate as relatively autonomous proxy-employers of the sessional teachers for the university. Without being paid to search for or review promising teachers, many of these proxy-employers save time through a 'first come, first served' approach to distributing jobs (May et al., 2013). Hence, just as the processes of the formal market make it true to its name, the processes associated with 'casual work' are, as Gunasekara (2007, p. 3) puts it, 'literally just that: casual'.

According to May et al. (2013, pp. 264–265), these informal processes have become the most common form of recruitment in Australian universities, with 90% of 3,160 casual academics surveyed having obtained their jobs through such 'personal approaches'. Similar reports are made by Junor (in Brown et al., 2006, p. 16), who, following a survey of 2,494 casual and fixed-term employed general and academic staff at five Australian universities, found that 80% of casually employed academics were employed 'by word of mouth', thereby 'contradicting university equal opportunities policies' (see Andrews et al., 2016; Coates et al., 2009). This is not limited to Australia, with informal recruitment processes becoming the norm for ever more academics in the United Kingdom (Bryson & Barnes, 2000), the Republic of Ireland (Courtois & O'Keefe, 2015), the United States of America (House Committee on Education and the Workforce, 2014) and Canada (Bauder, 2006).

Transitioning from one market to another involves a shift between employment processes, with the usefulness of social and academic capital between markets being mediated accordingly. For instance, it is conceivable that an experienced academic could be overlooked in the informal market in favour of the potential employer's postgraduate student, whose need for experience – and thus comparative inexperience – thereby becomes an advantage. This stands in stark contrast to the formal market, where experience quantified in journal publications, previous positions and research grants takes on more importance, and in which 'jobs for mates' is counted as nepotism. In both instances, we see the processes and conditions of one market allowing it to reproduce and distinguish itself it from the other, the mediation and evaluation of merit and resources, as well as the norms and expectations that underlie these processes. Such idiosyncratic conditions are open to exceptions and exploitation. For example, Rothengatter and Hil (2013, p. 56) tell the story of an Australian academic named 'Julia' who had taught at the same university for over 11 years on successive limited-term contracts, earned numerous awards for her teaching, and demonstrated her dedication by working six trimesters without breaks. However, when a continuing teaching-only position for a virtually identical role arose, the university repeatedly denied Julia's applications due to her unimpressive research record – even though the teaching-only role in question would not involve any research. Similar examples are provided by Gottschalk and McEachern (2010, p. 46), with one interviewed sessional who had worked at the same university for ten years stating: 'I used to labour under the theory that if you say "yes" to anything and everything in the way of casual work, and had appropriate qualifications and skills, eventually you would be rewarded. I feel naïve and duped'. For these sessionals, roles found through the informal market presented little by way of career development – rather, as Chalmers and Waddoups (2007) put it, such roles can present a trap rather than a bridge to the core.

So long as the situations of their proxy-employers remain the same, a sessional may find the informal market to be quite reliable and have no desire to do the extra work required by the formal market. However, it is worth noting that such supposedly reliable work can vanish if the unit is closed-down by the university, and that – unlike with ongoing staff – the university is not obligated to relocate or compensate the sessional who has had their job pulled out from under them. Likewise, poor communication and record-keeping between unit coordinators – that is, between the proxy-employers and benefactors of sessional staff – can cause teachers that might have years of experience with a unit to be replaced without ceremony when units change hands (Ryan et al., 2013, p. 168). This occurs in an informal fashion: for instance, the sessional emails their usual unit coordinator to check on their employment for the coming semester, only to be told that the coordinator is no longer running said unit and that their replacement has gone ahead and replaced the sessional. In short, whether their employment situation is drastically changed due to decisions made by administrators or other academics, the sessional is unlikely to be considered when such decisions are made, with the only recourse being to re-enter the informal market or go jobless. Thus, even for those with relatively reliable employment, the situations of those on the periphery ultimately depend on and are subject to the unaccountable decisions of the core.

Securities

The precariat includes those in employed short-term or casual contracts and thus insecure jobs and so face regular unemployment. Hence, when we discuss the precariat, we are discussing the routinely unemployed, casual and limited-term workers and, here in respect to higher education, the sessional academic. Accordingly, Standing (2011, p. 10) identifies the precariat by their lack of the following securities that the proletariat tended to have access to following the Second World War:

Labour market security – Adequate income-earning opportunities; at the macro-level, this is epitomised by a government commitment to 'full employment'.

Employment security – Protection against arbitrary dismissal, regulations on hiring and firing, imposition of costs on employers for failing to adhere to rules and so on.

Job security – Ability and opportunity to retain a niche in employment, plus barriers to skill dilution, and opportunities for 'upward' mobility in terms of status and income.

Work security – Protection against accidents and illness at work, through, for example, safety and health regulations, limits on working time, unsociable hours, night work for women, as well as compensation for mishaps.

Skill reproduction security – Opportunity to gain skills, through apprenticeships, employment training and so on, as well as opportunities to make use of competencies.

Income security – Assurance of an adequate stable income, protected through, for example, minimum wage machinery, wage indexation, comprehensive social security, progressive taxation to reduce inequality and to supplement low incomes.

Representation security – Possessing a collective voice in the labour market, through, for example, independent trade unions, with a right to strike.

These securities are ostensibly material, insofar that one either has or lacks secure employment, reliable income or transparent opportunities for advancement. For instance, a person employed on cash-in-hand jobs in the unregulated shadow economy might have none of the listed securities, while a member of the salariat has an ongoing salary, long-service leave, and can advance their career by applying for promotions and coveted positions according to clear criteria. That said, one can still be caught in the situations and experiences that characterise precarity while having some securities. A casual employee may be covered by safety regulations but have little or no protection from arbitrary dismissal or avenues for transferring to a secure position. Likewise, one can have employment and work security but have their lives routinely disrupted due to a lack of job security. Here Standing (2011, p. 11) gives the example of French Telecom's 'Time to Move' initiative, which required its employees to change workplaces and jobs every few years, and to which the suicides of 30 employees between 2008 and 2010 has been attributed. Albeit in a less deliberately orchestrated fashion, this lack of job security can also be observed in academia, for, despite their specialised expertise or experience teaching certain content, each new semester can mean a new discipline, colleagues and campus for the sessional academic. Hence, while Standing identifies the precariat by the lack of the seven securities listed earlier, this should not be seen as all-or-nothing binary but rather as one multi-faceted characteristic among many that we can use to orientate discussion and sociological analysis.

It is also worth noting that access to securities is not always clear-cut and can be inhibited by conditions that cannot be gleaned by employment categories and contracts alone. For instance, a person might formally have employment and job security insofar that they are protected from being arbitrarily fired or overlooked for promotion, as well as work security insofar that they are entitled to compensation for mishaps that lead to sickness or injury. However, if their relationship to the organisation takes the form of limited-term contracts, then they are only entitled to such securities throughout contracted periods that are short-lived and unreliable. One must also account for the factors that play into the renewal of an employment contract, as the employee's attempt to access potentially costly securities may jeopardise the employer's willingness to recruit them again, especially when there is an abundance of job seekers to replace them with.

These employment situations colour the work situations of precarious workers, vis-à-vis how they engage with their (potentially multiple) organisations and interact with their recurring employers. For instance, tension can arise between insisting on entitlements and being perceived as a 'good team player'. Drawing on the more secure members of the academic precariat as an example, the university might seek to reduce administrative costs by encouraging or simply telling annualised teachers to claim leave over the non-teaching period. Although such sessionals are entitled to choose when they claim leave or, alternatively, to take it in lieu at the end of their contracted period, the failure to meet this request might be viewed by the university as unnecessary costs and so undermine the chances of the teacher's contract being renewed. Another example regarding reappointment is provided by Rothengatter and Hil (2013, p. 55), who describe how a sessional who put in extra unpaid work to present data on sessional situations to his superiors '... was almost immediately cold-shouldered by his unit supervisor and the head of school. He was never reappointed and nothing was heard of him again'. For Rothengatter and Hil (2013, p. 56), this reveals how, for sessional academics in particular, 'to question institutional orthodoxies in relation to employment practices is, like much else in the university sector, to run the risk of being regarded as opposed to hegemonic corporate governance', with the consequence being the tacit-termination of disappearing without ceremony when the next contract period comes around. As Hassard and Morris (2018) observe, it is through these concerns over reemployment that precarity exerts disciplinary power.

Unpaid work-for-labour

Standing identifies regular unpaid work-for-labour as being central to the precariat. This is the unpaid work that a person does to attain paid employment. A basic example is job searching, which involves seeking out openings and completing numerous applications that may include all sorts of criteria, tailoring multiple resumes and cover letters, planning for transportation around interviews, and doing the research and preparation that can help a person to 'interview well'. While people have always had to work to find employment, the focus here is on the regularity and costs of such unpaid work-for-labour, for these can be time-consuming processes, especially for people in long stretches of job searching, and for those who must do so regularly due to the contingent nature of casual and limited-term employment. In keeping with his critique of current trends between higher education and industry, Standing (2015, p. 7) also emphasises the unpaid work that goes into increasing employment competitiveness, whereby people are expected to spend ever more time and money pursuing higher levels of educational attainment, credentials and work experience to secure positions that may not have anything to do with such expertise.

This can be seen in higher education, where, for example, academics seeking ongoing positions are expected to have increasingly lengthy publication lists (Hermanowicz, 2016; Pitt & Inger, 2016), even for teaching-only roles that involve no research (Rothengatter & Hil, 2013, p. 56). These increasingly steep expectations are described by Berry (2013, p. 63) with reference to the 'spectacle' of academic hiring and promotion committees rejecting applicants, when 'the majority, or at least many on the committee, could not pass the bar themselves'. Without being paid to do so, the savvy aspiring academic is expected to produce articles that can take many months or years to write and get published, with regular periods of unemployment meaning that they have no access to the scholarly resources and journals that provided for staff and students; contribute to panels and events to demonstrate their being a team player committed to service; and prepare papers to present at the networking opportunities of costly academic conferences (moreover, while attendance can be supported by scholarships, these can require the applicant to commit to producing publications and reports that may take weeks or months of unpaid work). This feeds into pressure to improve competitiveness in other ways, such as through potentially costly training courses and workshops (which, in relation to skill-reproduction security, sessional staff at some universities may have to pay for personally, unlike their more secure colleagues). As Osbaldiston et al. (2017) observe, a significant amount of the work that aspiring academics do is not viewed in terms of immediate reward but as a kind of professional investment, that is, unpaid hope labour undertaken in the present for a better position further down the road.

Being faced with unemployment made routine by structural conditions means that casual and limited-term workers must contend with ongoing uncertainty. This effects the ability to plan for beyond the near future, seek employment and to take advantage of opportunities. For instance, a team of university teachers might enter the period of unemployment following the conclusion of one semester without knowing who will be returning the next semester, what their workloads will be like or (for larger organisations) what campus (central or regional) they will be placed on. This is because the university itself may be unsure about student numbers, and thus the required number of teaching staff, right up until or even after commencement of the semester. The result is that the teachers who have reapplied for their limited-term contracts are now in the difficult situation of having to find a source of income over the teaching-break while also seeking out new jobs in case the reapplication is unsuccessful.

These structurally imposed uncertainties lead to pressures in respect to time and commitments: they are expected to commit to a job once offered, lest it undermine the unit coordinator's ability to determine who will be teaching for them, with tardiness or reneging on an arrangement reducing the chances that such work will be offered in the future. This is coupled with the time-pressure to reduce periods without an income by lodging contracts as soon as possible, as universities can take weeks to process such documentation, meaning that semesters can be well underway before the sessional receives their first payment. At the same time, however, a job that is appropriate in terms of subject area, allocation of paid-hours or distance from the home might be lost due to an earlier commitment to a less appropriate job – meaning that the sessional is also under pressure not to commit to anything too early. Thus, the sessional must be opportunistic when it comes to searching for work, and strategic when it comes to the possibility of arranging and accepting appropriate jobs. Unless the sessional knows an academic on whom they can depend for regular work, the stress of such processes becomes a routine process.

Relative deprivation and occupational identity

It is understandable that aspiring professionals who achieve a high level of educational attainment only to be caught in cycles characterised by such conditions would feel frustrated. It is notable then that Standing (2014, p. 30) treats a sense of *relative deprivation* as being particularly relevant to those who are 'plunged into a precariat existence after being promised the opposite' and become frustrated by the sense that they are 'not doing what they set out to do'. Such relative deprivation have been well documented in respect to academia. For example, Feldman and Turnley (2004, p. 285) note that sessionals may '… find their positions lacking relative to what they feel entitled to after several years of graduate school, relative to the jobs their peers received, or relative to the jobs many of their current colleagues possess'. Likewise, in a series on academic precarity in American anthropology, Kraemer (2018) notes that, in tandem with the extensive unpaid labour of competing for ongoing academic positions, '… many in the precariat experience a loss of selfhood along with deep shame at our perceived failures' and observes that 'graduate school does not prepare students for the dissonance of being recognized as an expert in one's specialization yet floundering on the market'.

One can get a sense of this by imagining a sessional teacher in their thirties. Due to their desire for an academic career, the encouragement they received from older academics, and the ignorance of, or unwillingness to account for, changes to the sector, they spent four years pursuing a doctorate. A further four years after completion, they are far from where they thought they would be, being stuck in cycles of low-paying jobs, their resumé being limited to university teaching, and their academic publications being less competitive each year. The time they can set aside to prepare publications is limited, and the distant conferences that cost non-students over $500 to attend, let alone travel to, are well beyond their budget. Due to their level-10 qualification, they cannot receive government support to reskill. And so, instead of 'settling down' in a home of their own as they gradually develop a career in their own discipline, they depend on cycles of contingent contracts, often in unrelated courses, are steeped in financial stress, and rent with other adults in similar situations. To be sure, with respect to education and the opportunities it is associated with, such an individual might be more privileged than someone who has never had a university education. However, this would not decrease their worries and frustration. Indeed, their level of education and academic ties may well be as salt in the wound.

For Standing, the precariat is also characterised by a lack of occupational identity, as in the ability for an individual to locate their work within a professional narrative that can be positively associated with their identity and aspirations. Members of the salariat can identify as lawyers, police, bankers, and professors, and in so doing identify with their sector, profession and career. They have been trained and educated to do their job, and so can connect it to past goals and the challenges and eventual accomplishments they involve. In other words, while some jobs are just a way to make money, some others can be viewed in terms of a 'bigger picture' or 'journey', with people becoming alienated from their occupation when this is absent. In contrast, a primary preoccupation among the precariat is finding work. For many among the precariat, this lack of occupational identity is twofold: it is tied to the insecurity of contingent employment situations, whereby regular unemployment and job changes undermine the lasting sense of a coherent occupational identity, and to work situations, via the marginality of being in a peripheral position. It is for this reason that Standing (2011, p. 14) likens the salariat to organisational citizens that typically have 'at least implicit voting rights in the firm, covering a range of decisions and practices' while describing 'the temps, casuals, dependent contractors and so on' as occupational denizens with 'a more limited range of rights than citizens do'.

Of course, this lack of occupational identity does not go for all members of the precariat and there are plenty of examples of people persisting in the cultural industries and academe precisely because of their vocational dimension (Bain & McLean, 2013; Gill, 2010; Miller, 2010). Moreover, occupational identity is not necessarily confined to one's occupational status at any given time: an unemployed academic can still attend university seminars, engage with scholarly discussions and attend conferences (i.e. if they have the free time and resources to do so). Even so, one can have a sense of occupational identity while still being akin to an organisational denizen in terms of situations and opportunities. For instance, drawing on in-depth interviews with 55 casually employed academics, Pocock et al. (2004) note how some sessionals described their experiences in terms of a perceived lack of 'workplace citizenship', which would presumably be reflected in the ability to have a say in the decisions that affect the workplace. Likewise, Brown et al. (2006, p. 19) report that, in Australia, 'such "workplace citizenship" is only available to 15% of academic casuals', with the rest being like the denizens described. For example, there are often occasions in which only those deemed real faculty are invited to staff meetings and events, even when the occasions are arguably relevant to all academic staff. Likewise, while continuing academic staff who are leaving a university often receive send-off ceremonies complete with refreshments and applause from their colleagues, there is no shortage of reports of sessional academics being unceremoniously 'disappearing' from a workplace, even after working at the university for many years (Brown et al., 2006; Rothengatter & Hil, 2013). Such oversights reveal the distinctions between the citizenry of the core and the denizens of the periphery, with the former having status such that their coming, belonging and leaving are acknowledged, while the latter can be around for years and leave without any such notice.

Discussion: formulating the academic precariat

For Standing, the precariat is defined by insecurity, limited opportunities, unpaid work-for-labour, and the sense of marginality, frustration and relative deprivation that comes with such situations. Drawing on literature primarily from Australia, North America and West Europe, this chapter illustrated how many of these characteristics are present among sessional academics as well as the structural conditions of precarisation that shape and reproduce these situations. Sessional university teachers may access securities during their limited periods of employment, but face regular periods of unemployment. These securities may protect them from arbitrary dismissal but are unlikely to cover the re-hiring processes that they are made to routinely apply for and which influence their relationships with other academics. In many universities, such contingent jobs present no avenues for attaining or transferring into more secure and upwardly mobile positions. For sessional teachers, this means a sense of disposability, routine unpaid work-for-labour, and ongoing and disruptive uncertainties over whether or where they will be working in the foreseeable future. For academia, such structural conditions mean a divide between the organisational citizenry and proxy-employers of the 'core' and the proletarianised denizens of the periphery. This divide can undermine the development, collegiality and consistency of academic communities, careers, courses and disciplines – and by extension, the quality of our universities.

This precarisation of academics around the world reflects the pervasiveness of the neoliberal trends and conditions to which the rise of the precariat – and the so-called 'progressives' in particular – is broadly attributed (Foti, 2017; Standing, 2011). To be sure, focussing on the experiences of workers may distract from the political and economic conditions behind the restructuring of institutions to which such individuals are subject. Likewise, there is the potential for self-interested discussions stemming from 'class-shock' to distract from more salient class-analysis. Here, Whelan (2015, p. 148) reminds us that the academic complaint that 'we shouldn't have to work and live like this' is not as compelling as the more inclusive argument that 'nobody should have to work and live like this'. Discussions of the academic precariat thus present a dual risk: first, of over-focussing on experiences rather than addressing the underlying structures; second, of clinging to elitist exceptionalism and entitlement. A more salient formulation of this highly educated sub-faction of the so-called 'progressive precariat' should aim for the opposite: first, to provide a basis from which academics can view their situations not just as personal troubles, but in terms of issues of social structure; second, it should serve as a reminder that such issues are not confined to universities, but reflect increasingly pervasive conditions and the potential for shared interests across institutional, national and professional contexts.

Note

1 While the market-metaphor is useful for describing different conditions and situations, Bousquet (2008) reminds us that such structural conditions are not the inevitable result of disinterested market processes, but of attempts by universities and governments to influence the conditions of work and employment. Hence, these market-metaphors are intended as ideal types that offer a general sense of the conditions and situations being addressed, rather than a fully detailed and idiosyncratic account. This is especially so for the formal market, where, despite its superior transparency, the often-hidden factors of 'who you know' can influence opportunities for employment and advancement.

References

Alberti, G., Bessa, L., Hardy, K., Trappmann, V., & Umney, C. (2018). In, against and beyond precarity: Work in insecure times. *Work, Employment and Society*, *32*(3), 447–457.

Andrews, S., Bare, L., Bentley, P., Goedegebuure, L., Pugsley, C., & Rance, B. (2016). *Contingent academic employment in Australian universities*. Melbourne, VIC: LH Martin Institute & Australian Higher Education Industrial Association.

Bain, A., & McLean, H. (2013). The artistic precariat. *Cambridge Journal of Regions, Economy and Society*, *6*(1), 93–111.

Bauder, H. (2006). The segmentation of academic labour. *ACME—An International Journal of Critical Geographies*, *4*(2), 227–238.

Berry, J. (2003). The new majority faculty: A class analysis for organizing. *Work and Days*, *21*(41–42), 57–69.

Bousquet, M. (2008). *How the university works: Higher education and the low-wage nation*. New York, NY: New York University Press.

Brown, T., Goodman, J., & Yasukawa, K. (2006). *Getting the best of you for nothing: Casual voices in the Australian academy*. South Melbourne: National Tertiary Education Union.

Brown, T., Goodman, J., & Yasukawa, K. (2010). Academic casualization in Australia: Class divisions in the university. *Journal of Industrial Relations*, *52*(2), 169–182.

Bryson, C., & Barnes, N. (2000). The casualisation of employment in higher education in the United Kingdom. In M. Tight (Ed.), *Academic work and life: What it is to be an academic, and how this is changing* (pp. 187–241). Bingley: Emerald Group Publishing.

Chalmers, J., & Waddoups, J. (2007). *Is casual employment a "bridge" or a "trap"?* Paper presented at the HILDA Survey Research Conference, The University of Melbourne.

Coaldrake, P., & Stedman, L. (1998). *On the brink: Australia's universities confronting their future.* St Lucia: University of Queensland Press.

Coates, H., Dobson, I., Goedegebuure, L., & Meek, L. (2009). Australia's casual approach to its academic teaching workforce. *People and Place, 17*(4), 47–54.

Courtois, A., & O'Keefe, T. (2015). Precarity in the ivory cage: Neoliberalism and casualisation of work in the Irish higher education sector. *Journal for Critical Education Policy Studies, 13*(1), 43–66.

Cryanoski, D., Gilbert, N., Ledford, H., Nayar, A., & Yahia, M. (2011). Education: The PhD factory. *Nature, 427,* 276–279.

Dearlove, J. (1997). The academic labour process: From collegiality and professionalism to managerialism and proletarianisation? *Higher Education Review, 30*(1), 56–75.Feldman, D., & Turnley, W. H. (2004). Contingent employment in academic careers: Relative deprivation among adjunct faculty. *Journal of Vocational Behavior, 64*(2), 284–307.

Foti, A. (2017). *General theory of the precariat: Great recession, revolution, reaction.* Amsterdam: Institute of Network Cultures.

Frase, P. (2013). The precariat: A class or a condition? *New Labor Forum, 22*(2), 11–14.

Gill, R. (2010). Breaking the silence: The hidden injuries of the neoliberal university. In R. G. Flood (Ed.), *Secrecy and silence in the research process: Feminist reflections* (pp. 228–244). London: Routledge.

Goldsworthy, D. (1990). Australian political science in the age of accountability. In H. Emy & A. Linklater (Eds.), *New horizons in politics: Essays with an Australian focus* (pp. 23–42). Sydney, NSW: Allen & Unwin.

Gunasekara, C. (2007). *It's an administrative thing: Positioning tutor identity through administrative practice in the academy.* Paper presented at the TASA and SAANZ joint conference, Auckland, New Zealand.

Harman, G. (2010). Producing PhD graduates in Australia for the knowledge economy. *Higher Education Research and Development, 21*(2), 179–190.

Hassard, J., & Morris, J. (2018). Contrived competition and manufactured uncertainty: Understanding managerial job insecurity narratives in large corporations. *Work, Employment and Society, 32*(3), 564–580.

Hermanowicz, J. (2016). Faculty perceptions of their graduate education. *Higher Education, 72*(3), 291–305.

House Committee on Education and the Workforce. (2014). *The just-in-time professor: A staff report summarizing eForum responses on the working conditions of contingent faculty in higher education.* Washington, DC: United States House of Representatives.

Ivancheva, M. (2015). The age of precarity and the new challenges to the academic profession. *Journal Studia Europaea, 60*(1), 39–47.

Jørgensen, M. (2016). Precariat – what it is and isn't – towards an understanding of what it does. *Critical Sociology, 42*(7–8), 959–974.
Junor, A. (2004). Casual university work: Choice, risk, inequity and the case for regulation. *The Economic and Labour Relations Review, 14*(2), 276–304.
Kalleberg, A. (2009). Precarious work, insecure workers: Employment relations in transition. *American Sociological Review, 74*(1), 1–22.
Kimber, M. (2010). The tenured 'core' and the tenuous 'periphery': The casualisation of academic work in Australian universities. *Journal of Higher Education Policy and Management, 25*(1), 41–50.
Kogan, M., Moses, I., & El-Khawa, E. (1994). *Staffing higher education: Meeting new challenges.* London: Jessica Kingsley and the Organisation for Economic Co-operation and Development.
Kraemer, J. (2018). *The invisible labor of the academic job market. Academic precarity in American Anthropology: A forum.* Retrieved from http://culanth.org
May, R., Peetz, D., & Strachan, G. (2013). The casual academic workforce and labour market segmentation in Australia. *Labour and Industry, 23*(3), 258–275.
McCarthy, G., Song, X., & Jayasuriya, K. (2017). The proletarianisation of academic labour in Australia. *Higher Education Research & Development, 36*(5), 1017–1030.
Miller, T. (2010). Culture + labour = precariat. *Communication and Critical/Cultural Studies, 7*(1), 96–99.
Munck, R. (2013). The precariat: a view from the South. *Third World Quarterly, 34*(5), 747–762.
Norton, A. (2012). *Mapping Australian higher education.* Melbourne: Grattan Institute. Retrieved from https://grattan.edu.au/report/mapping-australian-higher-education-2012/
Olssen, M., & Peters, M. (2005). Neoliberalism, higher education and the knowledge economy: From the free market to knowledge capitalism. *Journal of Education Policy, 20*(3), 313–345.
Osbaldiston, N., Cannizzo, F., & Mauri, C. (2017). Global perspectives on the postdoctoral scholar experience: Australia. In A. Jaeger & A. Dinin (Eds.), *The postdoc landscape: The invisible scholars* (pp. 203–226). London: Academic Press.
Percy, A., Scoufis, M., Parry, M., Goody, S., Hicks, A., Macdonald, I., ... Sheridan, L. (2008). *The RED report, recognition-enhancement-development: The contribution of sessional teachers to higher education.* Sydney: Australian Learning and Teaching Council. Retrieved from http://ro.uow.edu.au/
Pitt, R., & Mewburn, I. (2016). Academic superheroes? A critical analysis of academic job descriptions. *Journal of Higher Education Policy and Management, 38*(1), 88–101.
Pocock, B. A., Prosser, R. W., & Bridge, K. J. (2004). *Only a casual... How casual work affects employees, households and communities in Australia labour studies.* Adelaide: University of Adelaide.
PwC & AHEIA (Pricewaterhouse Coopers & Australian Higher Education Industrial Association). (2016). *Australian Higher Education Workforce of the Future.* Retrieved from http://www.aheia.edu.au
Rothengatter, M., & Hil, R. (2013). A precarious presence: Some realities and challenges of academic casualisation in Australian universities. *Australian Universities' Review, 55*(2), 51–59.

Ryan, S., & Bhattacharyya, A. (2016). Barriers to professional development among contingent academic employees: An Australian case study. *International Journal of Learning*, forthcoming. Available at https://ssrn.com/abstract=2729602

Ryan, S., Burgess, J., Connell, J., & Groen, E. (2013). Casual academic staff in an Australian university: Marginalised and excluded. *Tertiary Education and Management*, *19*(2), 161–175.

Standing, G. (2011). *The precariat*. London: Bloomsbury Academic.

Standing, G. (2014). *A precariat charter: From denizens to citizens*. London: Bloomsbury Academic.

Standing, G. (2015). The precariat and class struggle. *RCCS Annual Review*, *7*, 3–16.

Ward, S. (2012). *Neoliberalism and the global restructuring of knowledge and higher education*. New York, NY: Routledge.

Whelan, A. M. (2015). Academic critique of neoliberal academia. *Sites: A Journal of Social Anthropology and Cultural Studies*, *12*(1), 130–152.

Wright, E. (2015). Is the precariat a class? *Global Labor Journal*, *7*(2), 123–135.

Chapter 12

Living and working in the contemporary university

Sarah R. Davies

Introduction

In this chapter I want to consider the question: what is it like to live and work in academia today? More specifically, I want to explore what it is to exist within the changes that are unfolding in universities, and to examine how these changes are experienced from the inside. I ask how it feels to live at the heart of what have been claimed to be seismic (albeit multiple and at times conflicting) shifts in the nature and purpose of research, teaching and the university itself (see e.g. Ball, 2012; Collini, 2017; Shore, 2008).

This is of necessity a reflexive exploration. Over the past decade or more, since I completed my PhD, I have worked in universities in the United Kingdom, the United States and Denmark, first as a postdoc or research fellow, later as an assistant or associate professor.[1] At the same time I have been working within the discipline of Science and Technology Studies (STS) and have, among other things, studied researchers' experiences of academic life (e.g. Davies, 2013; Davies & Horst, 2015). These two aspects of experience, as participant and analyst, cannot be readily separated. The contemporary university is an area of study in which we, as scholars, are clearly implicated: we are of course always present in our research (Law, 2004), but here that research explicitly references our livelihoods, well-being, emotions and identities.

Perhaps that is why I have found this chapter difficult to write. I wanted to capture the ways in which the natural scientists I have worked with over the last years talked about working at the meeting point of multiple regimes, and to supplement this analysis with auto-ethnographic notes from my own experiences and observations. And indeed that is, in essence, the content that this chapter presents. But I have found it impossible, and perhaps even dangerously misleading, to construct a linear narrative or argument out of these empirical materials. Not only is my own experience too chaotic and complex to tell any neat story, but such a story would also misrepresent the interview data that I will draw on. It would not do justice to our ability, as subjects at the heart of the university system, to live in quite different realities at the same time, and thus to experience conflicting affects and tell, almost in the same breath, apparently contradictory stories. In presenting this material I have therefore chosen to draw on John Law's (2007) notion of juxtaposition as a means of acknowledging and depicting multiplicity. Rather than constructing a linear argument that progresses step by step, I use Law's metaphor of the pinboard as a means of structuring the text.

In what follows I offer a series of fragments and vignettes that mix a variety of materials, from interview extracts to curricula. The argument should be understood as impressionistic and cumulative rather than linear: I am aiming for a productive non-coherence (Law, 2002, 2007). To anchor this approach I start with some fragments that ground and frame juxtaposition and multiplicity as ordering devices.

Juxtaposition

In a 2007 essay STS scholar John Law reflected on the process of thinking, learning and teaching. The world, he said, is complex and multiple: 'spaces and times are enacted differently within different practices' (p. 128). Mainstream teaching is often an effort to force singularity on the world; to present one particular story of it. In practice this is never possible. We are all skilled at holding together diverse metaphysical assumptions – at dealing with the tensions that we encounter in the realities of the world (what Law and others would call ontological multiplicity; Mol, 2002). Law uses the example of Yoruba children being confronted with a European mathematics curriculum that is incommensurable with their numbering system. These students and teachers live, he says, within 'various partially overlapping realities and they weave these together in a kind of choreography: the curriculum; buying and selling in the street market; the need to make a lesson work' (p. 127). He is clear that those living in the global North similarly operate within 'overlapping realities'.

One sympathetic response to this multiplicity, Law argues, is to move away from static, singular narratives to a practice of juxtaposition. He is interested in techniques by which diverse ideas and ephemera can be held together and through which their tensions can be explored. Such juxtapositionary techniques might be technological: he cites a classroom project in which music, images, texts, video and other knowledge fragments are burned onto a CD-ROM, held together through a shared format. More prosaically, he also uses the pinboard as both physical prop and heuristic. A pinboard is a device which demonstrates 'the permissive possibilities of working on a surface, flexibly, and without a very strong system of classification about what it is that goes (or doesn't go) with what. It's about juxtaposition and difference' (p. 135). A pinboard collects fragments and allows their arrangement in different ways. Connections can be made and re-made and tensions highlighted. Importantly, it is non-hierarchical. Narratives may appear but are fragmented or readily rejected. Indeed, the pinboard as a whole is provisional, always subject to change as scraps are pinned up, taken down, covered up or re-arranged.

A real pinboard offers a flexible two-dimensional space in which connections can be made and re-made. An essay inevitably re-imposes a degree of hierarchy in that it is (usually) read sequentially, and is (usually) primarily composed of text. We might say, then, that this chapter is inspired by the spirit of the pinboard. It aims for some of its affordances (non-linearity, juxtaposition as a means of ordering) without fully realising its physical manifestation.

Multiplicity

I work with the understanding that reality is multiple. Divergences in narrative, materiality or experience – indeed in ontology – cannot be explained through different viewpoints or perspectives, but relate to the production of multiple and differing worlds (Law, 2004, 2007; Mol, 2002). In the context of studies of the academy, this view has led to a concern with the ways in which proliferating devices of evaluation and marketisation produce the realities that they purport to describe (Felt, 2017; Fochler & de Rijcke, 2017). Devices and developments, such as the H-index; citation counts; or, more widely, the 'projectification' of research (Fowler et al., 2015), are performative, bringing into being a system of valuation based upon citation practices, or a temporality of research that cycles through three year periods (Espeland & Sauder, 2007; Felt, 2017; Felt et al., 2017; Ylijoki, 2014). These realities are, however, only one of several that researchers may live within. No single performance of the academy is able to dominate, at least not all of the time (Fowler et al., 2015).

There are a number of conceptual tools for thinking about this multiplicity. Two such are Ulrike Felt's notions of epistemic living spaces and narrative infrastructures, the former referring to the social, epistemological and institutional spaces in which researchers live and which define what is knowable and thinkable (Felt & Fochler, 2012), and the latter being complexes of 'temporally stabilised narratives through which meanings and values of academic knowledge/work and its relation to society can be articulated' (Felt, 2017b, p. 56). Narrative infrastructures, we can say, produce epistemic living spaces. The stories that intertwine within them construct specific kinds of spaces that structure the behaviours, affects and expectations of researchers (these narratives, we should note, also interact with particular materialities and embodiments; Felt & Fochler, 2012). Felt (2017b) argues that university researchers today tend to exist within at least three distinct narrative infrastructures: one loosely framed around the logic of new public management (cf. Shore, 2008) which foregrounds evaluation and efficiency; one that involves 'reflexive work' and which relates to demands for public engagement, accountability and responsibilisation (de Saille, 2015); and a final 'cluster of narratives that strongly refer to past conditions of research' (Felt 2017b,

p. 60) and that thereby involve stories of nostalgia, academic independence and slowness (cf. Ylijoki, 2005). Importantly, these narrative infrastructures are not exclusive. It is not that some scholars or universities exist within one and not the others. Rather, a researcher sits at the centre of them all (and potentially others), at the heart of realities that perform the university, 'good' research, and the researcher themselves in diverse ways.

Which academy?

'A researcher'. But which researcher? Thus far my text has been universalising, ignoring the quite profound differences between countries, universities and individuals. In part this is because much of the literature on contemporary higher education agrees that a shift in the imagination and management of universities is taking place around the globe (Brown, 2015; Collini, 2017; Kenny, 2017; Ward, 2012). Though national contexts such as the United States, the United Kingdom or Australia may be the leading edge of the application of neoliberal values to the university, this process has also been documented in, for instance, Denmark, the Czech Republic, Austria and New Zealand (Amsler & Shore, 2017; Felt et al., 2017; Linkova, 2013; Young et al., 2017).

Despite this homogenisation, situatedness remains important: narrative infrastructures are inflected by local stories of the nation or region, specific cultural values and local concerns about global competition (Budd, 2017; Felt et al., 2017). So, it is important to note that I will largely be writing about my experiences in Denmark (where I have worked since 2012), and that I will be drawing on interview studies carried out in the United Kingdom, the United States and Denmark. Those interviews were carried out with natural scientists, working at universities, who were generally highly research active.[2] The stories I was told, and the possibilities for action that interviewees felt they had, might have been quite different if I had spoken to, say, part-time university teachers (Bamber et al., 2017) or PhD students (Hakala, 2009).

'Esben Lunde fjerner mål om social mobilitet fra KU-kontrakt' [Esben Lunde removes goal of social mobility from University of Copenhagen's contract]

The title is a headline from a 2015 news story in *Universitetsavisen*, the University of Copenhagen's internal newspaper,[3] which describes how the then Minister for Education – Esben Lunde – was removing the goal of social mobility from the university's 'development contract' with the Education Ministry. This of course raises the question: what are universities (and specifically, this university, my employer) for? Is social change part of their purpose?

More particularly, though, the news story served a specific function for me in that it alerted me to the fact that my employer, the University of

Copenhagen, had a 'development contract' with the Ministry at all. This was not something that had ever impinged on my experience of teaching or research at the university, and I was fascinated to discover that what the Danish government wanted from it was formalised in this way. I felt social mobility was a worthy aim – but, at the same time, did it even matter, given that the details of the contract clearly did not trickle down to the rank and file of university staff?

What is happening in universities?

What is happening in universities? Simplistically, we might use a kind of grab-bag of keywords as an answer to this question: marketisation; academic capitalism; neoliberalism; commodification; evaluation; precarity; responsibilisation; new public management; entrepreneurialism. These words come from different traditions, and describe slightly different phenomena – but taken collectively they give a flavour of the kinds of changes that are taking place (Amsler & Shore, 2017; Ball, 2012; Brown, 2015; Fochler & de Rijcke, 2017; Shore, 2008; Slaughter & Leslie, 1997; Ward, 2012).

We might also try and give such a flavour based on the affective components of these regimes. On the one hand, anxiety, neuroticism, contempt, shame, dissatisfaction (Lindgren & Rönnberg, 2018; Lorenz-Meyer, 2018; Loveday, 2018; Waaijer et al., 2017; Zábrodská et al., 2016). On the other (though often simultaneously), hope, excitement, pleasure, thrill, enthusiasm (Felt, 2017a; Lorenz-Meyer, 2018). Some of those pleasures derive from the satisfaction of beating the system, or of being 'happy when one fits, more or less, into the indicator game … and thus being able to produce a more or less coherent narrative' (Felt, 2017a, p. 60). Others are intrinsic to the contemporary academy, which operates, as Lorenz-Meyer (2018) suggests, according to 'clusters of promises' that both discipline and excite. In this respect to live in the university is to live under conditions of cruel optimism (Berlant, 2011), in a world where the promises we become attached to (tenure, stability, funding) can never be fully realised.

Responsibility

One regime that researchers exist within today is that of *responsibilisation*. This has two aspects. The first is the neoliberal move to individualise responsibility – a move that insists that academics must be entrepreneurs of their careers, assume 'leadership' and understand themselves as human resources in need of development (Amsler & Shore, 2017; Brown, 2015; Cannizzo, 2018a; Hakala, 2009). The second relates to the desire to responsibilise the academy in general and science and technology in particular (Davies & Horst, 2015; Felt, 2017b; de Saille, 2015). Such concerns, as Felt (2017b) describes them, circle around ideas of democratisation, public accountability, socially robust innovation and transparency; academics must, as well as carrying out teaching and research, 'fulfil their civic mission, care about service to communities, engage with citizens in diverse formats and much more' (p. 60). This narrative infrastructure is articulated through the language of 'academic citizenship' (Macfarlane, 2007), 'third mission' activities (Laredo, 2007) or 'responsible research and innovation' (RRI; Owen et al., 2012). In all cases public-facing activities, such as public communication or engagement, are key.

RRI, to take the example I am most familiar with (in part because it has been a key structuring device for European funding; de Saille, 2015), takes as its starting point the 'limitations of extant policy approaches to managing ethically-problematic areas of science and innovation' (Owen et al., 2012, pp. 751–752). Such problematic areas include genetically modified crops, synthetic biology, or geoengineering, but the notion has now been extended to cover all aspects of research and innovation, not merely the explicitly new or controversial. Unlike previous discussion of the need for public communication (Gregory & Lock, 2008), RRI's emphasis is on problematic academic communities rather than on problematic publics (Stilgoe, 2012). The aim is to open up scientific research and development to diverse perspectives, and to ensure that academic and innovation communities are responsive to societal values (Owen et al., 2012). In practice this has led to calls for increased reflection within academia, for dialogic public engagement, for openness and transparency, and for 'impactful' research (Koops et al., 2015).

As Felt and others have pointed out, despite their rather different premises narrative infrastructures of new public management and of reflexivity (including RRI) intersect in important ways, not least through the use of evaluative metrics and devices to try and measure, benchmark, and track academic reflexivity (Felt, 2017b; Glerup et al., 2017; de Saille, 2015). Similarly, both regimes construct past versions of the academy as insufficient: as unreflexive, lacking openness, inadequately entrepreneurial (Felt, 2017b). What these regimes thus produce, amongst other things, is a need for change. Researchers lack the right qualities for the way that contemporary research *should be*, and are called upon to discipline themselves accordingly: they are to be responsibilised.

Ulrik

Ulrik (whose name I have changed for the purposes of reporting) was a synthetic biologist working in the United Kingdom; he was highly successful – his research group, which he led, comprised some 15 people – and worked at a prestigious university. I interviewed him in 2013, asking in particular about responsibility. What responsibilities did he feel he, and others in his group, had, and to whom?[4]

In talking to Ulrik it became clear that multiple narrative infrastructures were layered upon how he described and imagined his activities. He talked about personal passion and excitement, about the sense of curiosity that took him into science and led him into synthetic biology where he felt like 'I could make a big contribution, to something that to me seemed exciting and new'. He wanted to 'deliver things that will have a benefit in general, economically or for the good of the world in some way' (though, strikingly, this was framed as a personal desire, rather than a public responsibility in the shape of RRI or similar directives). He was also clear that much of his time involved ensuring the survival of his group and line of research. Writing research proposals and publicising early findings to funders took up much of his working life and was a large part of why he felt pressed for time and why, as he said, he had 'so many things to worry about'. The practical and strategic activity of securing funding and disseminating results (which the scientists I have interviewed over the last years have almost uniformly experienced as an unwanted burden) was, however, filtered through the language of care for the group. Rather than – or, better, as well as – being framed as a purely utilitarian task, it was configured as an affective practice through which individuals affiliated to Ulrik were able to flourish:

> I feel very responsible for everyone in my team, that's the main thing; so I want them all to succeed and I want them all to get something out of their time here in terms of something they can go away and say, I've got my PhD and I've got publications that showed I did something novel, that's the main responsibility. More than anything else I feel like as a supervisor my responsibility is to my team to make sure that, they can do their work, they succeed in their work and they can go on and find jobs of their own elsewhere.

Ulrik wanted group members to feel nurtured and supported. He wanted them to feel that they had achieved something in their research, and ultimately he wanted to ensure that they could have a career outside of the immediate context of his team. Ulrik and other group leaders that I spoke to presented themselves as the lynchpin of their groups. They held things together, and some of the things that they held were contrasting dynamics of academia: they would deal with pressures for securing and accounting for research funding, and in this way they would protect their group from at least some of the stresses of academia. These were, Ulrik said, 'people who've given up the possibility of going and earning decent money … to instead do a PhD with you and it's important that they get a good experience'. They deserved protection from the worst excesses of the contemporary academy. Care was intertwined with more dangerous affects relating to pressure, (potential) failure or frustration.

Ulrik was not unaware of calls for the responsibilisation of science. Working in the United Kingdom and in synthetic biology – both key sites for the implementation of RRI – he was immediately familiar with policy pushes for responsibility when I raised them towards the end of the interview (though, as noted, he didn't choose to frame his own interest in science that 'will have a benefit' in these terms). 'Synthetic biology', he said, 'has been very proactive in making sure that it's not just scientists doing science', and he was a willing and interested participant in collaborations with social scientists, artists and activities that considered 'the social and sort of global implications' of his research. At the same time he had some concerns with the way that RRI was being developed. First there was the language of responsibility which, he pointed out, 'implies that all scientific research and innovation that doesn't do it this way is irresponsible', a judgement that he resisted. He was also keenly aware of the practicalities of integrating concern for societal implications of his group's work:

> I mean it's sad to say but, you know, how much my feeling of responsibility and caring prioritises the responsible aspect of our research and what that means for the whole world is, you know, is quite low in terms of the amount of time I can dedicate to thinking about that, just because I have to worry about so many other things.

Ulrik is clear here and elsewhere: his group is his priority. What their research 'means for the whole world' is important, but, realistically, it is fairly low down on his list of priorities. The reality is that he must manage multiple projects, attached to different individuals, all of which will come with a complex world of implications and responsibilities to wider society. While it might be nice to parse these out in detail, his experience of academia is that he simply has 'so many other things' to worry about that such thoroughness, such commitment to the ideals of RRI, is impossible. In his view the needs of his group – his desire to take care of them – trump wider and more abstract calls for responsibilisation. One comment on RRI is thus that it struggles, as an agenda, to speak to the language and experiences of scientists. It calls for responsibility but fails to acknowledge the responsibilities that are already enacted (Davies & Horst, 2015; Glerup et al., 2017).

Reading through the transcript of my conversation with Ulrik it becomes natural to picture him sitting at the centre of a web of narratives, each performing the academy slightly differently. His task is one of coordination: how to manage demands for responsibility to the wider world, the need for successful funding bids, his own curiosity, a sense of responsibility to the individuals in his group, publicising and disseminating his research? Importantly, these desires and demands cannot be readily deconstructed into distinct narrative infrastructures within the context of conversation. As analysts, we might trace them out, relating care for the group to older imaginations of the academy, or RRI to calls for scientific reflexivity (for instance). But in this interview they are intertwined, one running into the other. Ulrik sits within multiple versions of the university, and his role within it, but his experience seems to be that these run together. One becomes so used to living within competing regimes that their differences are forgotten or disappear.

Building a curriculum

In the summer of 2016 I coordinated a 7.5 ECTS summer school for Master's students, held in Copenhagen, part of a suite of courses in part designed to help Danish students 'catch up' with their ECTS points and finish their degrees on time.[5] This course, which focussed on science communication, was designed from scratch by myself and a group of colleagues from across the university. Here I want to consider one specific logistical issue relating to that process: building the course curriculum.

In Denmark a course curriculum, the *studieordning*, is a rather formal document, one that describes in binding detail the learning outcomes and structure of courses. When the summer school was confirmed our Faculty administration started to develop a draft for a *studieordning* for 'the elective at Master's level offered as a summer school in Science Communication'. They based this on a *studieordning* from another summer school; though this was on a very different subject (migration studies), most of the formal terms of the curriculum – things like the language the course was conducted in, or the admission requirements – would be the same. The draft was then handed over to my colleagues and I to customise, before being reviewed by department and faculty committees.

What I discovered during this process is that there are rather strict requirements as to how student learning can be imagined in a *studieordning*. These documents must use the language of knowledge and understanding (*viden og forståelse*), skills (*færdigheder*) and competences (*kompetencer*), a requirement derived from Danish legislation on university educations. A 2013 Ministerial Order further includes the statement that a Master's education must involve 'in-depth studies ... in the disciplines and methodologies of the subject area(s) in question ... that further develops the student's ability to work in a more specialised professional capacity'.[6] It is therefore a legal requirement that Master's programmes turn out skilled professionals. University educations are conceptualised in this legislation as forms of professional training through which subjects are able to put knowledge into practice, and, as I discovered as I worked on the *studieordning* for the summer school, this imagination of education works its way all the way from high level policy to the construction of curricula and the framing of learning outcomes.

It is worth noting that this idea of what a university education should do is not a given, and that there are other ways of imagining the purpose of Master's level training (Collini, 2017). But it's also important to tell the rest of the story of the summer school *studieordning*. Developing the right language and having it approved by different groups within the department and faculty took much time and energy over the course of several months – but, after the main text had been developed and signed off, it rapidly faded into the background of the practice of course development and teaching. Its language had been an uneasy fit with our collective imagination of the course and it was in many ways irrelevant to how it would be carried out, aside from providing a formal structure (in the event unused) by which we could pass or fail students. As it turned out, the teachers on the course rarely made use of it in their planning, and only one student – out of some 35 in the first year that the course ran – expressed any interest in seeing it. To offer an interpretative gloss on this experience, it seems that, despite bureaucratic requirements that seek to structure teaching and learning and to ensure that they serve particular purposes, there is substantial scope to operate outside of these – whilst simultaneously appearing to be fully aligned with them.[7]

International mobility

Academics have always moved between countries (Flanagan, 2015). But now international mobility is 'systemic' (Kim, 2017), a central aspect of the way in which national and global research systems function. These developments can at least in part be tied to the shifts in global science described earlier. Mobility is promoted by discourses of excellence that insist that internationalised scholars are necessary for competitive national economies (Ackers, 2013; Kim, 2017) but also enforced by a degree of competition that means that, in many disciplines and locations, there are far more qualified candidates than there are jobs (Müller, 2014). Insistence on the need for mobility has been framed as having adverse effects on, for instance, gender equity, or as shaping the kind of academic able to perform 'excellence' (Ackers, 2013; Leemann, 2010; Zippel, 2017).

The need to be internationally mobile – to have spent time working in a country other than the one that one trained in, and to maintain networks and connections with scholars around the world – can therefore be seen as one regime contemporary scientists live under. Indeed, in some countries funding structures essentially enforce mobility: in Denmark, for instance, it is now difficult to the point of impossibility to gain a tenured position or large scale funding without having spent time abroad (Davies, forthcoming; Ejlertsen, 2018; Wohlert et al., 2016).

Mattie

Mattie (again, not her real name) was a molecular biologist, originally from Australia but now working in Denmark. I interviewed her in 2017 as part of a research project looking at experiences of international mobility in the natural sciences.[8] We spoke in a café near where she lived, chatting over coffee as her young baby slept outside in a pram. She was bubbly and friendly, cheerfully tracing out for me the moves that she'd made and the choices she had arrived at.

Mattie had moved for her career. In Australia, she said, there was an awareness of being on the periphery that meant that researchers 'know that we're sitting all the way, away from everybody ... I wasn't even really in science that long, I hadn't even started my PhD before I knew I had to get out'. She always knew that if she wanted to work in science over the long term she would need international experience. Because she was ambitious she selected what she thought was the best lab in her field, taking the chance to talk to its leader at a conference and then securing Australian funding for a visit of a few months during her PhD. This period, she said, she saw as an 'extended job interview ... if I was good enough, [the lab leader] would want me back' for a postdoc. This was what happened. Over the next years she moved between Denmark and Australia, balancing a partner and life in Australia with what she saw as a key work opportunity in the form of a two year postdoc at the Danish lab before, after her relationship disintegrated, moving fully to Denmark and finding funding to stay on. When we spoke she was on parental leave (after meeting a new, Danish, partner) but was about to go and give a talk in her department because a key funder was visiting:

> He [her son] is ten weeks old, but I'm going and give a talk to 30 people about the project because I want the foundation to know who I am. I want them to remember me when I'm applying for a grant in another year's time.

Mattie was caught in a mass of competing affects. On the one hand she was frustrated by her precarity and the demands it placed on her: not just to go and give talks in a period when she was, theoretically, on leave, but to be constantly thinking about how to remain competitive. She was angry about what she saw as the gendered demand for constant mobility. Despite her successes she felt it was unlikely that she would get a permanent position in Denmark. There were, she said, others who were 'next in line' in her department who would probably be given positions ahead of her. She was currently looking for funding for collaborations in the United States and planning on spending time there, ideally with her family; fortunately, her partner 'likes travelling and he likes trying new things ... within the first week of us meeting I'm like uuh, would you move to Australia?'.

At the same time she was explicit about the pleasures of her position and even of the same transience that she could find so stressful. Indeed, challenges of mobility such as isolation or the 'energy' required to get to know people and 'start yourself up' in a new place could also be experienced as a kind of hedonism:

> It's very liberating when you don't have family commitments, and I- I miss my friends but then I don't have the friend commitments. It's like I said a very selfish way to push your career forward because it's- I only had to look after me.

Mattie was passionate about her work. Being transplanted to a new place had the benefit that it freed her from ties so that she could work long hours in the lab, focussing on her science and nothing else in a way that she framed as 'selfish' but also 'liberating'. While her situation had changed – now, she said, she couldn't 'just go to Australia for three months, with a baby' – she was still somehow torn between competing affects. Her work made her a 'better person' and 'energised' her, but she also, now, needed to care about other things as well.

What is striking in Mattie's account is what in Danish would be called its *dobbelthed*: 'doubleness', duality, the holding together of two opposing emotions or experiences in a way that goes beyond ambivalence or equivocation. Mobility is both pleasurable and an unwanted burden, something that Mattie both enjoys and desires and that she resents. To live under a regime that demands mobility is thus not, necessarily, to be completely subsumed by it. For Mattie international mobility was both a pleasure and 'a box I had to tick': in ticking that box – in her CV, grant applications and presentation of herself to funders – she managed to signal her alignment with policy notions of excellent (and marketable) science (Kim, 2017) while also allowing herself the possibility of resisting, subverting or distancing herself from the practices demanded of her (she might say she would be visiting a lab for three months, she told me, but in practice she might only go for a week). Narrative infrastructures of mobility simultaneously framed it as hedonistic opportunity and stressful burden. Mattie existed within both types of infrastructure, her experience mingling them so that they became indistinguishable.

Resistance and subversion

How do academics live in the contemporary university? Various strategies for resisting encroaching demands have been documented. Ball and Olmeda (2013) suggest (albeit primarily in the context of school education) that those caught within neoliberal technologies of governance may resist by practicing 'care of the self' that involves irresponsibility – disobedience – in the eyes of the governance system but that maintains one's own vision of good educational practice. A number of scholars have suggested that an ethics and practice of care is one concrete way that academics can intervene in their environments (Conesa Carpintero, 2017; Felt, 2017b; Lorenz-Meyer, 2018). Researchers may also take up hybrid identities that enable them to switch between different valuation systems (Lam, 2010), or decouple their personal or professional values from managerially oriented practices (Nielsen, 2016; Sauder & Espeland, 2009; Smith-Doerr & Vardi, 2015). Decoupling – strategies of 'lip service', distancing, or 'hiding' particular activities or values from systems of surveillance or evaluation – may, however, be difficult in the long term. As Sauder and Espeland (2009) write, '[c]hronic resistance is demoralizing' and the allure of alignment with managerial regimes may mean that the values associated with these are 'increasingly self-imposed and internalized' (p. 77). Indeed, Cannizzo (2018b) has argued that clear-cut distinctions between managerial and traditional academic norms and values are misleading. Today, 'academics' personal values and managerial norms are able to coexist because they are now mutually constituted' (p. 104).

Living in the university multiple[9]

The fragments I have drawn together in this chapter circle around the question of what it is to live and work in the university today, under diverse and at times contradictory narrative infrastructures. I have not attempted to construct a linear argument from this material. Rather, the aim has been to convey an impression of the affects and experiences that academics (including myself) have reported. In part this has been motivated by the belief that our modes of representation need to better reflect the complexities and dissonances of our empirical material (Law, 2004). If life in the contemporary university is experienced as multiple, fragmented and confusing (and it is, I believe, by many; Loveday, 2018), then perhaps our reporting of it should also be so.

But I have also sought, in both the material I have selected for this chapter and in my mode of presentation, to try and articulate some of the dynamics of what it is to live under competing regimes. That there are differing stories, and practices, of academia at work in the university today is well established (Cannizzo, 2018b; Felt, 2017b). Similarly well established are stories – both formal, in the shape of peer-reviewed literature, and informal, as gossip between colleagues – of resistance and subversion of regimes that are experienced as cruel, unnecessary or unethical according to personal values of academic practice (Sauder & Espeland, 2009). What I have sought to point to, in this chapter, is just how intertwined competing narrative infrastructures are within the bodies, experiences and careers of academics. The university is multiple: different practices of the academy construct it differently, but it is often individual academics who hold these differing realities together. Our bodies and career paths perform the acts of coordination and alignment that prevent universities from fragmenting into quite different entities. Both Ulrik and Mattie, for instance, sat at the centre of a web of diverse versions of academic life, mediated by techniques that sought to responsibilise or internationalise them, but managed to blend and make sense of these through their own narratives of care or pleasure. My own experience has been that there is constantly space for the insertion of one's own assumptions or beliefs about good academic practice within the interstices of bureaucratic regimes (the irrelevance of the *studieordning* to practice, my ignorance of the KU contract). Coordination occurs through individual sense-making, whether that is explicit or implicit. It is the mundane practice of making academic life liveable (Felt, 2017a).

This text is, of course, merely a sketch of these dynamics of alignment. If the university is multiple then we need further study of how its realities are coordinated, whether that is within the bodies of academics or through other techniques.

Notes

1 Danish job titles are approximately equivalent to the US system; it is therefore potentially relevant that, although I am now an associate professor, I am not tenured but remain dependent on project-based funding – a situation that may seem counterintuitive but is increasingly common in Denmark, where there are far more qualified scholars than permanent positions (Danish National Research Foundation, 2015).

2 I will draw on data from two studies in particular. The first is the project 'Scientific Social Responsibility', which was supported by a grant from the Danish Council for Independent Research, ran 2012–2015, and involved 29 interviews with principal investigators and research group leaders in Denmark, the United States and the United Kingdom about their ideas about and experiences of 'responsibility' in science (see Davies & Horst, 2015 for details of the research). The second is the project 'Impacts of International Mobility on Danish Research Integrity', which runs 2017–2019 and is funded by the Danish Ministry of Higher Education and Science. This research explores how science travels by looking at experiences of international mobility and different cultures around research integrity: it has involved 32 interviews with scientist of diverse backgrounds and training currently working in Denmark. Further details can be found in Davies (forthcoming).

3 Available at: http://universitetsavisen.dk/politik/esben-lunde-fjerner-mal-om-social-mobilitet-fra-ku-kontrakt

4 Again, there are more details about this research within Davies and Horst (2015).

5 'ECTS' stands for European Credit Transfer and Accumulation System: ECTS points are thus a standardised way of measuring work across (many) European universities. Each ECTS point represents 25–30 hours of student work.

6 http://ufm.dk/en/legislation/prevailing-laws-and-regulations/education/files/en_uddannelsesbekendtgorelsen-2013.pdf

7 This argument does, however, ignore the significant time and energy that may be required to perform such alignment and which may detract from other tasks, such as the practice of teaching itself. At least in the case of early career scholars, such 'bureaucracy' is likely to be experienced as an additional, unwelcome, burden (Müller, 2014).

8 Further details of the research can be found in Davies (forthcoming).

9 This heading draws on the title of Annemarie Mol's book The Body Multiple (2002), in which Mol argues that reality is enacted through practices, and that as those practices are multiple it is 'more than one – but less than many' (p. 55).

References

Ackers, L. (2013). Internet mobility, co-presence and purpose: Contextualising internationalisation in research careers. *Sociologia y Technociencia/Sociology and Technoscience*, *3*(3), 117–141.

Amsler, M., & Shore, C. (2017). Responsibilisation and leadership in the neoliberal university: A New Zealand perspective. *Discourse: Studies in the Cultural Politics of Education*, *38*(1), 123–137.
Ball, S. J. (2012). Performativity, commodification and commitment: An I-spy guide to the neoliberal university. *British Journal of Educational Studies*, *60*(1), 17–28.
Ball, S. J., & Olmedo, A. (2013). Care of the self, resistance and subjectivity under neoliberal governmentalities. *Critical Studies in Education*, *54*(1), 85–96.
Bamber, M., Allen-Collinson, J., & McCormack, J. (2017). Occupational limbo, transitional liminality and permanent liminality: New conceptual distinctions. *Human Relations*, *70*(12), 1514–1537.
Berlant, L. (2011). *Cruel optimism*. Durham: Duke University Press.
Brown, W. (2015). *Undoing the demos: Neoliberalism's stealth revolution*. Brooklyn, NY: MIT Press.
Budd, R. (2017). Undergraduate orientations towards higher education in Germany and England: Problematizing the notion of 'student as customer'. *Higher Education*, *73*(1), 23–37.
Cannizzo, F. (2018a). Tactical evaluations: Everyday neoliberalism in academia. *Journal of Sociology*, *54*(1), 77–91.
Cannizzo, F. (2018b). 'You've got to love what you do': Academic labour in a culture of authenticity. *The Sociological Review*, *66*(1), 91–106.
Collini, S. (2017). *Speaking of universities*. London: Verso.
Conesa Carpintero, E. (2017). '(No) Time for Care and Responsibility: From Neoliberal Practices in Academia to Collective Responsibility in Times of Crisis'. In B. Revelles-Benavente & Ana M. González Ramos (Eds.) *Teaching gender feminist pedagogy and responsibility in times of political crisis* (pp. 42–63). London: Routledge.
Danish National Research Foundation. (2015). *The post doc challenge*. Copenhagen: Danish National Research Foundation.
Davies, S. R. (2013). Research staff and public engagement: A UK study. *Higher Education*, *66*(6), 725–739.
Davies, S. R., & Horst, M. (2015). Crafting the group: Care in research management. *Social Studies of Science*, *45*(3), 371–393.
Davies, S. R. (forthcoming). An ethics of the system: Talking to scientists about research integrity. *Science and Engineering Ethics*. Advance online publication. Doi: 10.1007/s11948-018-0064-y.
Ejlertsen, M. (2018). Jeg gav alt, hvad jeg havde, da jeg kom hertil. *Magisterbladet*. Retrieved from https://www.magisterbladet.dk:443/news/2018/marts/jeggavalthvadjeghavdedajegkomhertil
Espeland, W. N., & Sauder, M. (2007). Rankings and reactivity: How public measures recreate social worlds. *American Journal of Sociology*, *113*(1), 1–40.
Felt, U. (2017a). 'Response-able practices' or 'new bureaucracies of virtue': The challenges of making RRI work in academic environments. In L. Asveld, R. van Dam-Miera, T. Swierstra, S. Lavrijssen, K. Linse, & J. van den Hoven (Eds.), *Responsible innovation 3* (pp. 49–68). Cham: Springer.
Felt, U. (2017b). Under the shadow of time: Where indicators and academic values meet. *Engaging Science, Technology, and Society*, *3*, 53–63. Online publication. Retrieved from https://estsjournal.org/
Felt, U., & Fochler, M. (2012). Re-ordering epistemic living spaces: On the tacit governance effects of the public communication of science. In S. Rödder,

M. Franzen, & P. Weingart (Eds.), *The sciences' media connection –Public communication and its repercussions* (pp. 133–154). Netherlands: Springer.

Felt, U., Fochler, M., Müller, R., & Nowotny, H. (2017). Re-imagining and relegitimising the university: Where past and future imaginaries meet. In Austrian Council for Research and Technology Development (Ed.), *Prospects and future tasks of universities* (pp. 25–42). Zürich: LIT Verlag.

Flanagan, K. (2015). International mobility of scientists. In D Archibugi, & A. Filippetti (Eds.), *The handbook of global science, technology, and innovation* (pp. 364–381). Chichester: Wiley.

Fochler, M, & de Rijcke, S. (2017). Implicated in the indicator game? An experimental debate. *Engaging Science, Technology, and Society, 3*, 21–40. Online publication. Retrieved from https://estsjournal.org/

Fowler, N., Lindahl, M., & Sköld, D. (2015). The projectification of university research: A study of resistance and accommodation of project management tools & techniques. *International Journal of Managing Projects in Business, 8*(1), 9–32.

Glerup, C., Davies, S. R., & Horst, M. (2017). 'Nothing really responsible goes on here': Scientists' experience and practice of responsibility. *Journal of Responsible Innovation, 4*(3), 319–336.

Gregory, J., & Lock, S. J. (2008). The evolution of 'public understanding of science': Public engagement as a tool of science policy in the UK. *Sociology Compass, 2*(4), 1252–1265.

Hakala, J. (2009). Socialization of junior researchers in new academic research environments: Two case studies from Finland. *Studies in Higher Education, 34*(5), 501–516.

Kenny, J. (2017). Academic work and performativity. *Higher Education, 74*(5), 897–913.

Kim, T. (2017). Academic mobility, transnational identity capital, and stratification under conditions of academic capitalism. *Higher Education, 73*(6), 981–997.

Koops, B.-J., Oosterlaken, I., Romijn, H., Swierstra, T., & van den Hoven, J. (2015). *Responsible innovation 2: Concepts, approaches, and applications*. Cham: Springer.

Lam, A. (2010). From 'ivory tower traditionalists' to 'entrepreneurial scientists'? Academic scientists in fuzzy university—Industry boundaries. *Social Studies of Science, 40*(2), 307–340.

Laredo, P. (2007). Revisiting the third mission of universities: Toward a renewed categorization of university activities? *Higher Education Policy, 20*(4), 441–456.

Law, J. (2002). *Aircraft stories: Decentering the object in technoscience*. Durham: Duke University Press.

Law, J. (2004). *After method: Mess in social science research*. Abingdon: Routledge.

Law, J. (2007). Pinboards and books: Juxtaposing, learning and materiality. In D. W. Kritt & L. T. Winegar (Eds.), *Education and technology: Critical perspectives, possible futures* (pp. 125–150). Plymouth: Lexington Books.

Leemann, R. J. (2010). Gender inequalities in transnational academic mobility and the ideal type of academic entrepreneur. *Discourse: Studies in the Cultural Politics of Education, 31*(5), 605–625.

Lindgren, J., & Rönnberg, L. (2018). The emotional politics of quality assurance reform: Shifting affective atmospheres in Swedish higher education policy. *Higher Education Policy, 31*(1), 55–73.

Linkova, M. (2013). Unable to resist: Researchers' responses to research assessment in the Czech Republic. *Human Affairs, 24*(1), 78–88.

Lorenz-Meyer, D. (2018). The academic productivist regime: Affective dynamics in the moral-political economy of publishing. *Science as Culture*, *27*(2), 151–174.
Loveday, V. (2018). The neurotic academic: Anxiety, casualisation, and governance in the neoliberalising university. *Journal of Cultural Economy*, *11*(2), 154–166.
Macfarlane, B. (2007). Defining and rewarding academic citizenship: The implications for university promotions policy. *Journal of Higher Education Policy and Management*, *29*(3), 261–273.
Mol, A. (2002). *The body multiple: Ontology in medical practice*. Durham: Duke University Press.
Müller, R. (2014). Postdoctoral life scientists and supervision work in the contemporary university: A case study of changes in the cultural norms of science. *Minerva*, *52*(3), 329–349.
Nielsen, M. W. (2016). Limits to meritocracy? Gender in academic recruitment and promotion processes. *Science and Public Policy*, *43*(3), 386–399.
Owen, R., Macnaghten, P., & Stilgoe, J. (2012). Responsible research and innovation: From science in society to science for society, with society. *Science and Public Policy*, *39*(6), 751–760.
de Saille, S. (2015). Innovating innovation policy: The emergence of 'responsible research and innovation'. *Journal of Responsible Innovation*, *2*(2), 152–168.
Sauder, M., & Espeland, W. N. (2009). The discipline of rankings: Tight coupling and organizational change. *American Sociological Review*, *74*(1), 63–82.
Shore, C. (2008). Audit culture and illiberal governance: Universities and the politics of accountability. *Anthropological Theory*, *8*(3), 278–298.
Slaughter, S., & Leslie, L. L. (1997). *Academic capitalism: Politics, policies, and the entrepreneurial university*. Baltimore, MA: The Johns Hopkins University Press.
Smith-Doerr, L., & Vardi, I. (2015). Mind the gap: Formal ethics policies and chemical scientists' everyday practices in academia and industry. *Science, Technology, & Human Values*, *40*(2), 176–198.
Stilgoe, J. (2012). Taking care of the future – the imperative of responsible innovation. *People and Science*, June 2012, 22.
Waaijer, C. J. F., Belder, R., Sonneveld, H., van Bochove, C. A., & van der Weijden, I. C. M. (2017). Temporary contracts: Effect on job satisfaction and personal lives of recent PhD graduates. *Higher Education*, *74*(2), 321–339.
Ward, S. C. (2012). *Neoliberalism and the global restructuring of knowledge and education*. New York, NY: Routledge.
Wohlert, J., Norn, M. T., Seidelin, C. A., & Klöcker-Gatzwiller, A. (2016) *From quantity to quality in international mobility and networks – international outlook of Danish research, part i*. Copenhagen: DEA.
Ylijoki, O.-H. (2005). Academic nostalgia: A narrative approach to academic work. *Human Relations*, *58*(5), 555–576.
Ylijoki, O.-H. (2014). Conquered by project time? Conflicting temporalities in university research. In P. Gibbs, O.-H. Ylijoki, C. Guzmán-Valenzuela, & R. Barnett (Eds.), *Universities in the flux of time* (pp. 108–121). London: Routledge.
Young, M., Sørensen, M. P., Bloch, C., & Degn, L. (2017). Systemic rejection: Political pressures seen from the science system. *Higher Education*, *74*(3), 491–505.
Zippel, K. S. (2017). *Women in global science: Advancing academic careers through international collaboration*. Stanford, CA: Stanford University Press.

Chapter 13

Fields of struggle

University work and global change

Raewyn Connell

The university world

Back in the 1960s, the US novelist John Barth wrote a doorstep-sized comedy called *Giles Goat-Boy*. With overtones of *Brave New World*, it told the story of a wild man, half goat, who comes into the modern urban world, is received as a great prophet, and finally becomes a sacrifice. Modern urban life, however, is slightly changed. The whole world has become a monster university, and life is an endless series of tutorials leading to the ultimate graduation.

At least that is the appearance; in fact the show is run from behind the scenes by a giant computer called WESCAC.[1] Strictly, there are two universities and two computers, one American and one Russian, though perhaps they are ultimately the same: the book is also a satire on the cold war and the Harvard-heavy Kennedy administration. The Western university world has a handsome leader who is recognisably a version of John F., in all his glamour and shallowness.

The novel's reputation has faded, but it had a certain prophetic flair. Today there are over 200 million higher education students in the world, more than the entire population of the United States in 1966, the year Barth's book was published. Scholars now speak of high-participation higher education systems where more than half the cohort of young people go to college or university.

That we live in a knowledge society has become a cliché of journalism and graduation addresses. The doctrine is proclaimed by no less an authority than the World Bank, which now declares itself to be a Knowledge Institution (World Bank, 2017, May 3) – somehow forgetting the cash that usually defines a bank. Our universities are indeed run via computers, though the giant IBM mainframes have been replaced by an apparatus of networks, platforms, proprietary apps, mobile devices and the Cloud, which is perhaps even scarier. The glamour in the political leadership seems to have faded, but the shallowness is still there…

Joking aside, the universities of the world, as the core of a higher education sector, have grown immensely in the last few generations and now form a considerable international industry. Governments and international agencies think them important for economic growth and technological development.

It is debatable how much universities really contribute to economic growth. The conventional view is that higher education forms human capital, the high-level skills and techniques needed for national prosperity in modern conditions. Australia's recent economic history, centring on open-cut mines and big ships full of minerals, meat and grain, might cast some doubt on that! In any case, universities are a particularly expensive way to get technical skills; some policy-makers in developing countries, seeing an unexpected level of graduate unemployment, have become sceptical. But there is no doubt that holding degree-level qualifications, especially from universities in English-speaking countries, gives personal advantages in the insecure labour markets of the current global economy. That logic still provides enough demand to drive university expansion (see the well-informed survey by Marginson, 2016).

Though most of the very-high-participation higher education systems are in the rich countries of the global North, much of the overall growth in enrolments has come in the developing countries of the global South. The biggest growth has been in China, India and Brazil; at the same time there is a very wide spread of universities across the Arab world, sub-Saharan Africa, east and south-east Asia, eastern Europe, south and central America, and the Pacific. Among the great universities of the world are UNAM in Mexico [National Autonomous University of Mexico] and al-Azhar in Egypt. Among the most interesting stories are those of Jawaharlal Nehru University in India and Makerere University in Uganda (Batabyal, 2014; Mamdani, 2009).

We cannot understand contemporary universities without paying serious attention to this world scene and its history. If one were looking for a typical university today, a provincial campus in India would provide a better answer than one in the mid-western United States.

The globalisation of universities is often talked about as if it were a very new thing. Far from it! The first colonial universities in European overseas empires were launched more than 450 years ago. They performed distinct functions in the imperial order, changing over time. Colonial universities and colleges trained religious and administrative workforces for the colonising powers; later, they educated indigenous elites in the culture and social practices of empire; later again, they produced the technical workforces wanted by postcolonial regimes to enter the neocolonial global economy.

Over the course of this history, cultural and institutional hierarchies arose which are a key feature of the global higher education scene today.

These hierarchies are embedded in the knowledge formation that is central to the universities' research effort, and to university curricula.

The work and the workforce

The main business of universities is intellectual labour, traditionally divided into teaching and research. The teaching part has the special role, in relation to a whole education system, of providing the most advanced levels of study. Research, the process of making a certain form of knowledge, is more than just data-collection. It also involves conceptualisation, methodology and a whole lot of organisational and technical work, and – very importantly – circulating the knowledge that is produced. The process of circulation has become, as the Open Access movement shows, a notable point of conflict in this work.

I emphasise that these activities are all forms of *labour*. Research is not done by magical inspiration, nor is teaching done by bolts of lightning. The university gets its results by patient, time-consuming labour. The university is a workplace, and the people in it are a workforce, now a large and complex workforce.

Though our cultural images of intellectual work still invoke personal genius – Albert Einstein, Stephen Hawking and so on – the production of knowledge has actually become more collectivised over time. It is not just that as researchers, teachers and learners we stand on the shoulders of giants – a humbling truth we all have to recognise, as Isaac Newton (recycling a mediaeval image) did. More and more of us are standing on the giants' shoulders, holding hands to keep our balance, at the same time.

Contemporary research, with few exceptions, now involves the coordinated effort of a variety of specialist workers. Research granting bodies, like the Australian Research Council, now normally fund research teams rather than individuals.

Further, the teams themselves rely on a larger workforce, comprised of those who supply the services (clerical, financial, technical, maintenance, transport) without which the people who have their names on the scientific papers could not operate at all. Much of this coordination exists before any particular research team is assembled, grant received or publication written. There has to be a library, an Information and Communication Technology (ICT) service, a journal for the publication to go into – and other universities, where there are other researchers, students, other libraries.

The same goes for teaching. Many courses are planned as team-teaching efforts. An academic may offer a one-teacher course and feel that she or he created it, curriculum, pedagogy and all. But in practice, for that course to happen depends on the labour of all the other academics in the degree programme. It also rests on the labour of a whole raft of other workers – cleaners, janitors, technical staff, grounds staff, office staff, finance workers, librarians and more (for the significance of these groups see Szekeres, 2011).

These workers, whom I call the operations staff as they are essential to making the university operate as an organisation, are generally worse paid than the academic workforce. They are more likely to be migrant workers, women (especially in gender-typed occupations) and to come from subordinated ethnic groups. In most universities, operations workers make up *more than half* of the workforce.

There is, in fact, a profound institutionalisation of the intellectual labour process, involving a large and complex workforce. To understand 'academia' we cannot speak of the academic fraction of this workforce or labour process in isolation; we have to think about the whole.

This collectivisation has become the necessary condition for every function that universities undertake, and every performance that contemporary metrics purport to measure. The performance metrics focus on what is most superficial about intellectual labour, and I think university staff sense that. Hence their usual scepticism about the ranking game that so excites university managers, journalists and Ministers of Education.

For reasons I will discuss later, recent university management has been engaged in cost-cutting; and in an institution like a university, where the biggest cost is workforce salaries, this translates into downward pressure on incomes and conditions of the less powerful parts of the workforce. Specifically, university management has followed two remarkably destructive workforce strategies: outsourcing of non-academic work and casualisation of academic work.

The casualisation of academic labour is much the better known; it is discussed in an earlier chapter of this book, and there is a valuable research literature treating it (Kniest, 2018; Morgan & Wood, 2017; Schwartz, 2014). Hard data on casualisation of teaching is difficult to come by; university managements and governments conceal the raw statistics, which would be damaging to their marketing strategies. In the Australian university system, somewhere between 50% and 70% of undergraduate teaching is now done by non-permanent staff, in a variety of insecure employment arrangements – fixed-term contracts, part-time contracts, hourly contracts or task-based contracts.

As casualisation has become an entrenched organisational strategy, a split has opened between a primary and secondary academic labour force. Tutoring, once rationalised as a limited period in an academic career with the flavour of apprenticeship, is turning into a mass experience of long-term insecurity and exploitation. The work of permanent academic staff is changed at the same time. Much more of it is now spent in being, in effect, lower managers – budgeting, finding and hiring casualised teachers, and coordinating the casualised labour across courses or programmes. It is not too much to say that the long-term sustainability of the academic workforce is now under threat.

The outsourcing of professional and support work is much less studied and debated, but it is equally important. A growing range of functions required for a university to work as an organisation are now arranged through contracts between a service-providing company and a university management. Printing, computer services, maintenance, professional services, campus policing and more. I remember standing on the picket line during the strike at the University of Sydney in 2013, talking to one of the security officers who turned up to glare at us, and finding that though he wore a University uniform, he was actually employed by a private security company.

The practice of outsourcing has two important effects. First, it brings an array of profit-making corporations into the everyday work of the university. This normalises profit-making and managerial culture *within* the university. It goes a long way to break down the organisational distinctiveness of the university, the sense (which used to be widespread among its workforce) of being partners in a unique public service of advanced education and knowledge-making.

Second, it affects the way the university can operate as an organisation. The complex coordination of a differentiated labour process is best achieved when the workers know each other and can develop working relationships over considerable periods of time. Outsourcing of services, and the rapid turnover of the workforce that is more likely with outsourcing, undermines this cooperation. Operations workers under such conditions cannot build up the everyday knowledge of how the organisation works, who to contact over different matters, how to make things happen informally, that is the normal way everyday life in organisations operates. With an outsourced workforce, the only remaining people who understand the organisation and its functions are – you guessed it – the managers.

Outsourcing, like casualisation, thus tends to de-skill the bulk of the university workforce. The everyday coordination is very imperfectly replaced by the managerial apparatus of goals, metrics, online templates and top-down directives. I have noticed this happening in practice: as particular functions in the university are taken over by central managers (a process that has accelerated recently), the actual work at the coal-face slows down and becomes more constrained and less flexible.

These restructurings are very uneven, across the global university workforce, and are to some extent counterbalanced by other features of intellectual labour. The classic work of Geoff Sharp, from the 1960s on, emphasised the technical features of intellectual labour that pointed in democratic directions. This labour was organised horizontally, there was reliance on other workers yet also on an intellectual culture and independence in intellectual judgment (Sharp & White, 1968; for an account of the development of these ideas, see Connell, 2016). The intellectually trained workforce, Sharp emphasised, was a matrix of autonomous workers linked by cooperation, not by command. The initial formulation of this thesis had a somewhat utopian idea, not unusual at the time, that intellectual workers were agents of a democratic socialist transformation. That has not come to pass, as we know.

But the features Sharp identified remain, and are an important source of resistance to the managerial transformation of universities.

Global economy and knowledge formation

The institutionalisation of knowledge production and circulation is worldwide. It is not enough to gesture towards this as a formless 'globalisation'. There is a global economy of knowledge, an extraction, production and circulation of materials, and it has a definite structure. Universities are the central, though never the only, institutions operating in this economy.

A key step in understanding this economy of knowledge was taken by the philosopher Paulin Hountondji (1997), who showed parallels with the imperial and postcolonial structure of the material economy. In particular, Hountondji explored the global division of labour within it. The South, the global periphery – where the majority of the world's people live – mainly serves this economy as a source of data. In fields ranging from climate change and epidemiology to gender studies and linguistics, a flood of information streams to the main world centres.

This has a history. The information was originally collected by the frontline forces of colonialism – the armed explorers, the conquistadores, the missionaries and the colonial officers, who sent accounts of what they were doing and the environments they encountered, in the form of official reports, letters, maps, memoirs, loot and curiosities. In time, this trade became professionalised; special data-collecting expeditions were sent out. Those headed by Captain Cook were particularly celebrated, though the later one that carried the young Mr Darwin around the world had the greater impact on science. As the colonial university system grew, it took over more of this function. Reports of colonial research published in the journals of the metropole were particularly prestigious for the colonials. They still are, in the postcolonial period: getting a paper into *Nature* or the *American Economic Review* is a tremendous career boost for any academic from the periphery.

In the knowledge institutions of the global North, especially the elite ones, data are not only collected but also accumulated, processed and theorised. Scientific societies, government offices, botanic gardens and specialised institutes were involved, but again, universities became central to this process. The concepts, methodologies, models and causal analyses used globally in the research world are mainly produced in the elite universities of the global metropole. It is not by chance that the most influential theorists of research-based knowledge, the Einsteins, Foucaults and their ilk, come from the global North. The Nobel Prizes in science overwhelmingly are awarded to researchers in Europe and North America; the prizes for creative literature, it is worth noting, are more widely distributed.

As a result of this structure, universities in the periphery are in a situation that has been called 'academic dependency' (Alatas, 2003). Universities Australia boasts that Australia produces nearly 3% of the world's academic publications, punching above our weight as usual. It would have been more informative to say that we are obliged to import 97%. Overwhelmingly, Australian universities import from Western Europe and the United States the theories, research paradigms and disciplinary frameworks that organise their curricula and research.

This is typical for the global periphery. I have seen an MBA curriculum from Sri Lanka, for instance, which could hardly be distinguished from one written in St Louis. Textbooks for university teaching in the periphery are often locally adapted versions of textbooks written in the metropole. Textbooks have a low value on the prestige scale in academia, but they are practically important, especially because of the casualisation of the teaching workforce. Teachers who scurry from one campus to another on multiple part-time contracts – they are called 'taxi professors' in Chile – don't have time to work up their own curricula. They are usually not funded to be part of the planning process for the courses they teach. Textbook-isation of undergraduate teaching, however dismal in educational terms, is a rational solution to the labour conditions in neoliberal universities.

What is usually missed by conventional accounts of the history of science, or the history of particular disciplines, is the exclusions on which the economy of knowledge was built. Colonialism impacted other knowledge formations as it impacted the societies that sustained them. Some were practically destroyed, in contexts of genocide or repression. The history of colonisation is littered with events such as the burning of the knowledge books of the Maya in the Yucatan, organised by the missionary bishop Diego de Landa in 1562.

Yet on a world scale, many knowledge formations survived the colonial and missionary onslaught, and some are very substantial indeed. They include indigenous knowledges, very much alive in the Americas, in Africa, in some parts of Asia, and in the Pacific (e.g. Odora Hoppers, 2002; Smith, 2012). They include alternative universalisms, such as the intellectual traditions of Islam, revived in intense debates about Islamic sciences and new applications of Islamic social thought (e.g. Alatas, 2014). They include, too, the knowledge formations I have called 'Southern theory', generated in the colonial encounter and from the experience of postcolonial societies (Connell, 2007).

Each of these alternatives is present in contemporary universities. This too has a history. It is a striking fact that the first two colleges set up by the British imperialists in India were, respectively, an Islamic and a Hindu college; later, the Raj swung towards Europeanising the curriculum. I don't have space in this paper to go into the issue of epistemic plurality in depth, but it is important to be aware that the world university system is not monocultural. Epistemes or knowledge systems are multiple and exist in complex relations with each other.

The episteme that is, nevertheless, dominant in the current economy of knowledge is what I call the research-based knowledge formation (RBKF). This is a way of organising knowledge that gives a central place to the research process, a process that can be understood as transforming an archive of knowledge, through time, by encounters with materials that exist outside the knowledge formation itself.

The materials are not necessarily objects in the material world, as in conventional empiricist accounts of knowledge; literary texts or philosophical concepts can also be approached this way. Whatever the materials of knowledge, the RBKF works through intellectual labour that engages with these materials, processes them in various ways (experimental manipulation, mathematical abstraction, literary interpretation, etc.), and through these encounters enables the critique and transformation of the existing body of knowledge, that is, the archive of previous research.

The RBKF as a whole is thus built by an endless series of successive transformations of its archive. Knowledge is never fixed in an ultimate form; researchers live in a permanent penultimate condition – their work will *always* be superseded in time. (In any discipline, it is instructive to go back to old journals and see what was being written in the field a hundred years ago – provided a super-efficient Chief Librarian hasn't yet discarded the old collections.)

These transformations are the epistemic side of the labour process of research. One can see here an important basis for the fundamentally collective character of academic labour; 'standing on the shoulders of giants' is a metaphor that expresses research work's relation to the archive, a collective product if ever there was one.

University teaching is also closely related to the archive of knowledge, though in a different way. A curriculum always involves a selection from the archive. It does not take research outputs and feed them raw to the student. Yet the teacher is also not a cook serving completed dishes to the student.

University education, working at the most advanced levels of an education system and working in the presence of the RBKF, requires the student herself to create knowledge, at least in her own mind. (In research higher degrees, further, the student has to create them for a public audience, through a thesis.) A good teacher is working on the edge of the students' understanding, helping them to build the concepts, structures of argument and bodies of relevant information that they need.

This requires, above all, a capacity to diagnose the current condition of a student's (or group of students') knowledge and devise paths forward from that condition. One can see why textbook-isation is a problem, and why casualisation of a teaching workforce, minimising the chance of teachers getting to know students well, undermines university education.

Into the corporate world

Recent changes in universities' decision-making, funding and the details of administration have often arrived in academic workers' lives feeling like random intrusions and aggressions, or – for the casualised – like irrational closing of opportunities and pathways. It is perfectly true that many of the lurches towards managerial power, fee-driven funding and corporate restructuring are uncoordinated and poorly thought out. University managements have often shown an extraordinary preference for the shallow prescriptions of corporate advisors, over the depth of knowledge and experience in their own workforce.

In a wider perspective, however, these trends are comprehensible, though by no means irresistible. They are part of a generation-long drive by the leadership of privileged classes and would-be elites to re-shape the public sector, in both the global metropole and in the periphery, on the model of profit-making corporations or as a field of profit-making for the corporate sector.

This logic plays out differently in different national contexts, producing lumpy policy trends and surprising political alliances. Discussions of the neoliberal impact on academia have mostly emphasised cases like the United Kingdom, where Tory governments, in two main waves, have shrunk public funding to universities and tried to impose 'market discipline' by inducing competition for the shrunken resource. In Australia, by contrast, the decisive policy shifts – re-introducing tuition fees, boosting managerial power and redefining universities as competing firms (rather than cooperating elements of a public system) – were introduced by a Labor Party government in the late 1980s as part of an attempt to expand the university system on the cheap.

The background is that Australia at the time was shifting from an economic development strategy based on import replacement industrialisation, to one based on the search for comparative advantage in global markets – the characteristic move in global-South neoliberalism. Deregulation of industries and corporatisation of the public sector were attempted very broadly, understood by Labor as a new kind of modernisation. The changes in the university sector were expected to shake up a static and privileged set of institutions, pushing them to amalgamate with colleges of advanced education and widen their intake (Lowe, 1994; Macintyre et al., 2017).

They did this, though not in quite the way intended. Within a few years the newly empowered managers were creating new hierarchies among universities, and had discovered that the fee regime gave them a rich source of profit in encouraging a flow of overseas students. The Australian university system now developed as a new kind of export industry, its institutional basis provided by the state, its managers (still mostly drawn from the academic workforce) working by a profit-and-loss logic which pushed them closer and closer to the techniques of corporate capitalism.

As the managers are now the group who make most of the significant decisions in university life, they are worth closer attention. Academics often experience the new regime as if it were an alien invasion. A hundred years ago, Veblen (1918/1957) took this view in his famous polemic, *The higher learning in America: A memorandum on the conduct of universities by business men*. In the new situation, Halffman and Radder (2015), authors of a striking 'Academic Manifesto' from the Netherlands, call market-oriented management The Wolf, against academics as the sheep.

But most university managers have risen within the university sector itself (Krücken et al., 2013). Those performing front-of-house roles, or managing universities' research and teaching efforts, are almost always former academics. Even those who have come in from other industries, with backgrounds in fields like marketing or accountancy, have taken university degrees. It is now possible to make a substantial career in university management – Deans becoming Provosts, Provosts becoming Presidents or Vice-Chancellors, and top executives of smaller and less prestigious colleges finding advancement by moving to bigger and better-known ones.

If contemporary managers are behaving like profit-seeking corporate executives, then it is because they have learned to do so. It is not hard to see the reasons why, nor some of the mechanisms: that is, policy shifts that redefine universities, in the eyes of the state, as competing firms; and insecure or declining public funding, making it imperative to scratch around for alternative sources of cash – fees, patents, consultancies, sponsorships, 'philanthropy' by rich people. These are strong pressures.

University managers, with business men and women on their Councils and surrounded by a business culture, have corporate models constantly before their eyes. It is notable how university managers' salaries have abandoned the connection with academic or operations workers' salaries, have crept up towards corporate-executive rip-off levels (a million dollars a year is now normal for Australian Vice-Chancellors), and have taken on corporate forms, such as the payment of 'bonuses' to executives when their subordinate workers reach particular 'targets'.

In the semi-privatised universities that public universities have become, outsourcing brings an array of other corporations, the providers of the outsourced services, into the organisational life of the university. Corporate logic, rather than public-service logic, is naturalised in everyday life. A cloud of profit-making companies now surrounds and penetrates the university sector, and some see it as good business to train the university managers in corporate ways.

For instance, every year university managers are invited to attend a World Academic Summit to discuss current issues and rub shoulders with global 'leaders' in the industry. An event run by UNESCO? No. The Bologna Process? No. It's venture capital's *Times Higher Education*, the owner of one of the global league tables, assisted by Elsevier, Microsoft, the *Wall Street Journal*, and other fine corporations (World Academic Summit, 2018).

The advertising for the World Academic Summit featured, as a great attraction, unveiling the next year's rankings on the *Times* league table. The multiplication of league tables, and the apparent credibility they have obtained with university managers and government policymakers, is one of the most striking developments in the market regime for universities. How do we understand this?

As the excellent survey by Usher (2017) shows, there is a history of attempts to evaluate university performance and rank universities. Some have been serious and sophisticated, though limited in their impact. But the ones that have attracted so much attention in the last 15 years are quick-and-dirty efforts that are impossible to take seriously as educational measurement. The criteria around which they have been designed automatically give the top place to the ruling-class institutions of the United States, and a few comparable ones in Western Europe.

What these ranking systems have going for them is high-powered publicity, and smooth articulation with a market-oriented world view. They treat universities as separate, independent firms, ignoring their embedding in local or national education systems. They assume a featureless, homogeneous global market in prestige, knowledge production and desirability, ignoring differences of audience or social need. And the firms that produce them cleverly produce a variety of sub-league-tables, for different categories, regions, disciplines, etc., maximising the chances that any given university will find something to boast about – greatly amplifying the publicity and giving undeserved credibility to the ranking system itself.

The league tables are the most visible part of a larger system of auditing, ranking and evaluation. Power's (1999) brilliant study *The audit society* shows how the neoliberal policy regime, in all fields where it has been at work, creates an imperative for organisations to make themselves auditable. This is presented as a moral demand for 'transparency' (quite striking in a regime where managerial decision-making occurs in secrecy and key decisions and agreements are held to be commercial-in-confidence). But it is enforced by a materialist system of financial rewards and punishments, laid down by policy-makers in the semi-government, semi-corporate space of the university system. The intended result, in this as in other areas of the former public sector, is a mechanism of control-at-a-distance. Representative bodies and policy implementation structures are no longer needed; ideally, after the policy settings are laid down by the state, universities will police themselves to conform.

Within universities, the ranking and audit mechanisms do not work so well, as different units in the organisation are not so easily regarded as competing firms – though some efforts are made to define them that way. In those parts of the world where managerial power is combined with the money to install elaborate computer systems, control in universities is now increasingly exercised through online templates.

I use the term 'templates' for management-controlled electronic systems that channel the way university staff do their work, including financial transactions, personnel processes, travel, use of rooms, research planning (including 'ethics' approvals), and, increasingly, teaching. The labour processes of teaching and research, formerly organised in a craft-like way with heavy reliance on a professional ethic and peer exchange, are increasingly organised in a top-down fashion with the front-line staff executing decisions made without their participation.

The format of courses, the heartland of academic control over university teaching, is now laid down by management-controlled templates. These systems are designed to be coercive: they are the only way that teachers can get rooms, assign staff, receive essays or record students' results. Templates prescribe teaching processes in ever finer detail, according to what managers, not teachers, decide is proper. The managerial imperative is to be able to sell access to a predictable, controllable product, with no surprises and no scandal. If the academic staff consider this undermines their judgement and know-how, and so undermines good teaching, they can go whistle.

These processes are not uniform across the university world. In many developing-country contexts, there are not enough computers, or trained personnel, to install this kind of control in anything but a fragmentary way. Older craft processes, bureaucratic forms of control, and in authoritarian states, ideological policing, are found instead.

Curiously, managerial control can also afford to be lighter at the very top of the prestige hierarchy, in the most elite universities of the United States. Here, resources are so abundant and demand is so strong that managers can afford to let successful academics operate on a loose rein, confident they will still produce research, grants and successful students. Indeed managers have little alternative, because in this specific milieu, an ethos of academic autonomy has remained relatively strong. It is lower down the hierarchy in the United States and Britain, and in middle-ranking countries, that the managerial revolution in universities seems to have had the strongest effects.

Contestations

One of the consequences of the technologies of control-at-a-distance is that senior managers do not need to be in frequent personal touch with their workforce. It's a paradox of managerialism that the managers seem to vanish, at least in terms of the everyday life of universities. Most university workers now rarely encounter members of the senior management group, except on a website, a news broadcast, or on ritual occasions such as graduations or 'consultations'.

Conversely, senior management rarely encounters the rank-and-file workers in any sustained way. The nearest thing to democratic decision-making in most universities today is a stylised event where senior managers front a lecture theatre full of staff, or a meeting with middle-managers, before the actual decision is announced. Since most university managers have come up through university careers, they are likely to think they understand the institution and its workers intimately. But as a group they show little understanding of the level of frustration and disillusion that is produced by a steady diet of casualisation, outsourcing, and intensifying surveillance and top-down control.

Though I am always wary of diagnosing crises – having seen too much of the Ongoing World Crisis in Everything over the past 60 or 70 years – I do think that these trends in university life are heading towards a crisis of a specific kind, eroding the sustainability of the university workforce. Training an expanding workforce to a high level of research expertise, at PhD level, and then finding for only a small minority a minimally secure career pathway, is not just wasteful of human resources, it is bloody cruel. The human cost of casualisation is growing. The human cost of outsourcing is much less visible, since operations staff generally don't have equivalent outlets for publicising their situation; but I should not think that this cost is any less. And most staff who remain in the university workforce are finding their scope for exercising judgement and expertise eroded by the ever-expanding network of managerial controls.

It is not surprising, then, that the university world has become a scene of frequent and sometimes very embittered struggles. They range from familiar forms of industrial conflict over wages and conditions of work, to struggles over whole-career issues such as the 2018 strike in England over cuts in the universities' pension scheme. There are also struggles over universities' relationships with their students: some that combine cultural and racial/caste issues such as the Rhodes Must Fall campaign at University of Cape Town in 2015–2016 or the caste-related struggle at the University of Hyderabad in 2016, some that concern the funding of universities and the economic difficulties of poor students, such as the Fees Must Fall campaign across South Africa.

It is not surprising that we see an interest in alternative universities and knowledge formations. Some of it is in the metropole, building on a tradition of alternative-university projects that go back at least a century. The New School in New York, and LSE in London, though now operating as conventional universities, are legacies of an early wave of alternatives. The contemporary Free University of NYC in best anarchist style uses public spaces through the city to conduct free educational activities. It builds on the Occupy movement and on the Freedom Schools tradition (see http://freeuniversitynyc.org/). The Freedom University in Georgia is more closely connected to mainstream universities, focussing on the education of undocumented students who are politically excluded by right-wing political policies (Muñoz et al., 2014). In Australia, there are Free University projects in Melbourne (http://www.melbournefreeuniversity.org) and Brisbane (https://brisbanefreeuniversity.org); the Brisbane project runs classes in a car park, produces podcasts and has a good set of links to similar projects. Many more examples can be found on the web, such as the impressive Social Science Centre in Lincoln, a not-for-profit co-operative (www.socialsciencecentre.org.uk) or the charming but now defunct University for Strategic Optimism (www.universityforstrategicoptimism.wordpress.com).

The major alternatives to the corporate research university are, however, found in the global periphery. The RBKF did not become dominant without struggle. It had to displace an older knowledge formation in the metropole, one based on the study of canonical texts and intended to form a religious and legal workforce. This displacement occurred in the metropole mainly in the nineteenth century, with the rise of a German model of the research university (Anderson, 2004). The struggle was over in the twentieth century, apart from occasional rear-guard actions in defence of a 'Great Books' or 'Western Civilization' curriculum. Bizarrely, these continue as a project of right-wing culture-war politics today. Several Australian universities have recently negotiated for money left by a dead conservative billionaire to re-install a Western Civilization programme.

As I noted earlier, the RBKF also had to establish itself in the colonised world against other knowledge formations. The Islamic tradition of great learning centres is older than the European universities, which in their early centuries drew on Islamic scholarship and organisational models from around the Mediterranean world. Across the modern Muslim world there are many examples of institutions that combine the two knowledge formations, sometimes teaching in parallel, and sometimes attempting syntheses. Al-Azhar University in Cairo is the best-known but far from the only one.

Local indigenous knowledges may seem harder to combine with the RBKF than alternative universalisms such as Islamic knowledge. But there is no lack of experimentation. The Kaupapa Maori project in Aotearoa New Zealand is known internationally and has given rise to a classic text, *Decolonizing methodologies*, by Linda Tuhiwai Smith (2012). The revival of indigenous culture in south, central and North America is now represented in higher education by multiple institutions. One is the Indigenous University of Bolivia founded under the Morales government, with three campuses, which awarded their first degrees in 2014 (http://revista.drclas.harvard.edu/book/bolivias-indigenous-universities). In 2008, seven institutions in the Central American region involved in indigenous education founded an association that is now called RUIICAY, the Network of Indigenous, Intercultural and Community Universities of Abya Yala (an indigenous name for the Americas). It seems that universities in the periphery, far more than those at the top of the international League Tables, currently have the opportunity for a great cultural enrichment of organised knowledge and higher education.

I am not predicting that this enrichment must happen, nor that the managerial university must collapse. The current global hierarchy corresponds to vast inequalities of material resources, and has political and social inertia in its favour. The economic change that is shifting global relations most – the rise of industrial capitalism in China – is associated with a politically controlled university system one would not want as a model anywhere. The US government has recently been taken over by a regime contemptuous of organised knowledge. Things could get worse.

But we have to live in the hope that they could get better. It is valuable to know that struggle in and around universities continues; that alternative knowledge formations exist; and that democratic experimentation in universities has not died. We are entitled to imagine good universities.

A good university, and a good university system, should be thinking a generation ahead. Universities need to be places where people feel valued, find scope, are not pushed about, and want to stay. Career structures need to offer, not spectacular rewards for a privileged minority, but decent conditions and security for the workforce as a whole. Organisational structures need to create space for cooperation, learning and decision-making from below. We already know how to do this. It's not rocket science.

Acknowledgements

This chapter draws on my book *The Good University* (Zed Books, and Monash University Publishing, 2019). I am grateful to many colleagues and comrades, especially Nour Dados and Kath Selkirk, for their help in this work.

Note

1 Fed by data on punch-cards. I remember them fondly. The wicked undergrads at UC Berkeley adjusted the standard punch-card warning on their enrolment cards to say: I am a student, do not fold, spindle or mutilate....

References

Alatas, S. F. (2003). Academic dependency and the global division of labour in the social sciences. *Current Sociology, 51*(6), 599–613.

Alatas, S. F. (2014). *Applying Ibn Khaldun: The recovery of a lost tradition in sociology*. London: Routledge.

Anderson, R. D. (2004). *European universities from the Enlightenment to 1914*. Oxford: Oxford University Press.

Barth, J. (1966). *Giles Goat-Boy or the revised new syllabus of George Giles our grand tutor*. New York, NY: Doubleday.
Batabyal, R. (2014). *JNU: The making of a university*. Noida, UP: HarperCollins.
Connell, R. (2007). *Southern theory: The global dynamics of knowledge in social science*. Sydney, NSW: Allen & Unwin.
Connell, R. (2016). Theorising intellectuals. In J. Hinkson, P. James, S. Cooper, A. Caddick, M. Hinkson, & D. Tout (Eds.), *Cold war to hot planet: Fifty years of arena* (pp. 12–27). Melbourne, VIC: Arena Publications.
Halffman, W., & Radder, H. (2015). The academic manifesto: From an occupied to a public university. *Minerva*, *53*, 165–187.
Hountondji, P. (Ed.). (1997). *Endogenous knowledge: Research trails*. Dakar: CODESRIA.
Kniest, P. (2018). How many casuals are out there? *Connect*, *11*(1), 22–24. Retrieved from https://issuu.com/nteu/docs/connect_11_01
Krücken, G., Blümel, A., & Kloke, K. (2013). The managerial turn in higher education? On the interplay of organizational and occupational change in German academia. *Minerva*, *51*(4), 417–442.
Lowe, I. (1994). *Our universities are turning us into the 'ignorant country'*. Sydney, NSW: University of New South Wales Press.
Macintyre, S., Brett, A., & Croucher, G. (2017). *No end of a lesson: Australia's unified national system of higher education*. Melbourne, VIC: Melbourne University Press.
Mamdani, M. (2009). *Scholars in the marketplace: The dilemmas of neo-liberal reform at Makere University 1989–2005*. Cape Town: HSRC Press.
Marginson, S. (2016). The worldwide trend to high participation higher education: Dynamics of social stratification in inclusive systems. *Higher Education*, *72*, 413–434.
Morgan, G., & Wood, J. (2017). The 'academic career' in the era of flexploitation. In E. Armano, A. Bore, & A. Murgia (Eds.), *Mapping precariousness, labour insecurity and uncertain livelihoods: Subjectivities and resistance* (pp. 82–97). London: Routledge.
Muñoz, S., Espino, M. M., & Antrop-González, R. (2014). Creating counter-spaces of resistance and sanctuaries of learning and teaching: An analysis of Freedom University. *Teachers College Record*, *116*(7), 1–32.
Odora Hoppers, C. A. (Ed.). (2002). *Indigenous knowledge and the integration of knowledge systems: Towards a philosophy of articulation*. Claremont: New Africa Books.
Power, M. (1999). *The audit society* (2nd ed.). Oxford: Oxford University Press.
Schwartz, J. M. (2014). Resisting the exploitation of contingent faculty labor in the neoliberal university: The challenge of building solidarity between tenured and non-tenured faculty. *New Political Science*, *36*(4), 504–522.
Sharp, G., & White, D. (1968). Features of the intellectually trained. *Arena*, *15*, 30–33.
Smith, L. T. (2012). *Decolonizing methodologies: Research and indigenous peoples* (2nd ed.). London: Zed Books.
Szekeres, J. (2011). Professional staff carve out a new space. *Journal of Higher Education Policy and Management*, *33*(6), 679–691.

Usher, A. (2017). A short global history of rankings. In E. Hazelkorn (Ed.), *Global rankings and the geopolitics of higher education* (pp. 23–53). London: Routledge.
Veblen, T. (1918/1957). *The higher learning in America: A memorandum on the conduct of universities by business men*. New York, NY: Sagamore Press.
World Academic Summit. (2018). Website at www.theworldsummitseries.com
World Bank. (2017, May 3). The World Bank – a knowledge institution, *The World Bank*. Retrieved from http://www.worldbank.org/en/news/feature/2017/05/03/the-world-bank-provider-of-knowledge

Index

For Product Safety Concerns and Information please contact our EU representative GPSR@taylorandfrancis.com
Taylor & Francis Verlag GmbH, Kaufingerstraße 24, 80331 München, Germany

www.ingramcontent.com/pod-product-compliance
Ingram Content Group UK Ltd.
Pitfield, Milton Keynes, MK11 3LW, UK
UKHW022026061126
477531UK00002B/63
9781138610125